Not Your Mother's®
CAST IRON SKILLET
Cookbook

MORE THAN 150 RECIPES
FOR ONE-PAN MEALS FOR
ANY TIME OF THE DAY

Lucy Vaserfirer

Contents

4

SIDES

5

SWEETS AND BAKES

6

SPICES AND SAUCES

Introduction: The Cast Iron Skillet, Both Timeless and New

Using a cast iron skillet is easy. There's nothing complicated about it, but cooking with and caring for a bare cast iron skillet does require a bit of knowledge that's not passed down from generation to generation as commonly as it once was.

If you have hesitated to use a cast iron skillet, trust me, I understand.

Cast iron cooking wasn't a tradition in my family growing up. I didn't learn it from my mother and grandmother, so I made every mistake in the book with my first two skillets, a 10¼ inch (26 cm) and 12 inch (30 cm), both from Lodge Manufacturing. I bought them when I moved into my first apartment my sophomore year of college. You see, I grew up in Texas loving Cajun food, and all I knew was any real kitchen had to have a cast iron skillet for making blackened fish. I found the recipe somewhere and endeavored to follow it. Now, this was back when cast iron skillets were sold coated in wax and before factory seasoning was a thing. I had absolutely no idea that I had to prepare the pan. I don't think I even knew

to remove the wax. I don't remember anything about the fish, but I do recall being certain that my now unevenly blackened pan was ruined after its first use. I stashed it away in the back of the pantry, too afraid to use it again. And there it stayed for several years with rust slowly taking it over.

I forgot about those two skillets, but somewhere along the line, I got wind of the notion that cast iron cookware required seasoning. I picked out a Lodge cast iron cactus pan on a trip to Arizona, and I resolved that I wouldn't make the same mistake of using an unseasoned pan again. So, I slathered that thing with as much oil as I could and put it in the oven at the recommended temperature for the recommended time. It came out sticky and gummy and gross. I tried to use it once, and of course, the cornbread stuck to it like glue. Into the back of the pantry it went, right beside my two rusty skillets.

I've already dated myself but realize this was all before the days of the Internet and I couldn't just ask Google how to deal with cast iron. I didn't even learn how to do it when I went to culinary school.

I turned to clad stainless steel cookware and relied on a couple of very expensive top-of-the-line nonstick frying pans for eggs and pancakes and the like. But after several years of use, the nonstick coating in those pricey pans began to fail. I didn't want to spend a lot of money on another set that would just wear out in time, and so I looked for a replacement that was healthier and longer lasting.

It was time to revisit the cast iron skillet.

This time, I schooled myself, learned what there is to know, and became a cast iron convert. And I became a cast iron cookware proponent and avid collector in the process.

So having learned it all the hard way, I truly get any trepidation you might have about using a cast iron skillet. You can have the benefit of learning from all of my early mistakes. Let me share with you what I know now.

Once you go cast iron, you'll never go back.

So What's So Special About the Cast Iron Skillet?

The bare cast iron skillet, which I like to call CI, performs like no other. It's as simple as that.

The CI skillet is the OG nonstick cooking vessel. An all-natural, chemical-free seasoning layer keeps even the most delicate foods like fish and eggs from sticking.

The CI skillet is the heavy-weight champion of heat capacity. The ability to retain heat means the temperature of the preheated pan will not plummet when cold ingredients are added and results in an unparalleled sear. Steaks cook up with a more substantial golden-brown crust, potatoes crispier, and fried foods lighter and less greasy. It also means that once you're "calibrated" for your pan and your stovetop, you can just set the heat and go. There's much less adjusting, tinkering, and futzing around with the heat than with lighter-weight cookware.

The CI skillet gets around. It's more versatile than any other and can be used on any heat source, including gas, electric, and induction. It'll work on glass stovetops if you're careful. It goes on the grill or in the smoker

in addition to the stovetop and oven. You can even use it over a campfire. Furthermore, you can cook just about anything in it. It handles simmered and braised foods as well as those that are seared and fried.

The CI skillet sits at the head of the table. It doubles as a great serving dish, keeping food warm throughout a meal.

The CI skillet is budget conscious. It's relatively inexpensive compared to other types of fine cookware. Generally speaking, it's just a fraction of the price of clad stainless steel and copper.

The CI skillet can take a beating. It's virtually indestructible and lasts several lifetimes. CI skillets are often handed down through generations as treasured family heirlooms.

And, if it's possible to use such a word to describe a frying pan, the CI skillet is downright sexy. With its timeless design and slick black patina, it's just as at home in a sleek, modern kitchen as it is in a country one.

A Very Brief History of the Cast Iron Skillet

Cast iron cookware, as the name implies, is made by a process of sand casting. It's a technology that's been used for thousands of years.

The early to mid-twentieth century was the heyday of American CI manufacturing, when brands such as Griswold, Wagner, Lodge, Birmingham Stove & Range, Favorite Stove & Range, Martin Stove & Range, Sidney Hollow Ware, Vollrath, and Wapak Hollow Ware were at their peak. These manufacturers employed skilled foundry workers to make their labor-intensive cookware products. In the 1960s and 1970s, the cast iron skillet fell out of favor as cheap, imported nonstick Teflon pans flooded the market. Of all of the American producers, only Lodge has survived to this day.

Collecting Antique and Vintage Cast Iron Skillets

Old-school cast iron skillets are revered for their low weight and smooth cooking surfaces and therefore highly sought after. It is this reputation that drives the unsuspecting home cook to seek out their first vintage CI skillet and start cooking with it. Said cook invariably becomes hooked and wants, no, needs, another skillet and then another and another. This cook has caught the collecting bug, or what is affectionately known as *castironitis*.

An addictive hobby, collecting cast iron cookware offers the thrill of the hunt, the joy of finding a bargain, and the romance of owning a piece of American history. There's also the fun of the restoration process, the surprise of uncovering the logo hidden beneath years of built up carbonization, and the sense of accomplishment when comparing the before and after.

Antique stores, secondhand and thrift shops, yard sales, and auction sites are all good places to score vintage and antique CI skillets. In general, American-made pans are considered collectible while imported pans are not. Warping and pitting decrease the value of a skillet even though warped and pitted pans can still be good daily "users." Rust, gunk, and built-up carbonization can all be dealt with in the restoration process, but avoid cracked skillets and those with a red or pink hue, which is indicative of fire damage. Seasoning will not stick to a fire-damaged skillet. Always check vintage and antique skillets of unknown origin for lead using a lead test kit from the hardware store before cooking in them.

The Book of Wagner & Griswold and *The Book of Griswold & Wagner* by David G. Smith and Chuck Wafford, which are known as the red book and blue book, are often referred to for establishing value of collectible cast iron cookware.

The Cast Iron Skillet Today

Today, the pendulum is swinging back again as chemicals used in nonstick coatings are linked to health risks, cooks are fed up with the short life spans of those lightweight Teflon pans and rejecting disposable goods that inevitably wind up in landfills, and almost all CI cookware now comes preseasoned from the factory. The cast iron skillet is making a comeback.

Modern mass-marketed CI skillets are generally heavier and have a rougher surface compared to vintage and antique skillets.

RECOMMENDED BRANDS OF CAST IRON SKILLETS

Good old made-in-the-USA Lodge and Victoria from Colombia are my personal favorites of all the widely available brands and they can be had on a budget.

Chinese-made brands of cast iron skillets abound. They work fine, but the casting quality can be inferior and they're extremely rough-surfaced even compared to brands like Lodge and Victoria. Chinese brands vary in price but are generally the market's cheapest.

IS ROUGH RUBBISH?

A rough cooking surface does not impact the way a cast iron skillet performs, but it certainly impacts how pleasant the skillet is to cook in. A fried egg won't stick to a rough surface any more than it'll stick to a smooth one. In fact, I've seen eggs slip and slide all around rough and pitted pans, and I even once saw someone turn a skillet upside down and fry an egg on the logo just to prove the point that texture doesn't matter. But a rough surface will make quite a clatter when you're cooking with a metal utensil. That scraping sound can drive you to distraction! And there's nothing more annoying than trying to flip your over-easy egg only to have your spatula stopped short by a bumpy casting flaw. So, while it works just fine, a CI skillet with a rough surface is just no fun.

RENAISSANCE OF AMERICAN CI COOKWARE MANUFACTURING

A growing number of small American companies are offering high-quality skillets that harken back to days of yore. These upstarts are producing smoother surfaced and, in some cases, lighter pans with a new sense of style. They are charging top dollar, as they lack economies of scale and their products are largely hand made in small batches. They firmly believe their products will stand the test of time and be passed down through generations, becoming the collectibles of the future, so much so that some of them offer warranties that will outlast you. Easily comparable to antique Griswolds and Wagners, some new artisan brands include: American Skillet Co., Borough Furnace, Butter Pat Industries, Field Company, FINEX, GRIZZLY Cast Iron Cookware, Lucky Decade Foundry, Marquette Castings, Nest Homeware, Smithey Ironware, and Stargazer Cast Iron.

As far as which brand to buy, it's about personal preference and budget. All of these brands perform beautifully well regardless of price. Ultimately, results depend more on the skill of the cook than the brand of iron.

Cast Iron Skillet Cooking

WHAT CAN YOU COOK IN A CAST IRON SKILLET?

Short answer: just about anything! The CI skillet is good for simmering, sautéing and stir-frying, baking and roasting, broiling, braising, pan-roasting, toasting and dry-roasting, and especially searing and frying. Perhaps the only thing to avoid is long-cooked acidic foods, such as tomato sauce, which can potentially react with a pan with a less developed seasoning layer. Then again, there are plenty of cast iron cooks out there who wouldn't consider making their marinara in any other pan.

THE VARIOUS CAST IRON SKILLETS AND THEIR USES

- **3 inch (7.5 cm):** This size skillet is best used for frying up perfectly round eggs for a breakfast sandwich on a biscuit or English muffin or for mini individual portions.
- **4, 5, and 6 inch (10, 13, and 15 cm):** These size skillets are best used for individual portions and appetizers.
- **8 inch (20 cm):** This size skillet is best used for eggs, small batches, and individual portions. It is a frequently used size.

- **9, 10, and 12 inch (23, 25.5, and 30 cm):** These size skillets are best used for most recipes serving 2 to 6 and are the most useful and practical sizes for most home cooks. The 9-inch (23-cm) skillet happens to have the same capacity as an 8-inch (20-cm) square baking dish.
- **13, 15, 17, and 20 inch (33, 38, 43, and 51 cm):** These size skillets are best used for feeding a small to large army.
- **Chef Skillet:** This skillet shape is best used for the ease of flipping foods when sautéing and stir-frying and sliding out foods such as omelets and hash browns.
- **Deep Skillet (a.k.a. Chicken Fryer):** This skillet is best used for deep-frying.
- **Small Square Skillet:** This skillet shape is best used for grilled sandwiches made with sliced bread.
- **Large Square Skillet:** This skillet shape is best used for fitting more strips of bacon or when you're just feeling square.

There's also a wide range of specialty skillets, such as the divided bacon and eggs skillet and a cornbread wedge pan.

USEFUL TOOLS AND UTENSILS FOR CAST IRON SKILLET COOKING

- **Tongs:** For flipping and manipulating food

- **Tweezer Tongs:** For flipping and manipulating small, delicate foods **(A)**

- **Solid and Slotted Cooking Spoons:** For stirring and tossing **(B)**

- **Basting Spoon:** For basting with fat and pan juices

- **Heatproof Silicone Spoonula (Spoon/Spatula Hybrid):** For scraping up every last drop of sauces and gravies **(C)**

- **Flexible Bladed Spatula and Fish Spatula:** For flipping and tossing **(D)**

- **Flat Whisk:** For making roux and pan gravy **(E)**

- **Wire Skimmer:** For removing fried foods from hot oil **(F)**

- **Candy/Jelly/Deep-Fry Thermometer:** For monitoring fry oil temperature **(G)**

- **Meat Thermometer:** For taking internal temperature of meats to judge doneness **(H)**

- **Salt Pig:** For having kosher salt at your fingertips for seasoning to taste

- **Pepper Mill:** For freshly ground black pepper for seasoning to taste

- **Tasting Spoon:** For tasting in order to make adjustments **(I)**

- **Mesh Breading Baskets:** For shaking off excess coating ingredients when breading and dredging small foods for frying **(J)**

- **Fine-Mesh Sieve:** For straining fry oil for reuse **(K)**

- **Grill Press:** For pressing grilled sandwiches and weighing down chicken under a brick

- **Lids:** For covered cooking

- **Roasting Rack:** For ensuring air circulation during roasting

- **Splatter Screen:** For keeping down the grease splatter

- **Pot Holders, Hot Handle Holders, and Pinch Mitts:** For protection from hot handles— beware as these are not meant to be left in the oven.

- **Trivets and Underliners:** For using hot CI skillets at the table as serving dishes

And don't forget sharp knives, a honing steel, a generously sized cutting board, a Microplane, and bowls of all sizes for prepping food with safety and ease!

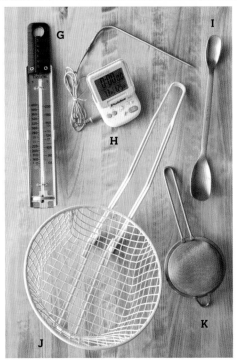

A FEW THINGS TO KEEP IN MIND BEFORE COOKING

Because of its tremendous heat capacity, cast iron requires lower heat settings than other types of cookware and is still harder to overcrowd.

While cast iron maintains heat well, it is not the most conductive material. That means it's very important to choose the right burner for the right skillet. A small burner should be used for a small pan and a large burner should be used for a large pan. A pan that's too large for the burner that it's on will heat up in the center and stay relatively cool around the edges, even if the heat is cranked up. If you've ever seen a warped CI skillet or one that's discolored in the center, it's likely from being heated on a burner that's too small.

Cast iron is susceptible to thermal shock. Heat a cold skillet relatively slowly over low to medium heat. Similarly, let a hot skillet cool on the stovetop. Never throw a cold cast iron skillet directly over high heat or dunk a hot pan into cold water to avoid the risk of cracking.

Cast iron is brittle relative to other metals. It can take a beating, but it can break if dropped.

Cast iron is not porous. If it were porous, oil would seep right through.

SO CAN WE HURRY UP AND GET TO SEASONING ALREADY? WHAT IS SEASONING?

Seasoning is a layer of polymerized fat and carbonized, or burned, residue. It protects the cast iron skillet from oxidation, a.k.a. rust, and keeps it from reacting with food. In other words, it's nature's nonstick coating.

Contrary to popular belief, seasoning has nothing to do with flavor and does not add flavor to the food that comes in contact with it. If it has nothing to do with flavor, then why use such a misleading word? I can only guess that it's "season" as in the sense of passing time. Perhaps it has to do with something that happens over the course of time or develops over many seasons.

Seasoning is a hard and durable coating and chemically bonded to the iron. Stainless steel utensils are not only acceptable but recommended for use as they help to scrape off bits of carbonized food that may be stuck inside the skillet.

Having said that, seasoning is ever changing. Some recipes add to the seasoning layer, some recipes may subtract a bit from the seasoning layer. This is normal. So don't worry too much about it and just carry on cooking! This is discussed in more detail starting on page 29.

WHAT IS POLYMERIZATION?

My resident science guy, a.k.a. my husband, who just happens to be a chemical engineer, describes polymerization as "a chemical reaction in which simple molecules bond together to form larger molecules, typically in the shape of a chain." He explains that in the case of cast iron seasoning, "simple fat molecules bond together to form progressively heavier and stickier molecules when heated. The polymer will eventually start to resemble a chemically resistant or inert coating, like a natural version of Teflon."

PREPARE TO COOK

First things first—do your *mise en place*. That's French for "put in place" and chef-speak for "everything you need should be in its place before you begin to cook." It refers to mental as well as physical preparation. Read through your entire recipe once or twice to familiarize yourself with the ingredients and the procedure. Chop, slice, and measure everything before you put the skillet to the heat. I even go so far as to arrange all of my ingredients by the stovetop in the order of use. If necessary, have ready a clean platter as a landing pad for the cooked food and a piece of foil for tenting it to keep it warm. You'll scarcely have time to do any of this once you start cooking.

THE RULES

To keep seared and fried foods from sticking, follow these rules:

Choose the right size skillet for the job. The skillet should be large enough to avoid overcrowding but not so large that it will be filled too sparsely. Hmmm, which skillet would Goldilocks have chosen? (If you don't have a skillet that's large enough, cook in batches.)

Choose the right size burner for the skillet. Use a small burner for a small pan and a large burner for a large pan.

Preheat the skillet slowly over low to medium heat*.

Check that the skillet is sufficiently preheated. There are three tests to see if it's hot enough:

- Cautiously and lightly touch the handle. The skillet is hot enough when the handle becomes too hot to handle.

- Flick a few water droplets into the skillet. If the water sizzles, the pan needs to preheat more.

- The skillet is hot enough if the droplets dance. (If you use this test, quickly and carefully wipe out any water droplets with a clean kitchen towel before proceeding.)

- Watch carefully. The skillet is hot enough at the first wisps of smoke.

Immediately add the cooking fat to the skillet and swirl to coat the inside. Use plenty of fat and add more if the skillet begins to look dry.

If you have followed all of the preceding rules and the food seems stuck, resist any temptation to move it and let it cook undisturbed. Just wait a minute or two and check it again. The food will release from the skillet easily when it's ready to be turned.

Always heed these rules but especially for potatoes and eggs. Also, to keep potatoes from sticking when fried, rinse off the starch with cold water, drain, and dry thoroughly on paper towels before cooking. Alternatively, par-cook potatoes by steaming, boiling, or microwaving them.

*An alternative to preheating the skillet on the stovetop is preheating it in a very hot oven. This method works well, better even, as the skillet preheats more evenly in the oven, but it seems to be a practical choice only if a number of skillets are being preheated at the same time or if there's another reason to have the oven on. For instance, if the food is started on the stovetop and then transferred to the oven, or if the oven is in use for another purpose, preheating the skillet in the oven can make sense.

CAST IRON SKILLET COOKING METHODS DEFINED

As you cook the recipes in this book, refer to these definitions for a better understanding of the mechanics of the various cooking methods.

Poaching/Simmering/Boiling

Poaching, simmering, and boiling are closely related moist, low-heat, zero-fat cooking methods. Poaching is used for small, naturally tender or delicate foods (such as eggs and fish fillets), which would toughen at higher temperatures, while simmering can be used for either small, naturally tender or large foods that are high in connective tissue and therefore relatively tough. Boiling is generally reserved for vegetables and starches. The three cooking methods are distinguished by temperature, or the rate at which bubbles break the surface of the cooking liquid. Poaching is the lowest at 160 to 180°F (71 to 82°C) and the gentlest with only an occasional bubble breaking the surface, and simmering is in the middle range of 180 to 200°F (82 to 93°C) with a number of small bubbles breaking the surface at a lively pace. Boiling is the hottest at approximately 212°F (100°C), the boiling point of water at sea level, with many large bubbles breaking the surface and roiling the cooking liquid. (My resident science guy points out that the boiling point of water can vary depending on altitude and weather.) The temperature with any of these cooking methods cannot exceed the boiling point of water no matter how high the burner is set. The cooking liquid ought to be well flavored. Food is completely submerged in this bubbling flavorful liquid in a cooking vessel on the stovetop and left there until done. The vessel is usually covered loosely to maintain the cooking temperature, and additionally, a piece of parchment paper or cheesecloth may be placed directly on the surface of the cooking liquid to keep the cooking food from bobbing up. Doneness of the food is determined by color and tenderness.

For simmering and poaching, it's difficult to know in advance precisely what the correct burner setting will be. So it's most efficient to first bring the cooking liquid to a boil and then immediately reduce it to a simmer. This is far easier and in the long run requires less adjusting than trying to bring the liquid directly to a simmer.

A CI skillet is a good choice for poaching, simmering, and boiling because the heat capacity ensures that the temperature will be kept stable within the correct range. These methods, however, are a little harder on the seasoning, so when cleaning the skillet afterward, go ahead and do the final optional step of heating it until it smokes.

Steaming

Steaming is a moist, relatively low-heat, zero-fat cooking method for small, naturally tender foods. The temperature exceeds 212°F (100°C), the boiling point of water at sea level. Food is placed on a steaming rack over simmering water in a cooking vessel on the stovetop and left there until done. The vessel is covered to capture the steam and maintain the cooking temperature. The heat is moderated by increasing or decreasing the rate at which the water is simmering. In some cases, food is steamed in a skillet with a bit of water in the bottom and the water may be allowed to reduce out. Doneness of the food is determined by color and tenderness.

A CI skillet is a good choice for skillet steaming because the heat capacity ensures that the temperature will be kept stable within the correct range. But due to the simmering water, this method is a little harder on the seasoning, so when cleaning the skillet afterward, go ahead and do the final optional step of heating it until it smokes.

Sautéing/Stir-Frying

Sautéing and stir-frying are different terms for very similar dry, direct-, high-heat, minimal-fat cooking methods for small, naturally tender foods. "Sauté" comes from the French verb "sauter," meaning "to jump." Food is added to a hot round-sided sauté pan on the stovetop and, as the name implies, flipped or tossed until done. Stir-frying is essentially the same as sautéing, but it's done in a wok over an extremely powerful wok burner.

Doneness of the food is determined by color and tenderness.

A CI skillet is an excellent choice for sautéing and stir-frying because the heat capacity ensures the temperature will stay high when food is added. If the weight of the skillet prevents you from picking it up and tossing the food, simply stir and flip using a spoon or spatula.

Searing

Searing is a dry, direct-, high-heat, minimal-fat cooking method for small, naturally tender foods. It can also be used as a first flavor-building step for large foods or foods high in connective tissue that will subsequently be simmered, as for braising, or roasted, as for pan-roasting. Food that has been patted dry is added to a very hot skillet or sauté pan on the stovetop and cooked on each side until done, or if it is to be finished by braising, roasting, or pan-roasting, until golden brown all over. The food should be started presentation-side down for the most attractive results. Foods such as steaks, chops, and fish fillets may be flipped once or they may be flipped constantly. Foods of varying and irregular shapes, such as cubes of stew meat and large roasts, may be flipped a number of times until they are seared on all sides. The cooking fat may be used to baste

▶ **What's the Difference Between a Skillet, Fry Pan, and Sauté Pan?**

- A skillet or fry pan has straight sides to facilitate pan-frying.
- A sauté pan has rounded sides to facilitate sautéing and flipping or tossing food.
- A skillet holds a larger volume of food than a sauté pan of equivalent diameter.

Having said that, these terms are often used the opposite way, with skillets being referred to as sauté pans and sauté pans being referred to as skillets. Ultimately, the name doesn't matter as long as you understand the use.

the food as it cooks. Doneness is determined by color and tenderness. If the food is to be carved, it must be rested first so that it can retain its juices.

A CI skillet is an excellent choice for searing because the heat capacity ensures the temperature will stay high when food is added.

Blackening

Blackening, often associated with Cajun cuisine, is a very quick, dry, direct-, extremely high heat, minimal-fat cooking method for small, naturally tender foods. It is most frequently used for fish, especially redfish, but it is also great for other types of fish as well as steaks and chops. Food is coated with melted butter, then coated with Cajun Spice (page 250) or a similar blend, added to an extremely hot, smoking cast iron skillet on the stovetop, and cooked on each side until done. The food should be started presentation-side down for the most attractive results. The food is flipped only once, and a bit of additional butter is drizzled over the food as it cooks. Doneness of the food is determined by color, which is charred or blackened on the surface, and tenderness. Much smoke is generated with this cooking method.

Only a CI skillet will do for blackening. No other material can withstand the extremely high heat, and of course, the heat capacity ensures the temperature will stay extremely high when food is added.

Baking/Roasting

Baking and roasting are two terms for the same dry, indirect-heat cooking method. It can be used both for small, naturally tender foods and for large foods that are high in connective tissue, depending on the cooking temperature. In general, oven temperatures below 300°F (150°C, or gas mark 2) are considered low, temperatures from 300 to 400°F (150 to 200°, or gas marks 2 to 6) are considered medium, and temperatures above 400°F (200°C, or gas mark 6) are considered hot. Lower temperatures are likely to be used for larger, tougher foods, while higher temperatures are likely to be used for smaller, more tender foods. Food on a roasting rack or on a bed of vegetables in an oven-safe cooking vessel is placed into the middle of a preheated oven and left there until done. The food may be trussed to ensure even cooking, and pan juices and rendered fat may be used to baste the food as it cooks. Doneness of the food is determined by color, tenderness, and internal temperature. If the food is to be carved, it must be rested first so that it can retain its juices.

"Baking" usually refers to baked goods such as cakes and cookies and "roasting" usually refs to meats and vegetables, but the two terms are often used interchangeably. For instance, it is common and acceptable to say "baked fish" or "baked chicken."

A CI skillet is a good choice for baking and roasting as it is entirely oven-safe.

Broiling

Broiling is a dry, direct-, high-heat, minimal-fat cooking method for small, naturally tender foods. Food in a shallow oven-safe cooking vessel is placed beneath a hot broiler or salamander and left there until done. The heat is moderated by moving the food closer to or further away from the broiler. The food should be started presentation-side up for the most attractive results, and it may be flipped once. Doneness of the food is determined by color and tenderness. If the food is to be carved, it must be rested first so that it can retain its juices.

A CI skillet is a good choice for broiling as it is entirely oven-safe.

Braising

Braising is a combination cooking method in which food is first seared and then simmered. It is most often used for large foods that are high in connective tissue, but it can also be appropriate for small or naturally tender foods, depending on the cooking time. The searing step takes place in a skillet, a sauté pan, or a large, broad pot known as a *rondeau* on the stovetop. The simmering step takes place in a flavorful liquid in a covered cooking vessel either on the stovetop or in a 350 to 375°F (180 to 190°C, or gas mark 4 to gas mark 5) oven, and the food is simmered until done. The food may be completely submerged by the liquid, or the food may be partially submerged and flipped periodically, which allows steam to help the cooking process along. Doneness of the food is determined by tenderness, which is said to be "fork tender, well done." The food is done when it is meltingly tender, and a fork or paring knife inserted in the center will meet little or no resistance. The cooking liquid is usually thickened and served as the sauce. Stews and pot roasts are classic examples of braises.

▶ Deglazing

After a food has been cooked by sautéing, searing, baking or roasting, broiling, pan-roasting, or pan-frying, browned remnants remain in the skillet. While it may not seem like much, this browned matter, known as the *fond*, the French word for "foundation," is loaded with flavor and should be taken advantage of to make the base of a sauce or gravy. This is done by dissolving the browned bits into a flavorful liquid, usually wine or something else acidic, and is known as deglazing. To deglaze a skillet, simply add the flavorful liquid and bring it to a boil while scraping up the browned bits using a whisk or heatproof spatula.

► **Reducing**

"Reducing" means simmering to evaporate water in order to thicken the cooking liquid or sauce and concentrate flavor.

A CI skillet is an excellent choice for braising as is excels at both searing and simmering. But due to the simmering step, this method is a little harder on the seasoning, so when cleaning the skillet afterward, go ahead and do the final optional step of heating it until it smokes.

Pan-Roasting

Pan-roasting is a combination cooking method in which food is first seared and then roasted. It is most often used for small, naturally tender foods, but it can also be appropriate for large foods or foods high in connective tissue, depending on cooking temperature. It is especially appropriate for tender foods that would not be sufficiently cooked through by searing alone, such as bone-in chicken breasts or double-cut steaks and chops. The searing step takes place in a skillet or sauté pan on the stovetop, and it should be started presentation-side down for the most attractive results. The food is then transferred into a preheated oven right in the same skillet or sauté pan and roasted until done. A roasting rack is not used as it is desirable for the food to continue searing on the side that's in contact with the pan as it cooks in the oven. The food may be trussed to ensure even cooking, and pan juices and rendered fat may be used to baste the food as it cooks. Doneness of the food is determined by color, tenderness, and internal temperature. If the food is to be carved, it must be rested first so that it can retain its juices.

A CI skillet is an excellent choice for pan-roasting as is excels at both searing and roasting.

Pan-Frying

Pan-frying is a dry, direct-, moderate-heat, abundant-fat cooking method for small, naturally tender foods. Food is added to a relatively shallow amount of hot oil in a skillet on the stovetop and cooked on each side until done. The depth of the oil used for pan-frying is too shallow to get an accurate reading with a

► **Uneven Coloring**

Have you noticed pan-fried foods that cook up golden brown near the center of a cast iron skillet and pale near the edges of the skillet? This happens because cast iron is not the best conductor of heat and so the skillet is hotter in the center in the area that is directly over the burner and cooler around the edges. But the solution to the uneven coloring problem is easy: simply rotate the food 180 degrees ⅔ to ¾ of the way through the cooking time.

▶ Cooking Bacon

Bacon is often the very first thing people think of when they hear the words "cast iron skillet." But, and here's one enormous "but," as much as I love to cook everything in a CI skillet, the chef in me still prefers to cook bacon on a sheet tray in the oven. I know it sounds like heresy but hear me out: When it comes to cooking quantities of a pound (455 g) or more, cooking bacon strips in the oven is faster, requires less attention, ensures more even results, and keeps down the mess. It's much more efficient, and that's why the oven method is the one used in restaurant kitchens. It also keeps your CI skillet free for the other tasks it does best, like cooking up a big batch of crunchy, brown home fries and some runny eggs to go with all that bacon.

HOW TO BAKE BACON

First, use thick-cut bacon. Because, really, why bother with those strips that are so thin you can almost see through them? We're talking bacon here!

Preheat the oven to 375°F (190°C, or gas mark 5).

Arrange the bacon strips in a single layer on a foil-lined sheet tray. Bake, flipping once or twice, until golden brown, crispy, and rendered, 40 to 45 minutes. Remove the bacon to a paper towel–lined sheet tray, let it drain for a moment, and serve.

For par-cooked bacon, bake the bacon until partially rendered but not yet crispy, 20 to 25 minutes.

While the bacon fat is still warm, strain it through a fine-mesh sieve. Store in a tightly sealed container in the refrigerator for several weeks. Use for fried eggs, for potatoes, and in any dish to which you'd like to add a hint of smoky, porky flavor.

Some people prefer to bake bacon on a rack, but I find that bacon cooks more evenly right in the rendering fat on the sheet tray, and excess fat gets blotted away later when the bacon is drained on paper towels. Anyway, who wants to have to scrub a bacon-encrusted rack, the single most hard to clean piece of cooking equipment in the kitchen?

candy/jelly/deep-fry thermometer, so the oil is deemed ready when a small quantity of the food to be fried sizzles immediately when added. The oil should maintain a lively sizzle for the duration of the cooking time. If the sizzle is too slow, it indicates the oil it too cold; if the sizzle is too loud or fast or if the oil begins to smoke, the oil is too hot. The food being pan-fried is almost always dredged or breaded (but not battered, as it would develop a flat spot). The food should be started presentation-side down for the most attractive results. It should be submerged in oil only half to three-quarters of the way. It is flipped only once. Doneness of the food is determined by color, tenderness, and if necessary, cutting open a sample piece. In general, the bubbling will subside when the food is close to being done. If the food is golden brown but not yet done, it can be finished on a rack on a sheet tray in a hot oven. Immediately upon removing it from the hot oil, the food should be drained of excess fat on a rack or paper towels and seasoned with salt or rolled in sugar, as the case may be.

A CI skillet is an excellent choice for pan-frying because the heat capacity ensures the temperature will stay high when food is added.

To avoid a safety hazard, after frying, leave the skillet of hot oil on the stovetop undisturbed to cool completely and only then clean up.

Deep-Frying

Deep-frying is a dry, moderate-heat, abundant-fat cooking method. It is most often used for small, naturally tender foods, but it can also be appropriate for large foods that are high in connective tissue, such as whole turkeys, depending on the cooking temperature. Food is added to a relatively deep amount of hot oil in a deep fryer, deep skillet, or pot on the stovetop and cooked until done. The cooking vessel must have enough headspace to allow for the displacement and bubbling of the oil. Depending on the food, the oil should register 350 to 375°F (180 to 190°C) on a candy/jelly/deep-fry thermometer before the food is added. The oil should not fall more than 30 to 60°F (17 to 33°C) when the food is added and should maintain a lively sizzle for the duration of the cooking time. The food being fried is almost always dredged, breaded, battered, or otherwise coated, but some foods like chicken wings

may be cooked naked. The food should be fully submerged in oil, and it should be flipped occasionally once it begins to float. Doneness of the food is determined by color, tenderness, and if necessary, cutting open a sample piece. In general, food will float at the top of the oil and the bubbling will subside when it is close to being done. If the food is golden brown but not yet done, it can be finished on a rack on a sheet tray in a hot oven. Immediately upon removing it from the hot oil, the food should be drained of excess fat on a rack or paper towels and seasoned with salt or rolled in sugar, as the case may be. If the food is to be carved, it must be rested first so that it can retain its juices.

A deep CI skillet is an excellent choice for deep-frying because the heat capacity ensures the temperature will stay high when food is added.

To avoid a safety hazard, after frying, leave the skillet of hot oil on the stovetop undisturbed to cool completely and only then clean up.

Regular versus Deep Skillets for Deep-Frying

I almost always reach for my deep 10¼-inch (26-cm) skillet when deep-frying. Personally, I like its proportions: the diameter makes it a good match for my largest burner, the depth allows it to hold a large volume of oil and still have plenty of headspace for displacement and bubbling, it's easy to clip on a candy/jelly/deep-fry thermometer, and it actually fits in my sink, which makes washing up a lot easier. But it is certainly possibly to deep-fry small foods and foods that float to the surface of the oil in a shallower amount of oil in a regular 12-inch (30-cm) skillet. In fact, the extra surface area

▶ Coatings for Frying

Dredges, breadings, and batters protect fried food from drying out as it cooks.

DREDGES

Dredges are typically the lightest and simplest of all of the coatings. They often consist of nothing but seasoned flour or meal, such as all-purpose flour, cornmeal, masa harina, cornstarch, or rice flour, and food is coated in a single step. Dredges made from cornstarch, rice flour, and similar ingredients tend to be crispier than those made from all-purpose flour. In general, excess flour or meal should be shaken off the food before frying.

In one particular style of dredge used commonly in the South for fried chicken and "chicken-fried" foods, food is first coated with seasoned flour, then seasoned buttermilk (possibly with a bit of egg mixed in), and then seasoned flour or meal again. Sometimes, the food is marinated for a time in the seasoned buttermilk since it has tenderizing properties; if this is the case, the food is not coated with seasoned flour first. It is actually desirable for there to be a shaggy coating with lots of dry flour clinging to the food for it to cook up with an irregular crispy and craggy texture. In fact, stirring a small quantity of the buttermilk mixture into the final quantity of flour before dredging the food will help to build up the crust. Some cooks like to set aside freshly dredged food for a short period of time before frying it to allow the flour to hydrate and the coating to set for a significant, thick crust. Some cooks, including me, prefer to dredge and fry immediately for a lighter, airier crust.

To coat, roll large foods in dry dredging ingredients and dip in wet dredging ingredients. Gently toss or, using a large fork, stir small foods with dry or wet dredging ingredients.

THREE-STEP BREADING PROCEDURE

To bread foods for pan-frying or deep-frying, they must be coated with flour first, then egg wash, and finally breading. This three-step procedure is necessary for most foods to make the breading adhere. Foods that are naturally sticky, such as meatballs, can go directly into breading.

Flour

All-purpose flour is the glue for breading. If you've ever had a breaded food where the breading comes off in large swaths, the flour step was likely skipped.

Egg wash

Egg wash is simply eggs blended with enough milk, water, or other liquid to coat food lightly. Egg wash ingredients should be beaten until no visible streaks of whites remain but not so much that they begin to foam.

Breading

Breading can consist of bread crumbs, cracker crumbs, ground nuts, whole seeds (such as sesame seeds), shredded cheese, shredded coconut, or a wide variety of other ingredients.

Each of the three components of the three-Step Breading Procedure should be generously seasoned. To coat, roll large foods in seasoned flour and then dip in egg wash. Gently toss or, using a large fork, stir small foods with seasoned flour and then egg wash. Then, roll foods in breading, patting so that it adheres. Excess coating should be shaken off the food after each step, and then the food should be arranged on a rack on a sheet tray as it is breaded. Though it's not strictly necessary, freshly breaded food benefits from being set aside for a short period of time before being fried to allow the flour to hydrate and the breading to set.

THE LITTLE-KNOWN FOUR-STEP BREADING PROCEDURE

After being coated with breading, food can be dipped into or brushed with oil or melted butter and baked in a cast iron skillet in a hot oven rather than being pan-fried or deep-fried. The food should be flipped once during the cooking time. I'm not going to claim that "oven-frying" in this manner is a healthier alternative, but it does yield crispy, golden-brown, and delicious results while keeping the splatter down.

THE SET UP

The components for dredging and breading should be placed into separate shallow dishes or bowls and arranged side by side to make the process easy and efficient.

DRY HAND, WET HAND

To prevent dredges and breadings from building up on your fingers, use one hand for the wet steps and the other hand for the dry steps.

MESH BREADING BASKETS

Transferring food between dredging and breading steps can be messy business. Pieces stick together, excess flour and bread crumbs go everywhere, and you inevitably wind up breading your fingers in the process. For hassle-free and efficient coating, especially when preparing small foods such as onion rings or calamari, use a separate coarse mesh basket in each step of the breading or dredging procedure. The baskets make shaking off excess coating ingredients and transferring foods from step to step much easier. If you don't have coarse mesh baskets, wire fry baskets and large wire skimmers work just as well.

BATTERS

Batters may be made from flour or meal, such as all-purpose flour, cornmeal, cornstarch, or rice flour, and liquid, such as milk, beer, or soda water. They may or may not contain eggs and leaveners such as yeast or baking powder, and they may be thick or thin. Batters made from cornstarch, rice flour, and similar ingredients tend to be crispier than those made from all-purpose flour, and batters made from carbonated liquids tend to be lighter than those made without. In general, excess batter should be shaken off the food before frying.

Food must be fried immediately upon being coated with batter, and it must be lowered into the hot oil slowly enough to allow the batter a few moments to set. This helps prevent the food from developing a flat spot when it sinks to the bottom of the cooking vessel.

EXCESS DREDGE, BREADING, AND BATTER INGREDIENTS

When coating foods, an excess of flour, bread crumbs, or batter must be used to get a good coating on the food. Excess ingredients should be discarded for food safety purposes.

would make a 12-inch (30-cm) skillet a particularly good choice for floating foods. The moral of the story is use whichever skillet you are more comfortable with.

In a 10¼-inch (26-cm) deep skillet, which is about 3 inches (7.5 cm) deep, 1½ quarts (1.4 L) of oil comes to a depth of 1½ inches (3.5 cm) and leaves 1½ inches (3.5 cm) of headspace.

In a 12-inch (30-cm) skillet, which is just over 2 inches (5 cm) deep, 1½ quarts (1.4 L) of oil comes to a depth of 1 inch (2.5 cm) and leaves just over 1 inch (2.5 cm) of headspace.

Reusing Fry Oil

Oil used for deep-frying can be cooled and then strained through a fine-mesh sieve and reused a number of times, though there is no hard-and-fast rule as to how many. Whether the oil is good to reuse depends on the frying time and temperature, the type of food that was fried, and how many food particles were left in the oil during frying. Oil used to fry flour-dredged foods will have a shorter life span because of the flour particle sediment left behind. Oil that got too hot or exceeded the smoke point should not be reused. Oil that foamed or became dark or discolored during frying should also be discarded. And of course, oil that has a rancid odor should not be used again. Use your senses and your good judgment to determine if used oil is still good to use for another frying session and always remember the chef mantra, "When in doubt, throw it out."

If you really want to get the most life out of your fry oil, you can pass it through a coffee filter after straining it through a sieve. Though filtering it in this manner is a slow process, it removes even the small food particles that

made their way through the sieve. Personally, I don't have the patience, so I just let the food particles settle before straining through the sieve and then I stop pouring short of the sediment layer.

To avoid imparting off flavors to other foods, oil that was used for fish should be reserved for frying seafood only.

Store fry oil in a tightly sealed container in the pantry for several weeks.

By the way, the frying properties of oil change with use. Oil that's been used once or twice fries better than fresh oil. This is because fresh oil is more hydrophobic than older oil. Too fresh, or hydrophobic, and the oil doesn't maintain enough contact with the frying food, resulting in longer fry times and less even and good color. Too old, or hydrophilic, and it is more readily absorbed into the food.

Toasting, Dry-Roasting, Griddling, and Charring

"Toasting," "dry-roasting," "griddling," and "charring" are different terms for very similar dry, direct- or indirect-heat, zero-fat cooking methods for small, naturally tender foods, such as spices, seeds and nuts, coffee beans, and tortillas and other flatbreads. Griddling and charring are done on the stovetop, whereas toasting and dry-roasting may be done on the stovetop or in the oven. For griddling and charring, food is added to a hot griddle on the stovetop and flipped or tossed until done. For toasting and dry-roasting, food may be added to either a hot or cold pan and flipped or tossed until done, or food in an oven-safe cooking vessel may be placed into a preheated oven and left there until done. Regardless, there is no additional fat used and food must be monitored closely to

► Firing Up the Grill?

- You can put your cast iron skillet right on the grill grate.
- Use direct heat with the grill open to simulate the stovetop.
- Use indirect heat with the grill closed to simulate the oven.

avoid burning. Doneness of the food is generally determined by color, aroma, and in the case of spices or coffee beans, sound.

A CI skillet is a good choice for toasting, dry-roasting, griddling, and charring because the heat capacity ensures the temperature will stay high when food is added and it is entirely oven-safe. If the weight of the skillet prevents you from picking it up and tossing the food, simply stir and flip using a spoon or spatula.

"REVERSE SEARING"/"REVERSE BRAISING"

The term "reverse searing" is used for food that is first cooked at a relatively low temperature in the oven and then seared. Likewise, the term "reverse braising" is sometimes used for food that's first simmered and then browned. Steak is often reverse seared and Pork Carnitas (page 144) are a good example of a food that's reverse braised.

IS IT DONE YET?

It is not necessary to peek inside a food to tell if it's done. Be observant and use all of your senses when you cook, and you will quickly develop your ability to judge doneness.

Your first clue is aroma. You will notice that food starts to smell done when it's almost ready. (Others may start to notice the aroma, too, and converge upon the kitchen.)

Listen for the sound. Notice if the rate of the sizzle changes or if it becomes softer or louder.

Watch closely. Monitor the color and the progress of browning. Look for meat shrinking away from bones. Note when bubbling subsides, especially during frying, and when foods begin to float during boiling and frying. Observe the amount of moisture on the surface, especially for steaks and chops. A rare food barely glistens. Moisture will begin to appear on the surface when the food is medium-rare. Juices actually start to pool on the surface when the food is medium.

Feel for texture and firmness. Simply use a finger and poke! Foods feel soft, mushy, and almost gelatinous when they are rare, and they feel firmer and firmer the longer they cook. (Some cooks use the fleshy area of their palms beneath the thumb to compare to as a rough guide. Bringing the index finger and thumb together simulates rare texture, the thumb to the middle finger is like medium-rare, the thumb to the fourth finger is like medium, and the thumb to the pinky finger is like well-done.) Eventually with long-cooking foods, connective tissue breaks down, making them tender again. Insert a fork or paring knife and gauge the amount of resistance. Wiggle drumsticks on birds to check if they are loose in the joint. Test if a bit of pressure makes fish begin to flake.

Insert a paring knife into the center and then carefully touch it to your lip to test if it's hot.

Measure internal temperatures with a meat thermometer, particularly for larger cuts and roasts. Rare is 120 to 125°F (49 to 52°C), medium-rare is 130 to 135°F (54 to 57°C), medium is 140 to 145°F (60 to 63°C), medium-well is 150 to 155°F (66 to 68°C), and well-done is 160°F (71°C). Chicken and turkey must be cooked to 160°F (71°C) and allowed to carryover to 165°F (71°C) by traditional cooking methods to be safe to eat.

Be aware of all of these sensory cues and indicators of doneness, and you will develop your cook's intuition in no time at all. Until then, feel free to nick and peek!

CARRYOVER, RESTING, AND CARVING

Many seared, blackened, baked and roasted, broiled, and pan-roasted foods must be rested before being served. This is particularly true of large roasts, birds, and certain cuts with long muscle fibers, such as flank, which must be carved (but even individual steaks benefit from resting).

Resting before carving is important because once a food is done it will continue to cook for a period from residual heat, which is referred to as carryover cooking. If you slice a food without letting it rest, all of the delicious juices will run right out onto the carving board. Juices leak from cooking meats because heat causes proteins and muscle fibers to contract and force out moisture, much like wringing out a wet towel. Resting allows proteins and fibers relax and retain juices better since they aren't as tightly bound. Resting time is therefore just as important as any other cooking step.

To rest food, tent it loosely with foil to keep warm. Resting 5 to 10 minutes is sufficient for small items such as steaks and chops. Rest large roasts 20 to 30 minutes before carving.

After the food has rested, slice it against the grain for the most tender results.

Cast Iron Skillet Maintenance

Though it may seem a little intimidating at first, caring for a cast iron skillet is quick and easy and forgiving. Washing up after cooking a meal, routine maintenance, and seasoning are all simple and straightforward if you follow these basic guidelines.

CLEANING UP

Cleaning up is easiest while the skillet is still warm, before food has a chance to congeal. You can start by scraping up any bits of food with a metal spatula. That's often enough to dislodge anything that's stuck on, and then you can simply wipe out the skillet with a dry dish cloth or paper towel. If that doesn't take care of it, wash the skillet with dish soap and water and your choice of non-scratch dish sponge, dish brush, plastic pan scraper (**A**), or stainless steel chain mail scrubber (**B**). And don't believe the myth that you shouldn't use dish soap on seasoned cast iron. Modern dish soaps do not contain lye and are perfectly safe to use. Personally, I avoid citrus dish soap. I choose to use Seventh Generation Free & Clear Natural

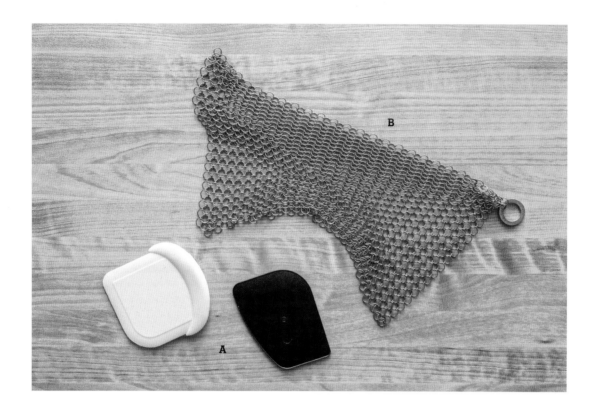

Dish Liquid because it also happens to be safe for my marble pastry board, while many other cast iron aficionados choose Dawn.

To clean your skillet of badly cooked-on or burned-on foods or caramelized sugar, you can employ the old chef's trick of deglazing the skillet with water. Simply add 1 to 2 cups (235 to 475 ml) of water to your dirty skillet and bring it to a boil while scraping with whatever heatproof utensil you have handy, be it a spoon, spatula, or whisk—you can even use a chain mail scrubber and swirl it around inside the skillet using a pair of tongs. Then, finish up with a quick rinse.

If you don't believe me that dish soap is safe on seasoned cast iron, just think of the little brown splatters that never come off the sides of the roasting pan after you roast a chicken, or potatoes, or anything else for that matter, the little splatters that are nearly impossible to scrub off no matter how much elbow grease you use. Not even a trip through the longest cycle of the dishwasher will dislodge them. Those little brown splatters are polymerized fat, essentially the same thing as the seasoning on a cast iron skillet. So you see, modern dish soap ain't got a thing on seasoning!

Towel dry the skillet immediately after washing it and then heat it on the stovetop on low or in a warm oven until bone dry. It's a good idea to set a timer for 5 or 10 minutes as a reminder to turn off the heat. Many a skillet has had its seasoning burned up because it was left on the heat on the stovetop to dry and forgotten there.

Whether or not the skillet has pour spouts, make a habit of wiping up any drips or dribbles immediately after pouring from the skillet to prevent a layer of gunk from building up on the outside of it.

Then, rub a minimal amount of fat or beeswax/fat blend, marketed under the brand name Crisbee (page 32), all over the warm skillet, inside and out, using a lint-free cloth or paper towel. Pay particular attention to the cooking surface. This coating step protects any areas of the skillet that may have a less than perfect seasoning layer.

Finally, if you like, add a quick layer of "stovetop seasoning." Heat the skillet slowly over medium heat on the stovetop until it just begins to smoke. This optional step for the meticulous among us serves to reinforce the seasoning layer. I don't bother with it with every single use of my skillet, but I do make a point of doing it if I've used my skillet for applications that tend to be hard on the seasoning, such as simmering and making acidic pan sauces. Also, I've noticed that with repeated use and sliding across burners and oven racks, the seasoning on the bottom of skillets tends to get scuffed off. If I can see the shiny silver of bare iron peeking through the seasoning on the bottom of a skillet, I give the skillet some love and do this step.

LIMITING THE LINT

Wipe a dish cloth or paper towel across the rough surface of your modern cast iron skillet, and you're sure to see a trail of lint left behind. It's not exactly appetizing. Cast iron cooks have tried everything from flour sack towels to coffee filters to bandanas to old T-shirts trying to avoid that loathsome lint. Some have learned to live with it, but if it's a problem for you, pick up some Scott Shop Towels from the hardware store. These blue paper towels absorb plenty of grease, last for several uses, and are the only material that I've found that virtually eliminates the lint. Do not use microfiber cloths as they are made of plastic and will melt on contact.

THE MUCH-HYPED SALT SCRUB

You may be wondering about the often-mentioned salt method of cleaning up. The idea is to scrub the skillet with a relatively large quantity of salt, which will act as an abrasive. Personally, I find this method to be a bother. It seems so messy, and it only works on greasy skillets. If there's moisture in the skillet, say from a sauce or gravy, salt can actually do more harm than good as dissolved salt can be corrosive.

RUST SPOTS

If you find a spot or two of rust on your skillet, never fear, it can be touched up. Scrub the spot with a few drops of vinegar or a product containing oxalic acid such as Bar Keepers Friend or simply scour it with #0000 super fine steel wool. Then, wash thoroughly with dish soap and water, dry thoroughly, and finally apply a thin coat of vegetable oil to the spot. The seasoning layer should heal over with use.

▶ Never, Ever

- Plunge a hot cast iron skillet into cold water.

- Leave a cast iron skillet to soak.

- Wash a cast iron skillet in the dishwasher.

- Store food in a cast iron skillet.

STORAGE

Keep your cast iron skillet in a dry place with plenty of air circulation to avoid rust. Store stacked CI skillets and lids separated by paper towels or pot protectors so that moisture cannot get trapped between them. If you store your CI skillet in your gas oven, remove it before preheating the oven as gas ovens generate a lot of moisture when heating up.

SEASONING

Modern cast iron skillets almost always come preseasoned, or seasoned from the factory, which means that they're ready for use straight out of the box. But if you ever notice your pre-seasoned skillet is imparting a metallic flavor to food, or if you see the shiny silver color of bare iron glinting through, you need to season it again. Of course, on the rare occasion that you do acquire an unseasoned skillet or if you undertake a restoration project and strip a skillet of its old seasoning, you will have to season it before use.

Some cast iron cooking enthusiasts turn their noses up at factory seasoning and prefer to strip it and apply their own seasoning according to their own protocols, but that's a strictly personal decision.

▶ Enamel-Coated and Nickel-Plated Cast Iron Skillets

Enameled and nickel-plated cast iron skillets are inherently nonreactive and rust-free and require no seasoning; but of course, that also means they lack the natural nonstick properties of seasoning. Coated and plated CI is favored by people who don't care to spend time maintaining a bare CI skillet. Attractive enameled cast iron skillets are relatively popular and widely available in a variety of bright colors, but they should not be heated as aggressively and care must be exercised to avoid scratching, cracking, crazing, and chipping. Nickel-plated cast iron skillets are more difficult to find but they are durable and perform much more like bare cast iron.

It's possible to spend countless hours researching the science of seasoning, but the truth is it's not necessary to don a lab coat and learn all about chemical reactions to be successful. Previous generations certainly didn't and they still enjoyed nonstick eggs for breakfast. Here's all you really need to know to season your skillet.

Seasoning Your Cast Iron Skillet Step-by-Step

1. Ignore the product label. Product labels often include bad information that can only get you in trouble when it comes to seasoning. (For example, my cast iron muffin pans came with a label recommending seasoning at 350°F [180°C, or gas mark 4], and I know from personal experience with a certain cast iron cactus pan that that temperature will just result in a sticky mess.)

2. Preheat the oven to 200°F (93°C).

3. Wash the skillet with dish soap and cold water.

4. Dry the skillet using a lint-free cloth or paper towel.

5. Heat the skillet in the oven until bone-dry, about 20 minutes.

6. Using oven mitts, as the skillet will be quite warm having been dried in the oven, rub a small amount of vegetable oil, canola oil, corn oil, grapeseed oil, peanut oil, light olive oil, soybean oil, sunflower oil, or used and strained fry oil all over the skillet using a lint-free cloth or paper towel.

7. Now, wipe it all off again with a dry lint-free cloth or paper towel.

   Wax on, wax off, for as thin a layer of fat as possible to ensure drip-free, puddle-free results and to avoid sticky spots.

8. Place the skillet back in the 200°F (93°C) oven and increase the heat to 500°F (250°C, or gas mark 10).

9. Once the oven reaches 500°F (250°C), bake for 1 hour. There may be a bit of smoke.

10. Turn off the oven and let the skillet cool in the oven undisturbed.

11. Check that the skillet feels dry to the touch. If it feels sticky, repeat steps 8 and 9.

12. Repeat this process one or two more times if desired.

13. Use the skillet. The best way to season a skillet is to cook in it. A freshly seasoned pan will look bronze or brown and will color unevenly at first. The characteristic black patina develops with use over time.

14. Keep calm and carry on cooking! There's no need to worry or fret if you notice changes

▶ What Can Go Wrong?

Slathering on too thick a layer of oil or baking it at too low a temperature during seasoning will result in a sticky skillet.

in the appearance of the seasoning or spend undue time trying to keep it looking perfect. Just remember, what matters is not what the skillet *looks* like but what it *cooks* like. So long as you avoid sticky buildup and rust, everything will be fine.

CHOOSING A FAT FOR YOUR BASE LAYER SEASONING

Smoke Point

The smoke point is the temperature at which a particular fat begins to smoke (as opposed to the flash point, which is the temperature at which the fat catches fire). It's often said that it's necessary to exceed the smoke point of the seasoning fat when selecting the oven temperature for the seasoning process for polymerization to take place. But the truth is that many fats polymerize at temperatures well below the smoke point. Just think of the sticky dribbles on the outside of the bottle of canola oil that's been in the pantry for a few months—that's an example of oil beginning to polymerize at room temperature. The truth is it's important to have a general idea of smoke points in order to choose a seasoning fat with a relatively high smoke point if you want a durable, high heat-resistant seasoning for your CI skillet. Low smoke–point fat seasonings will fail if the skillet is exposed to high heat, and of course, your CI skillet will surely be exposed to high heat. For instance, if you use a seasoning fat with a smoke point of 350°F (180°C) and you frequently use your skillet to bake cornbread at 425°F (220°C, or gas mark 7), your seasoning is likely to deteriorate and flake off with time.

Vegetable Oils

Oils such as vegetable oil, canola oil, corn oil, grapeseed oil, peanut oil, light olive oil, soybean oil, and sunflower oil have relatively high smoke points in the range of 400 to 500°F (200 to 250°C), making them good choices for seasoning your CI skillet.

Used Fry Oil

Vegetable oil, canola oil, corn oil, grapeseed oil, peanut oil, light olive oil, soybean oil, and sunflower oil previously used for frying and then strained through a fine-mesh sieve are great choices because they have relatively high smoke points and have the advantage of contributing carbonized residue to the seasoning of your CI skillet.

Lard and Tallow

Despite the fact that some CI users swear by animal fats, pork lard and beef tallow have relatively low smoke points in the range of 370 to 400°F (188 to 200°C). Also, saturated fats tend to polymerize less readily than unsaturated fats.

Coconut Oil

Coconut oil has a smoke point of just 350°F (180°C), it's a saturated fat, and it's relatively expensive, so there are far better choices.

Flaxseed Oil

Much has been made of how good a choice flax oil is for seasoning, but with a smoke point of just 225°F (107°C), it's not a question of if flax oil will fail but when. It's only a matter of time before a flax oil seasoning begins to flake and needs to be stripped off. I know from personal experience, so trust me when I say flax oil is to be avoided.

▶ Crisbee

A relatively new product on the market, Crisbee is a blend of soybean oil, palm oil, and beeswax and has a smoke point of approximately 350°F (180°C). I tried it out as I was searching for a way to maintain my steel skillets, which unlike CI are notoriously difficult to keep seasoned because of their extremely slick, mirror-like cooking surfaces. I discovered that Crisbee does not bead like oil does when rubbed onto the surface of a skillet. So while it has a relatively low smoke point for seasoning, it's my favorite choice for sealing a skillet that's just been washed and dried. It's also great for sealing lids, which are difficult to keep perfectly seasoned because they are constantly subjected to steam and condensation. Beeswax is of course food safe, and interestingly, it's traditionally used blended with butter to season the little copper molds for baking French canelés.

Cast Iron "Seasoning Spray"

The best-known brand of seasoning spray contains only one ingredient: canola oil. Why pay a premium for what's nothing but a spray bottle full of canola oil?

Vegetable Shortening and Cooking Spray

The most widely available brand of vegetable shortening on the market contains hydrogenated fat, and the most common brand of cooking spray contains preservatives and other chemicals. As far as I'm concerned, there's just no good reason to have products like these in the kitchen at all.

Choosing an Oven Temperature for Seasoning

Set your oven temperature to 25 to 50°F (14 to 28°C) above the smoke point to account for variations in the composition of the oil and differences in oven calibration.

What It All Boils Down to (or More Precisely, Bakes Down To)

Just pick a refined vegetable oil and set your oven to 500°F (250°C) for seasoning your CI skillet.

Stovetop Seasoning

Cast iron skillets with wooden handles and other oven-unsafe parts can be seasoned on the stovetop. Heat the skillet over low heat until warm, apply the seasoning oil using the wax on, wax off method, and then heat the skillet slowly over medium heat until it smokes. Let the skillet cool on the stovetop undisturbed, check that it's dry, and repeat to build up as many seasoning layers as desired.

What to Cook in a Freshly Seasoned Skillet

Consistent use it the surest way to develop the seasoning on a cast iron skillet. Conventional wisdom has it that frying bacon is the best way to break in a new or freshly seasoned pan, but most of the bacon on the market today has high sugar and moisture content, making it sure to stick and a poor choice. Instead, bake and sear in your skillet to start it out right. Whip up a batch or two of cornbread and then sear a couple of steaks or chops. Save the bacon for later and certainly hold off on cooking any long-simmering acidic foods, such as tomato sauce, until the seasoning is well established.

CAST IRON SKILLET RESTORATION

When to Strip and Reseason a Cast Iron Skillet

If you have a cast iron skillet with a thick layer of sticky gunk that won't wash off, if the seasoning starts flaking off, if there are large areas of rust, if you've discovered an antique or vintage treasure you'd like to restore, or if you've purchased a new skillet and you'd like to replace the factory seasoning with your own, you must do what's known as stripping and re-seasoning your skillet. Cast iron skillets may be nonstick, but the one thing that's really difficult to remove is the seasoning layer itself.

Stripping Old Seasoning

To strip off the existing seasoning layer from a cast iron skillet, there's no avoiding it—chemicals must be deployed, and usually that means the use of some form of lye.

Keep in mind that lye is a highly caustic substance and can cause serious injury, including burns and blindness if proper safety precautions aren't taken. Use eye protection, cuffed, long, heavy-duty rubber gloves, and a rubber apron. Work in a well-ventilated area. If you get so much as a single drop on your skin, flush it with plenty of water. Keep any lye out of reach of children and pets. Most importantly, follow all safety precautions on the product label.

Oven Cleaner Method

The most straightforward and accessible option for home use is to coat the skillet to be stripped thoroughly with a foaming lye-based oven cleaner such as Easy-Off Heavy Duty, the one with the yellow cap, and seal it in a plastic trash bag to keep the oven cleaner from drying up. Place the bagged skillet into a plastic tub to catch leaks and set aside in a warm place for a few days or a week. Check on it periodically—the skillet is ready when the seasoning seems to have melted off into a black sludge. Once the seasoning has dissolved, rinse the skillet off in the sink with plenty of water. Take care to flush it thoroughly and keep in mind that it might be slippery from the lye. Then, proceed directly to rust removal.

Lye-Bath Method

If you would like a more economical and efficient option for stripping a number of skillets, look into using a lye bath. This method requires a large tub of pure sodium hydroxide lye crystals dissolved in water and a solid understanding of and careful adherence to the proper safety protocols of working with highly caustic chemicals.

Fire and Self-Cleaning Oven Methods

It is possible to strip seasoning off a cast iron skillet by running it through an oven's self-cleaning cycle or by throwing it into a fire. These methods ought to be avoided, however, because they can cause irreparable damage to cast iron. If a skillet gets hot enough, it can warp, crack, and take on a red or pink hue. A skillet damaged by excessive heat is known as fire damaged and it will no longer take seasoning. Worse yet, using the self-cleaning oven to strip a skillet can be a fire hazard.

Removing Rust

Only after the old seasoning has been completely removed can rust be addressed. If there is minor rust, scrub it with #0000 super fine steel wool and a product containing oxalic acid, such as Bar Keepers Friend. If the rust is extensive, submerge the skillet completely in a mixture of equal parts distilled white vinegar and water for half an hour and then try scouring off the rust. Repeat the vinegar bath and scouring steps as many times as necessary to remove all of the rust but never soak the skillet more than 30 minutes at a time or the vinegar can begin to eat away at the cast iron.

Do not attempt to grind, sand, or otherwise machine your cast iron skillet in order to remove rust or smooth its cooking surface as it may damage its ability to hold a seasoning.

Electrolysis

If you would like to remove old seasoning and rust from your cast iron skillet in one fell swoop, look into electrolysis. This method requires a car battery charger, a large vat of sodium carbonate washing soda dissolved in water, a piece of steel or iron to serve as a sacrificial anode, lots of wires, the desire to undertake a bit of a science project, and a solid understanding of and careful adherence to the proper safety protocols of working with electricity. It's employed by dealers of antique and vintage cast iron and others who have reason to restore cast iron cookware by the numbers quickly and efficiently. I have yet to convince my resident science guy to build me an electrolysis setup.

Reseasoning

Once both the old seasoning and rust have been completely removed, immediately wash the cast iron skillet thoroughly with dish soap and cold water, dry it thoroughly, and proceed with reseasoning right away. Do not be dismayed at the appearance of flash rust, the very thin layer of rust that can appear on the surface of your naked skillet. It will come off as you wipe on the oil to begin the seasoning process.

About the Recipes

In selecting cast iron skillet recipes to include in this book, it would have been easy to come up with countless fried and seared dishes, but I didn't want it to be predictable like that. I strived to find a balance of cooking methods, ingredients, ethnic dishes, and seasonality, and I tried to include ideas for as many surprising and unexpected uses for the CI skillet as possible. I also incorporated main and side dishes that would pair well together for complete meals.

I've organized the recipes loosely according to the cuisine that inspired them. The recipes are in a sort of world-tour order, which proceeds as follows: US, US regional, Mexican, English, French, Italian, Spanish, German, Northern European, Russian, Middle Eastern/North African, Chinese, Japanese, Vietnamese, Thai, Korean, Indian, and finally Island. I also considered type of dish, main ingredient, and seasonality to some degree.

I developed and tested every single recipe using Lodge skillets on my stovetop and in my conventional oven for consistency. (I chose Lodge simply because they are the most widely available.) Your stovetop or oven may run hotter or colder than mine, so make adjustments to the cooking times as necessary. And remember that the cooking times are just general guidelines. Rely more on the sensory cues than the cooking times as indicators of doneness.

Each recipe lists a recommended skillet size, which is the size I used when developing it. Feel free to adjust as you see fit and use the size skillet you have at your disposal. I tried to always select the smallest skillet that could be used successfully for each recipe so as not to heft unnecessary weight.

Each recipe also lists the main cooking method used in case you'd like to read up on it in the section titled "Cast Iron Skillet Cooking Methods Defined" (page 14).

FOR THE RECORD

For those of you who may be curious: I purchased one new 9-inch (23-cm), one new 10¼-inch (26-cm), and one new 12-inch (30-cm) Lodge cast iron skillet specifically for developing and testing the recipes in this book. For creating recipes requiring smaller skillets, I used two 6½-inch (16-cm) and two 8-inch (20-cm) Lodge skillets I already owned. All these skillets came preseasoned from the factory, and I cared for them *exactly* as described in "Cast Iron Skillet Maintenance: Cleaning Up" (page 26). I put new skillets to immediate (and heavy!) use after giving them a quick rinse. I cooked with stainless steel utensils. I scraped the skillets with stainless steel spatulas and, when necessary, a chain mail scrubber, and I washed them regularly with dish soap and water using a non-scratch dish sponge. After washing, I wiped them with a towel and then heated them dry on a burner, I applied a very thin coat of Crisbee or whatever oil happened to be handy, and if the skillet was used for a simmered dish, I heated it on the stovetop briefly until it smoked. I did not baby these skillets at all, and I never stripped and reseasoned them. Nothing sticks and all of these skillets continue to serve me well.

SCALING THE RECIPES

To double a recipe, cook the food in two or more batches or use two skillets.

ABOUT THE INGREDIENTS

Always select the freshest and best-quality ingredients possible; the dish will only be as good as the ingredients that go into it.

Salt and Pepper

I prefer the clean flavor and coarse grain of kosher salt. The size of the crystals makes kosher salt convenient to pinch and sprinkle, and it is visible on the surface of food, making it easier to gauge how much to use for seasoning. Kosher salt is inexpensive and available in supermarkets. I recommend Diamond Crystal kosher salt.

Flaky sea salt, such as fleur de del or Maldon, can be used as a finishing salt when a little crunch and zing is desired.

Do not use iodized salt, which has a harsh metallic flavor.

Ground pepper loses its flavor and potency quickly, so keep black peppercorns in a mill and grind them as needed.

What Does Season to Taste Mean?

Aside from recipes for baked goods, most recipes don't prescribe quantities of salt to allow for variation in ingredients, differences in cooking (and especially reduction), and also personal taste.

So how do you determine how much salt to add?

Salt is added to food to bring out its inherent flavors and make it taste better, not to make it taste salty. Food that doesn't have enough salt tastes flat and uninteresting, so it's important to know how to season correctly. Add a little salt at a time and always taste as you go. When the flavors pop and you can taste each individual component, the dish is seasoned perfectly. If you are unsure, simply remove a small amount of the food to a separate bowl and season it. Once you think it's perfect, add a little more salt and taste again. Does it taste better now, or is it just too salty? Now, you have trained your palate and you know exactly how the food should taste. Return this small amount to the rest of the food and season the entire quantity. Keep in mind that you can always add more salt to a dish but you cannot take it out once you've added too much.

Adding pepper to taste isn't so technical; it's even more a matter of personal preference. So just go ahead and add as little or as much as you'd like.

What Is a Generous Pinch?

To give you a point of reference, my three- to four-finger "generous pinch" of kosher salt measures in at somewhere between a heaping 1/4 teaspoon and 1/2 teaspoon. My "generous pinch" of cayenne pepper is about 1/8 teaspoon.

Seasoning Marinades, Dredges, Breadings, and Batters to Taste

Marinades, dredges, beadings, and batters should be seasoned aggressively—after all, the amount of salt and pepper they contain must be enough to season the food that's in them. You can season them to taste like any other food, just taste before any raw meat, chicken, or seafood is added, and they should be a bit on the salty side. And yes, you can taste a little pinch of raw flour in a dredge—it won't kill you!

Seasoning Ground Meat to Taste

Obviously, you should not taste ground beef, pork, chicken, or turkey in its raw form to check for seasoning. So how can you check that foods made with these have the right amount of salt and pepper? Simply take a small quantity, perhaps a teaspoonful, cook it off (the microwave is the quickest and most efficient option for this), and then taste. It's not a lot of trouble, and it's worth doing to make sure your sausages and meatballs are seasoned to perfection before cooking.

Butter

Unsalted butter has the freshest, sweetest flavor and allows you control over how much salt is in your finished dish. It is a better choice than salted butter for cooking and baking.

Milk

Milk is whole and pasteurized. Avoid ultra-pasteurized milk.

Cream

Cream is heavy and pasteurized. Avoid ultra-pasteurized cream.

Eggs

Eggs are large grade AA.

Flour

Flour is measured by the scoop-and-sweep method.

Sugar

Sugar is white granulated unless otherwise specified.

Wines and Spirits

Select wines and spirits that are good enough to drink. Steer clear of those marketed as cooking wine.

1

EGGS AND BREAKFASTS

Individual Dutch Babies

These puffy, oven-baked pancakes are surprisingly quick and easy to make, and they are a treat any time of day for breakfast, lunch, or brinner (breakfast for dinner).

Dutch Babies rely on steam generated by high heat for their dramatic expansion. This means the cast iron skillets, along with the butter used to grease them, must be thoroughly preheated in a very hot oven. When the skillets are ready, the butter will be nutty and brown and the batter should be added without delay. It will sizzle when it hits the pans. Bake the Dutch Babies until they are quite dark and caramelized and the crust is set. Go darker than you might think— they'll taste amazing and they won't fall when they come out of the oven.

Cast iron skillets are by far the vessel of choice for the puffiest and tastiest Dutch Babies. Those made in stainless steel pans or glass or ceramic baking dishes lack the deeply caramelized crust and deflate as soon as they come out of the oven.

You can serve the Dutch Babies right in their skillets, or you can slide them out onto plates. The cast iron keeps them warm longer, but of course it melts toppings like whipped cream faster too. Top them simply with a spoonful of preserves or a drizzle of maple syrup or honey, or take them from simple to spectacular with a topping of seasonal fruit and lightly sweetened vanilla whipped cream. A favorite summertime combination at my house is strawberries and cream.

The batter can be prepared the day before and kept refrigerated until use. You'll likely find batter rested in this manner rises even higher when baked. // *Yield: 2 servings*

- **RECOMMENDED SKILLETS:** two 6½ inch (16 cm)
- **COOKING METHOD:** Baking

(continued)

½ cup (63 g) all-purpose flour
¼ cup (50 g) sugar
¼ teaspoon kosher salt
3 large eggs
¾ cup (175 ml) milk

1 teaspoon pure vanilla extract
1 ounce (2 tablespoons, or 28 g)
    unsalted butter, cut into 1-tablespoon
    (14-g) pieces

Preheat the oven to 450°F (230°C, or gas mark 8).

Whisk together the flour, sugar, and salt in a medium bowl. Whisk together the eggs, milk, and vanilla in another medium bowl. Add the egg mixture to the flour mixture in thirds, whisking after each addition until smooth. If you add the wet ingredients to the dry ingredients all at once, you'll inevitably wind up with a lumpy batter.

Place ½ ounce (1 tablespoon, or 14 g) of the butter into each of two cast iron skillets and bake until browned, about 6 to 8 minutes. Once the butter is brown, work quickly: Remove the skillets from the oven, swirl each one to coat the inside with butter, give the batter one final whisk, and divide it among the hot skillets. Bake until puffed, dark golden brown, and set in the center, 22 to 24 minutes. Serve immediately.

Dutch Baby to Share Variation: Use a single 8-inch (20-cm) skillet to make one large Dutch Baby. It will take 7 to 9 minutes to brown the butter and 24 to 26 minutes to bake an 8-inch (20-cm) Dutch Baby.

Chocolate Variation: Whisk 3 tablespoons (15 g) of cocoa powder into the flour mixture. Serve with chocolate sauce and/or caramel sauce rather than maple syrup.

Peanut Butter Variation: Place 3 tablespoons (48 g) of creamy peanut butter in a medium bowl. Add the egg mixture to the peanut butter a little bit at a time, whisking after each addition until smooth. Serve with jelly, of course. Chocolate sauce is also fantastic with these.

Baked Banana Pancake

A baked pancake is typically made with apples; here's a new variation you're sure to go bananas over! It has the custardy center of a clafoutis, the puff of a Dutch Baby, and a hint of spice. Serve with warm maple syrup, if desired. // *Yield: 4 to 6 servings*

- **RECOMMENDED SKILLET:** 10¼ inch (26 cm)
- **COOKING METHOD:** Baking

¾ cup (94 g) all-purpose flour
⅓ cup (67 g) sugar
¼ teaspoon baking powder
¼ teaspoon kosher salt
5 eggs
1 cup (235 ml) milk
1 teaspoon pure vanilla extract

2 ounces (4 tablespoons, or 55 g)
   unsalted butter, cut into 1-tablespoon
   (14-g) pieces
3 ripe bananas, cut into ½-inch
   (1-cm) slices
¼ teaspoon ground cinnamon
⅛ teaspoon freshly grated nutmeg

Preheat the oven to 450°F (230°C, or gas mark 8).

Whisk together the flour, sugar, baking powder, and salt in a medium bowl. Whisk together the eggs, milk, and vanilla in another medium bowl. Add the egg mixture to the flour mixture in thirds, whisking after each addition until smooth. If you add the wet ingredients to the dry ingredients all at once, you'll inevitably wind up with a lumpy batter.

Preheat a cast iron skillet over medium heat. Add the butter, swirl to coat the inside of the skillet, and heat until the butter is melted and the foam subsides. Add the bananas and sauté until soft, about 2 minutes. Add the cinnamon and nutmeg and stir through. Give the batter one final whisk and add it to the skillet. Transfer the skillet to the oven and bake until puffed, golden brown, and set in the center, 18 to 20 minutes. Cut into wedges and serve immediately.

Cheese Yorkshire Puddings with Sunny-Side Up Eggs, Bacon & Mushrooms

Generously sized individual Yorkshire puddings, also known as popovers, topped with fried eggs and all the fixings make a hearty meal that's good any time of day.

Feel free to substitute cheddar or Swiss for the Gruyère. Store-bought bacon may be substituted for homemade. // *Yield: 2 servings*

- **RECOMMENDED SKILLETS:** two 8 inch (20 cm) plus 10¼ inch (26 cm)
- **COOKING METHOD:** Pan-Frying/Baking

1 cup (125 g) all-purpose flour
Kosher salt
Generous pinch of mustard powder
Generous pinch of cayenne pepper
5 eggs, divided
1¼ cups (295 ml) milk
Several drops of Worcestershire sauce
2 ounces (56 g) shredded Gruyère
   (about ⅔ cup)
½ ounce (15 g) shredded Parmigiano-
   Reggiano (about 2 tablespoons)

2½ ounces (5 tablespoons, or 70 g)
   unsalted butter, cut into 1-tablespoon
   (14-g) pieces, divided
3 thick-cut strips of Andrew's Uncured
   Bacon (page 51), halved
4 ounces (112 g) button or cremini
   mushrooms, sliced (about 2 cups)
1 clove of garlic, minced
Freshly ground black pepper

Preheat the oven to 450°F (230°C, or gas mark 8).

Whisk together the flour, ½ teaspoon of salt, mustard powder, and cayenne in a medium bowl. Whisk together 3 of the eggs, milk, and Worcestershire sauce in another medium bowl. Add the egg mixture to the flour mixture in thirds, whisking after each addition until smooth. If you add the wet ingredients to the dry ingredients all at once, you'll inevitably wind up with a lumpy batter. Add the Gruyère and Parmigiano-Reggiano and stir through.

Place ¾ ounce (1½ tablespoons, or 21 g) of the butter into each of two cast iron skillets and bake until browned, 7 to 9 minutes. Once the butter is brown, work quickly: Remove the skillets from the oven, swirl each one to coat the inside with butter, give the batter one final whisk, and divide it among the hot skillets. Bake until puffed, golden brown, and set in the center, 22 to 24 minutes.

(continued)

Meanwhile, preheat a cast iron skillet over medium-low heat. Add the bacon and fry, flipping occasionally, until golden brown, crispy, and rendered, 10 to 14 minutes. Remove the bacon to a paper towel–lined plate, let drain for a moment, and stack to keep warm. Add the mushrooms to the skillet and cook, stirring once or twice, until golden brown and soft, 4 to 5 minutes. Add the garlic and stir through. Season the mushrooms to taste with salt and pepper and remove to the plate with the bacon. Add the remaining 1 ounce (2 tablespoons, or 28 g) of butter to the skillet, swirl to coat the inside, and heat until the butter is melted and the foam subsides. Add the remaining 2 eggs one at a time and fry until the whites are nearly set and the yolks are still runny, 2 to 3 minutes. Season with salt and pepper.

Divide the bacon and mushrooms among the Yorkshire puddings and then top with the fried eggs. Serve immediately.

Fluffy Omelet

So of course a cast iron skillet can make all sorts of hearty, crusty, deeply browned food, but did you know that it has a gentle side too? Use it over low heat to turn out this tenderest, most delicate omelet.

Personally, I like the pure simplicity of this omelet, but feel free to embellish it with a few minced tender herbs. // *Yield: 1 serving*

- **RECOMMENDED SKILLET:** 8 inch (20 cm) with lid
- **COOKING METHOD:** Pan-Frying

2 eggs
2 tablespoons (16 g) all-purpose flour
½ cup (120 ml) milk
¼ teaspoon kosher salt

Freshly ground black pepper
2 tablespoons (28 g) butter
Flaky sea salt, such as fleur de sel
    or Maldon

Lightly beat the eggs in a medium bowl. Place the flour into another medium bowl. Add the eggs to the flour in thirds, whisking after each addition until smooth. If you add the eggs to the flour all at once, you'll inevitably wind up with a lumpy mixture. Add the milk, kosher salt, and a generous pinch of black pepper and whisk until smooth.

Preheat a cast iron skillet over medium-low heat. Add the butter, swirl to coat the inside of the skillet, and heat until the butter is melted and the foam subsides. Add the egg mixture, cover the skillet, decrease the heat to low, and cook until set, 14 to 16 minutes. Sprinkle with a generous pinch of sea salt and serve immediately.

Corn Fry Cakes with Jalapeño-Maple Butter

These cornmeal pancakes, inspired by the Southern favorite johnnycakes, are crispy on the outside and tender within and served with a sweet and spicy butter for slathering.

Feel free to fold a handful of fresh corn kernels into the batter in the summertime when corn is in season. // *Yield: 4 servings*

- **RECOMMENDED SKILLET:** 12 inch (30 cm)
- **COOKING METHOD:** Pan-Frying

2 ounces (4 tablespoons, or 55 g)
    unsalted butter, softened
1 large jalapeño, roasted, peeled, seeded,
    and minced
1 tablespoon (15 ml) maple syrup
Flaky sea salt, such as fleur de sel
    or Maldon
1½ cups (210 g) fine cornmeal

1 cup (125 g) all-purpose flour
1½ teaspoons sugar
¾ teaspoon baking powder
1 teaspoon kosher salt
3 eggs
2 cups (475 ml) buttermilk
½ cup (120 ml) canola oil

Mix together the butter, jalapeño, and maple syrup in a medium bowl and season to taste with the sea salt. Cover and set aside.

Whisk together the cornmeal, flour, sugar, baking powder, and kosher salt in a medium bowl. Whisk together the eggs and buttermilk in another medium bowl. Add the egg mixture to the cornmeal mixture and whisk until just combined and all of the ingredients are moistened.

(continued)

Pour the oil into a cast iron skillet and preheat over medium heat until a drop of batter sizzles immediately when added. Scoop the batter into the skillet by the scant ¼ cup (60 ml), spacing the corn cakes 2 inches (5 cm) apart. Fry the corn cakes until golden brown, set around the edges, and bubbles begin to rise to the surface, 2 to 3 minutes. Using a slotted spatula, flip the corn cakes and fry until golden brown and cooked through, 1 to 2 minutes. Remove the corn cakes to a paper towel–lined sheet tray, let drain for a moment, and stack to keep warm. Fry the remaining batter in the same manner, decreasing the heat a bit if they seem to be browning too quickly after the first batch.

Serve the corn fry cakes hot with the jalapeño-maple butter.

Apricot Cream Cheese–Stuffed French Toast

Stuffed French toast may sound like a fancy special you'd order when going out for brunch, but really it's no more complicated than making plain French toast. You just have to build some cream cheese sandwiches to start, and then you soak them in custard and fry them up like usual. Of course, the cream cheese gets warm and melty as the toast cooks, and everyone is always delighted and surprised by the hidden filling when they dig in!

Serve with warm maple syrup and Andrew's Uncured Bacon (page 51) or Homemade Sage Breakfast Sausage (page 56) patties. // *Yield: 4 servings*

- **RECOMMENDED SKILLET:** 12 inch (30 cm)

- **COOKING METHOD:** Pan-Frying

3 ounces (85 g) dried apricots
   (about 26 halves)
8 ounces (225 g) cream cheese, softened
¼ cup (60 g) packed brown sugar
¼ teaspoon ground cinnamon
Pinch of ground cardamom
Kosher salt
6 eggs
2 cups (475 ml) milk

3 tablespoons (45 ml) brandy
2 teaspoons pure vanilla extract
1 large loaf (1¼ pounds, or 570 g) challah,
   cut into ½-inch (1-cm) thick slices
½ cup (120 ml) canola oil
2 ounces (4 tablespoons, or 55 g)
   unsalted butter, cut into 1-tablespoon
   (14-g) pieces

Place the apricots in a medium bowl and add enough boiling water to cover. Let soak until rehydrated and pliable, 10 to 15 minutes. Drain the apricots and blot dry on paper towels. Transfer to a cutting board and mince.

Mix together the cream cheese, brown sugar, cinnamon, cardamom, apricots, and a generous pinch of salt in a medium bowl until thoroughly combined.

Lightly beat the eggs in a medium bowl. Add the milk, brandy, vanilla, and a generous pinch of salt and whisk until thoroughly combined. Pour into a shallow dish.

Divide the cream cheese mixture among half of the slices of challah and spread it evenly and then top with the remaining half of the slices, pressing down gently to sandwich them.

Pour the oil into the cast iron skillet, add the butter, and preheat over medium-low heat until a drop of custard sizzles immediately when added. Just before the oil comes to temperature, add as many sandwiches as will fit in a single layer in the skillet to the custard and soak, flipping once or twice, until soaked through, about 2 minutes. Transfer to the skillet, shaking off any excess custard, and fry until golden brown, 4 to 5 minutes. Using a slotted spatula, flip the French toast and fry until golden brown, slightly puffed, and cooked through, 3 to 4 minutes. Remove the French toast to a paper towel–lined sheet tray, let drain for a moment, and stack to keep warm. Soak and fry the remaining French toast in the same manner and serve hot.

Andrew's Uncured Bacon

My little brother Andrew is a butcher, charcutier, and gifted chef in his own right. He developed this bacon recipe with the home cook in mind. The recipe is 100 percent accessible and requires no sodium nitrite curing salt and no smoker. But the results are legit! It's nearly impossible to tell that this bacon is uncured and unsmoked when you see it and taste it. It has both the characteristic pink color and characteristic smoky flavor of "real" bacon.

The term "uncured" refers to the fact that no nitrites are used in the curing process. This bacon is, in reality, a salt-cured product made with a simple salt and sugar rub. It relies on a combination of smoked salt, smoked Spanish paprika, and Chinese Lapsang souchong smoked black tea to lend a permeating smoky flavor since most home kitchens are not equipped with a smoker.

Because of the relatively high sugar content, this bacon browns fast. Be careful not to let it burn before it gets crispy and rendered. Decrease the heat if it seems to be browning too quickly as it fries.

Serve this bacon with fried eggs and Home Fries (page 208), tuck it into a BLT, or use it to make Cheese Yorkshire Puddings with Sunny-Side Up Eggs, Bacon & Mushrooms (page 45). Chop it up and put it in Skillet Roasted Brussels Sprouts with Chestnuts, Shallots & Bacon (page 204), or Kale & Butternut Squash with Bacon & Toasted Garlic (page 202). If you have homemade bacon in your refrigerator, you'll doubtless think of a myriad of ways to use it.

Smoked salt and sweet Spanish paprika, also known as pimentón dulce, can be found at gourmet markets and online. Loose leaf Lapsang souchong is available wherever fine teas are sold. // *Yield: about 3¾ pounds (1,706 g)*

- **RECOMMENDED SKILLET:** 12 inch (30 cm) with roasting rack
- **COOKING METHOD:** Roasting/Pan-Frying

(continued)

▶ Grams and Percentages

Professionals prefer to use grams and percentages when making recipes for the most ease, accuracy, and flexibility. Andrew and I recommend you do the same. As long as you have a scale that works in grams, it's very simple to do and you don't even need to know any conversions. All of the ingredients are expressed as a percentage of the weight of the pork belly. For example, if you have a 1-pound (455-gram) piece of pork belly, you can calculate that you need 9.1 grams of smoked sea salt by multiplying 455 grams by 2%. Using percentages allows you to figure out exactly how much of each ingredient you need whatever the weight of the piece of pork belly you start with.

Using a gram scale is certainly preferred. But since not everybody has one and since a 4-pound (1,820-g) piece of pork belly just happens to fit perfectly inside a gallon-size (3.8-L) zip-top bag, I have included the amount of each ingredient in both weight and approximate volume measurements to use for 4 pounds (1,820 g).

PERCENTAGE	AMOUNT FOR 4 POUNDS (1,820 G) OF PORK BELLY	
100%	1,820 grams/4.00 pounds	skinned pork belly
0.5%	9.1 grams/0.32 ounces/2½ tablespoons	Lapsang souchong tea leaves
0.125%	2.3 grams/0.07 ounces/1¼ each	star anise
2%	36.3 grams/1.27 ounces/3 tablespoons	smoked sea salt
2%	36.3 grams/1.27 ounces/3½ tablespoons packed	light brown sugar
0.25%	4.5 grams/0.18 ounces/1 tablespoon	sweet Spanish paprika
0.25%	4.5 grams/0.18 ounces/1 tablespoon plus 1 teaspoon	red chile flakes
2%	36.3 grams/1.27 ounces/2 tablespoons	molasses

Using a spice mill, grind the tea leaves and star anise to a powder. Whisk together the smoked sea salt, brown sugar, Spanish paprika, red chile flakes, and tea leaf mixture in a small bowl.

Sprinkle the pork belly evenly with the salt mixture, patting so that it adheres, and then drizzle all over with the molasses. Transfer the pork belly to a vacuum sealer bag, add any loose salt mixture, and vacuum seal. (If you don't have a vacuum sealer, use a gallon-size [3.8-L] zip-top bag and press out as much air as possible as you seal it.) Refrigerate and let cure for 4 days.

Preheat the oven to 200°F (94°C).

Remove the bacon from the bag, rinse off the cure, blot dry with paper towels, and roast on a roasting rack in a cast iron skillet until a meat thermometer registers 140°F (60°C), 2¼ to 2¾ hours. Let cool completely and then refrigerate until chilled and firm, about 4 hours, before slicing.

Using a very sharp knife, cut the bacon against the grain into ³⁄₁₆- to ¼-inch (5- to 6-mm) thick slices as needed. To maximize keeping time, store the rest unsliced and vacuum sealed in a clean vacuum sealer bag in the refrigerator. Uncured bacon stored in this manner will keep for a week or two. Alternatively, slice all of the bacon and keep individual portions vacuum sealed in clean vacuum sealer bags in the freezer for up to 3 months. (If you don't have a vacuum sealer, use zip-top bags and press out as much air as possible as you seal them.)

To cook, preheat a cast iron skillet over medium-low heat. Add the bacon strips and fry, flipping occasionally, until golden brown, crispy, and rendered, 10 to 14 minutes. Transfer to a paper towel–lined sheet tray, let drain for a moment, and serve hot.

While the bacon fat is still warm, strain it through a fine-mesh sieve. Store in a tightly sealed container in the refrigerator for several weeks and use wherever you would ordinarily use bacon fat.

Andrew's Insta-Lardons

When you want the taste of homemade bacon without the four-day wait, these quick-curing lardons are the answer!

"Lardon" is culinary speak for diced fried bacon. According to the rules of classical French cuisine, lardons are cut into small strips and blanched to tame the saltiness and smokiness be-fore frying. The size and shape gives lardons a nice meaty chew when they are cooked.

Usually, lardons are cut from cured bacon, but in this case, raw pork belly is cut into small pieces and then cured. Exposing that much surface area allows the salt to penetrate the meat completely in a matter of hours instead of days. As Andrew puts it, "You can skip the curing of a whole belly and cut raw pork lardons, cure, and cook a couple hours later right in the cast iron skillet. There's no real wait. I haven't seen the instant lardon recipe in print yet, but I've used it in a pinch many times." And there you have it, a closely guarded chef's secret revealed!

Using a gram scale is certainly preferred. But since not everybody has one, I have included the amount of each ingredient in both weight and approximate volume measurements to use for 1 pound (455 g) of pork belly.

One pound (455 g) of these lardons is enough for a batch each of Frisee aux Lardons (page 78) and Loaded Crispy Smashed Potatoes (page 209), plus some extra for scrambling into eggs, folding inside of an omelet, sprinkling over salad, or tucking into baked potatoes. Use them in any recipe that calls for bacon lardons—no blanching required—or wherever you would ordinarily use crumbled bacon. // *Yield: about 1 pound (455 g)*

- **RECOMMENDED SKILLET:** 10¼ inch (26 cm)
- **COOKING METHOD:** Pan-Frying

PERCENTAGE	AMOUNT FOR 1 POUND (455 G) OF PORK BELLY	
100%	455 grams/1.00 pound	skinned pork belly, cut into ¼ by ¼-inch by 1- to 1½-inch pieces
2%	9.1 grams/0.32 ounces/1½ teaspoons	smoked sea salt
2%	9.1 grams/0.32 ounces/2¼ teaspoons packed	light brown sugar
0.3%	1.4 grams/0.05 ounces/½ teaspoon	sweet Spanish paprika
0.3%	1.4 grams/0.05 ounces/¾ teaspoon	freshly ground black pepper
2%	9.1 grams/0.32 ounces/1¼ teaspoons	molasses

Whisk together the smoked sea salt, brown sugar, Spanish paprika, and pepper in a small bowl.

Place the pork belly in a large bowl, sprinkle with the salt mixture, drizzle with the molasses, and toss gently to coat. Refrigerate and let cure for 3 to 4 hours.

Transfer the lardons to a fine-mesh sieve and gently rinse off the cure. Transfer to a paper towel–lined sheet tray and let drain. Blot dry with paper towels.

To cook, preheat a cast iron skillet over medium-low heat. Add ¼ to ½ pounds (115 to 225 grams) of lardons at a time and fry, stirring occasionally, until golden brown, crispy, and rendered, 8 to 10 minutes. Transfer to a paper towel–lined plate, let drain for a moment, and use as desired within a couple of days.

While the lardon fat is still warm, strain it through a fine-mesh sieve. Store in a tightly sealed container in the refrigerator for several weeks and use wherever you would ordinarily use bacon fat.

Homemade Sage Breakfast Sausage

This highly seasoned, flavorful sausage can stand alone or serve as the base for other recipes. Cook up patties to serve along with eggs, pancakes, or waffles or tuck into breakfast sandwiches on croissants or Buttermilk Biscuits (page 228) or use crumbles to make Biscuits & Sausage Gravy (page 60) or Sausage & Herb Cornbread Dressing (page 207). It's also perfect in bulk for Scotch Eggs (page 80).

When making fresh sausage, do not try to use ground pork with a lower fat content. Keep all equipment and ingredients well chilled and mix until thoroughly blended and visibly sticky to ensure proper emulsification. Stickiness is a sign that the proteins have bound with the liquid in the meat and the emulsion is set. The result when cooked is juicy sausage that holds together because the fat won't render as readily.

Using a gram scale is certainly preferred. But since not everybody has one, I have included the amount of each ingredient in both weight and approximate volume measurements to use for 2 pounds (900 g) of ground pork.

You can cook the sausage as soon as it is mixed, but the flavor benefits from being refrigerated overnight. Raw sausage may be kept tightly sealed in the refrigerator for 3 to 4 days or in the freezer for several weeks. Portion bulk sausage into zip-top or vacuum sealer bags and flatten to a thickness of no more than ¾ inch (2 cm) before sealing for speedy freezing and thawing.

// *Yield: about 2 pounds (900 g)*

- **RECOMMENDED SKILLET:** 12 inch (30 cm)
- **COOKING METHOD:** Pan-Frying

▶ Cooking Sausage Crumbles

For sausage crumbles to cook up golden brown on the outside and juicy on the inside, break up the raw sausage into small bits before putting it into a thoroughly preheated skillet. Then, stir the sausage only occasionally as it cooks, about two or three times is sufficient. Adding a single large mass of sausage to the skillet and trying to break it up as it cooks will result in sausage that stews in its own juices. When that happens, all of the juices must cook off before any browning can take place, and the end result is dry sausage.

The same is also true of cooking raw ground meat.

PERCENTAGE	AMOUNT FOR 2 POUNDS (900 G) OF GROUND PORK	
100%	900 grams/2.00 pounds	20 to 30% fat ground pork, broken up
1.75%	15.9 grams/0.56 ounces/2 tablespoons plus 1 teaspoon	kosher salt
0.75%	6.8 grams/0.24 ounces/3 tablespoons lightly packed	minced fresh sage
0.4%	3.6 grams/0.13 ounces/2¼ teaspoons	freshly ground coarse black pepper
0.15%	1.4 grams/0.05 ounces/¾ teaspoon	red chile flakes

TO COOK:
2 tablespoons (30 ml) canola oil

Whisk together the salt, sage, pepper, and red chile flakes in a small bowl.

Place the pork into a stand mixer bowl, sprinkle with the salt mixture, fit onto the mixer with the paddle attachment, and mix on low speed until thoroughly blended and visibly sticky, about 2 minutes.

To cook crumbles, break the raw sausage into small bits.

Preheat a cast iron skillet over medium-low to medium heat. Add the oil and swirl to coat the inside of the skillet. Add 12 to 16 ounces (340 to 455 g) of broken-up sausage at a time and cook, stirring occasionally, until golden brown, 4 to 6 minutes for partially cooked and 6 to 10 minutes for completely cooked, depending on the final use.

To cook patties, divide the raw sausage into 3-ounce (85-g) portions and gently form each portion into a ball. Gently pat each ball into a 3¼-inch (9.5-cm) patty that's slightly thinner in the center and thicker around the edges; doing this prevents the patty from cooking up into a ball shape.

Preheat a cast iron skillet over medium-low heat. Add the oil and swirl to coat the inside of the skillet. Add 5 to 6 patties at a time and cook without disturbing until golden brown, 5 to 6 minutes. Flip the patties and cook until golden brown and just cooked through, 4 to 5 minutes. Moisture will pool on the surface of the patties and they will feel firm to the touch when they are just cooked through. Serve hot.

Homemade Mexican Chorizo

This chorizo is highly seasoned but not spicy hot, as both varieties of chile used in it are relatively mild. Mexican chorizo is typically used in crumbled form as a flavoring. Having lived most of my life in Texas where chorizo is nearly as common as breakfast sausage, I don't think I've ever seen a chorizo sausage patty. But there's no reason why it can't be done—a chorizo patty would make a fantastic sausage, egg, and cheese breakfast sandwich, especially with the addition of roasted Anaheim or New Mexico green chiles (page 142). Use crumbles to scramble into eggs for Homemade Mexican Chorizo & Egg Breakfast Tacos (page 61) and for Chicken with Peppers & Mexican Chorizo (page 143).

Mexican oregano has a unique floral character. Do not substitute Greek or Italian oregano. Look for Mexican oregano, pure mild New Mexico chile powder, and pure gaujillo chile powder at Mexican markets or order them online.

When making fresh sausage, do not try to use ground pork with a lower fat content. Keep all equipment and ingredients well chilled and mix until thoroughly blended and visibly sticky to ensure proper emulsification. Stickiness is a sign that the proteins have bound with the liquid in the meat and the emulsion is set. The result when cooked is juicy sausage that holds together because the fat won't render as readily.

Using a gram scale is certainly preferred. But since not everybody has one, I have included the amount of each ingredient in both weight and approximate volume measurements to use for 2 pounds (900 g) of ground pork.

You can cook the sausage as soon as it is mixed, but the flavor benefits from being refrigerated overnight. Raw sausage may be kept tightly sealed in the refrigerator for 3 to 4 days or in the freezer for several weeks. Portion bulk sausage into zip-top or vacuum sealer bags and flatten to a thickness of no more than ¾ inch (2 cm) before sealing for speedy freezing and thawing.

// *Yield: about 2 pounds (900 grams)*

- **RECOMMENDED SKILLET:** 12 inch (30 cm)
- **COOKING METHOD:** Pan-Frying

PERCENTAGE	AMOUNT FOR 2 POUNDS (900 G) OF GROUND PORK	
100%	900 grams/2.00 pounds	20 to 30% fat ground pork, broken up
1.75%	15.9 grams/0.56 ounces/2 tablespoons plus 1 teaspoon	kosher salt
1%	9.1 grams/0.32 ounces/1 tablespoon plus 1½ teaspoons	mi⬛⬛o ch⬛
1%	9.1 grams/0.32 ounces/1 tablespoon plus 1½ teaspoons	gu⬛⬛wder
0.2%	1.8 grams/0.06 ounces/¾ teaspoon	gr⬛
0.2%	1.8 grams/0.06 ounces/1 tablespoon plus 1 teaspoon	Mexican oregano
0.02%	0.2 grams/0.01 ounces/1/16 teaspoon	ground cloves
1%	9.1 grams/0.32 ounces/1 tablespoon plus 1 teaspoon	minced garlic
2%	18.2 grams/0.64 ounces/1 tablespoon plus 2 teaspoons	cider vinegar

TO COOK:
2 tablespoons (30 ml) canola oil

Whisk together the salt, New Mexico chile powder, guajillo chile powder, cumin, Mexican oregano, and ground cloves in a small bowl.

Place the pork into a stand mixer bowl, sprinkle with the salt mixture, garlic, and cider vinegar, fit onto the mixer with the paddle attachment, and mix on low speed until thoroughly blended and visibly sticky, about 2 minutes.

To cook crumbles, break the raw sausage into small bits. Preheat a cast iron skillet over medium-low to medium heat. Add the oil and swirl to coat the inside of the skillet. Add 12 to 16 ounces (340 to 455 g) broken-up sausage at a time and cook, stirring occasionally, until golden brown, 4 to 6 minutes for partially cooked and 6 to 10 minutes for completely cooked, depending on the final use.

To cook patties, divide the raw sausage into 3-ounce (85-g) portions and gently form each portion into a ball. Gently pat each ball into a 3¼-inch (19.5-cm) patty that's slightly thinner in the center and thicker around the edges; doing this prevents the patty from cooking up into a ball shape.

Preheat a cast iron skillet over medium-low heat. Add the oil and swirl to coat the inside of the skillet. Add 5 to 6 patties at a time and cook without disturbing until golden brown, 5 to 6 minutes. Flip the patties and cook until golden brown and just cooked through, 4 to 5 minutes. Moisture will pool on the surface of the patties and they will feel firm to the touch when they are just cooked through. Serve hot.

Biscuits & Sausage Gravy

Homemade Sage Breakfast Sausage (page 56) and homemade Buttermilk Biscuits (page 228) star in this version of the classic stick-to-your-ribs comfort food.

The amount of fat that renders from the sausage as it fries can vary slightly, so the flour needed to make the roux might need to be adjusted accordingly, give or take 1 tablespoon (8 g). Add enough flour to soak up the fat in the skillet. It shouldn't look greasy, and it shouldn't look too pasty either. This recipe results in a fairly thick savory, buttery gravy to coat the biscuits. You can alter the thickness to suit your taste by simmering it a little more or less time. If you find that it got too thick, simply whisk in a splash of milk to thin it out again. Store-bought sausage may be substituted for homemade. // *Yield: 4 to 6 servings*

- **RECOMMENDED SKILLET:** 12 inch (30 cm)
- **COOKING METHOD:** Pan-Frying/Simmering

2 ounces (4 tablespoons, or 55 g) unsalted butter, cut into 1-tablespoon (14-g) pieces
1 pound (455 g) uncooked Homemade Sage Breakfast Sausage (page 56), broken up
½ cup (63 g) all-purpose flour

1½ teaspoons freshly ground coarse black pepper
1 quart (946 ml) milk
Kosher salt
6 warm Buttermilk Biscuits (page 228)

Preheat a cast iron skillet over medium heat. Add the butter, swirl to coat the inside of the skillet, and heat until the butter is melted and the foam subsides. Add the sausage and cook, stirring occasionally, until golden brown but not necessarily cooked through, 5 to 6 minutes. Add the flour and slowly stir through until no dry flour remains and then add the pepper and stir through. Add the milk and bring to a boil, stirring constantly and scraping up the browned bits from the bottom of the skillet with a heatproof spatula. Simmer, stirring constantly, until thickened, 7 to 9 minutes. Season to taste with salt.

Using a serrated knife, cut the biscuits in half horizontally. Arrange the biscuits cut-side up on individual plates and top with the gravy. Serve immediately.

Homemade Mexican Chorizo & Egg Breakfast Tacos

In Texas, breakfast tacos are an institution. They're filled with scrambled eggs and bacon, steak, or my favorite, chile-laden chorizo, and enjoyed any time of day. The best ones are made with fresh flour tortillas and loaded with avocado slices and spicy salsa, though Tabasco makes a good substitute when there's no salsa on hand.

Store-bought chorizo and tortillas may be substituted for homemade. // *Yield: 4 servings*

- **RECOMMENDED SKILLET:** 12 inch (30 cm)

- **COOKING METHOD:** Pan-Frying

8 eggs
2 ounces (4 tablespoons, or 55 g)
    unsalted butter, cut into 1-tablespoon
    (14-g) pieces, divided
12 ounces (340 g) uncooked Homemade
    Mexican Chorizo (page 58), broken up
Kosher salt

8 warm Flour Tortillas (page 216)
4 ounces (115 g) shredded sharp cheddar
    (about 1 cup)
1 large avocado, thinly sliced
Charred Tomatillo Salsa (page 256) or other
    salsa or hot sauce, for serving

Lightly beat the eggs in a medium bowl.

Preheat a cast iron skillet over medium-low heat. Add 1 ounce (2 tablespoons, or 28 g) of the butter, swirl to coat the inside of the skillet, and heat until the butter is melted and the foam subsides. Add the chorizo and cook, stirring occasionally, until golden brown and cooked through, 7 to 8 minutes. Remove the chorizo to a bowl. Add the remaining 1 ounce (2 tablespoons, or 28 g) of butter to the skillet, swirl to coat the inside, and heat until the butter is melted and the foam subsides. Add the eggs and cook until scrambled but not dry, 2 to 3 minutes. Season to taste with salt. Return the chorizo to the skillet and stir through.

Arrange the tortillas on individual plates. Divide the egg mixture and then the cheese and avocado among them. Serve immediately with the salsa.

Over-Easy Egg, Bacon, Taleggio & Arugula Breakfast Sandwiches

This breakfast sandwich is a nice change of pace from the usual. It's actually a BLT of sorts, with peppery arugula subbing for the lettuce and tomatoes in the form of sundried tomato mayo. Taleggio, which is an Italian washed rind cheese, melts beautifully and holds the whole thing together.

Store-bought bacon may be substituted for homemade. // **Yield: 2 servings**

- **RECOMMENDED SKILLET:** 10¼ inch (26 cm)
- **COOKING METHOD:** Pan-Frying

2 halves sundried tomatoes
2 tablespoons (28 g) mayonnaise,
   preferably Best Foods
1 clove of garlic, grated on a Microplane
Kosher salt
4 thick-cut strips of Andrew's Uncured
   Bacon (page 51)
2 eggs

Freshly ground black pepper
2 ounces (55 g) taleggio, cut into
   ¼-inch (6-mm) thick slices
2 artisan-style ciabatta rolls,
   warmed and split
2 ounces (55 g) baby arugula
   (about 2 handfuls)

Place the sundried tomatoes in a medium bowl and add enough boiling water to cover. Let soak until rehydrated and pliable, 10 to 15 minutes. Drain the sundried tomatoes and blot dry on paper towels. Transfer to a cutting board and mince.

Mix together the mayonnaise, garlic, sundried tomatoes, and a generous pinch of salt in a medium bowl.

Preheat a cast iron skillet over medium-low heat. Add the bacon and fry, flipping occasionally, until golden brown, crispy, and rendered, 10 to 14 minutes. Remove the bacon to a paper towel–lined plate, let drain for a moment, and stack to keep warm. Add the eggs to the skillet one at a time, decrease the heat to low, season with salt and pepper, and fry until the whites are half set. Flip the eggs, top each one with a slice of the taleggio, cover the skillet, and fry until the whites are set, the yolks are still runny, and the taleggio is melted, about 2 minutes.

Arrange the ciabatta bottoms cut-side up on individual plates. Divide the sundried tomato mayo and then the eggs, bacon, and arugula among them and then top with the ciabatta tops cut-side down. Serve immediately.

Shakshuka

Shakshuka is a dish of eggs poached in a spicy tomato sauce. It's popular in the Middle East, North Africa, and around the Mediterranean. This version is warm with jalapeño and Aleppo pepper, which is available at Mediterranean and Middle Eastern markets, spice shops, and at most gourmet grocers.

Serve it for breakfast or at any time of day with plenty of warm pita bread. // *Yield: 2 servings*

- **RECOMMENDED SKILLET:** 10¼ inch (26 cm) plus lid

- **COOKING METHOD:** Simmering/Poaching

¼ cup (60 ml) extra virgin olive oil, divided
½ of a yellow onion, diced
1 jalapeño, minced
2 cloves of garlic, minced
1 tablespoon (3.6 g) Aleppo pepper
1 teaspoon ground cumin

1½ cups (368 g) Charred Tomato Sauce (page 257)
Kosher salt
4 eggs
3 tablespoons (3 g) minced cilantro
2 tablespoons (8 g) minced Italian parsley

Preheat a cast iron skillet over medium-low heat. Add 2 tablespoons (30 ml) of the olive oil and swirl to coat the inside of the skillet. Add the onion and sauté until soft, 4 to 5 minutes. Add the jalapeño and sauté until it begins to soften, about 1 minute. Add the garlic and stir through and then add the Aleppo pepper and cumin and stir through. Add the Charred Tomato Sauce, bring to a boil, and simmer until slightly thickened, 6 to 8 minutes. Season to taste with salt. Make 4 wells in the tomato sauce, crack an egg into each one, and season each egg with salt. Cover the skillet and simmer until the whites are nearly set and the yolks are still runny, 6 to 8 minutes. Drizzle with the remaining 2 tablespoons (30 ml) of olive oil and then sprinkle with the cilantro and parsley. Serve immediately.

DIY-CI Dark Roasted Coffee Beans

Please be aware that you must be extremely careful when roasting coffee. My resident science guy cautions, "You are essentially heating cellulose to just below its burning point." Coffee beans are flammable, so never, ever walk away from the stove while they're are on the heat. Smoke is generated during the roasting process and coffee bean skins, known as chaff, go everywhere, so consider doing it outdoors. Be prepared to remove the extremely hot beans from the skillet the moment they're done—spilling them onto a sheet tray will immediately arrest the cooking and allow for quick cooling, preventing any carryover cooking.

Coffee goes through various stages as it roasts. First, there's a drying stage during which time the beans go from green to yellow. Next is browning when most of the Maillard reactions, the chemical change in which proteins and sugars brown and take on distinctive caramelized flavors, take place. Then first crack and second crack occur. First crack sounds like popcorn popping while second crack is more of a crackling, and the beans expand noticeably. Finally come the various levels of dark roast, with Vienna being the lightest dark roast, followed by French, followed by Italian, which is nearly carbonized and extremely bitter. Start evaluating doneness shortly after you hear first and second crack, which happen in quick succession or even overlap when skillet roasting coffee. For a nice Vienna/light French roast, look for the beans to turn the shade of brown right between milk and dark chocolate.

Green coffee beans are available through a variety of mail order sources. My resident science guy, a.k.a. my resident coffee roaster, recommends Sweet Maria's at sweetmarias.com.

// **Yield: 6 to 7 ounces (170 to 200 g)**

- **RECOMMENDED SKILLET:** 9 inch (23 cm)
- **COOKING METHOD:** Toasting

8 ounces (225 g) green coffee beans

Place the coffee beans into a cast iron skillet. Place over medium-low heat and toast, stirring constantly, until the shade of brown between milk and dark chocolate, 3 to 5 minutes after the majority of the popping and crackling starts and about 21 to 22 minutes total. Immediately transfer to a sheet tray and let cool completely.

Take the pan of coffee outdoors and give it a little shake. The chaff will float away with the slightest breeze. Transfer to a container with a one-way valve to allow the coffee to degas and age for 3 to 4 days for the flavor to develop before brewing. Store in a tightly sealed container in the pantry for up to 3 weeks.

2

STARTERS AND SNACKS

French Onion Dip

Try this homemade dip once and you may never be able to eat the store-bought stuff again. It's simple to make, but caramelizing onions does take a bit of time. The flavors improve with time, so if at all possible, make it the day before you plan to serve it. Store in a tightly sealed container in the refrigerator for several days.

This classic dip is great with chips, of course, but it also makes a great topping for steak and spread for roast beef sandwiches. // *Yield: about 2 cups (320 g) or 6 to 8 servings*

- **RECOMMENDED SKILLET:** 10¼ inch (26 cm)
- **COOKING METHOD:** Sautéing

2 ounces (4 tablespoons, or 55 g)
    unsalted butter, cut into 1-tablespoon
    (14-g) pieces
2 yellow onions, diced
Kosher salt
1 small clove of garlic, minced, optional
¼ teaspoon minced fresh thyme

1 cup (230 g) sour cream
⅓ cup (75 g) mayonnaise, preferably
    Best Foods
Freshly squeezed juice of 1 lemon
¼ teaspoon Worcestershire sauce
Freshly ground black pepper

(continued)

Preheat a cast iron skillet over medium-low heat. Add the butter, swirl to coat the inside of the skillet, and heat until the butter is melted and the foam subsides. Add the onions and a generous pinch of salt and cook, stirring frequently, until the onions are golden brown, 55 to 60 minutes. Add the garlic, if desired, and stir through and then add the thyme and stir through. Transfer the onion mixture to a bowl and let cool slightly.

Mix together the sour cream, mayonnaise, lemon juice, Worcestershire sauce, and onion mixture in a medium bowl. Season to taste with salt and pepper. Serve chilled or at room temperature.

▶ Caramelized Onions

For golden-brown, deeply caramelized, sweet, and meltingly tender results, onions must be cooked low and slow. Yellow and sweet onions are best for caramelizing. Dice or julienne the onions uniformly for even cooking and keep in mind that what seems like a huge heap of raw onions will cook down considerably. One medium onion yields about ½ cup (80 g) caramelized onion. Cook the onions in an ample amount of oil and/or butter, about 2 tablespoons (30 ml or 28 g) per onion, and a generous pinch of salt in a cast iron skillet over medium-low heat, stirring often. You should hear a soft, slow sizzle for the duration of the cooking time. If you hear a lively sizzle, as in sautéing, turn the heat down slightly—the onions will burn before they caramelize if the heat is too high. At first, the onions will sweat, or exude moisture. Once most of the moisture cooks off, they will begin to brown. The color and flavor take time to develop. Caramelized onions can be prepared up to several days in advance and kept tightly sealed in the refrigerator.

Spicy Carnival Corn

Did you know that you can use your cast iron skillet to make popcorn? In another vessel, this would be known as kettle corn.

Once the popping starts, don't peek or remove the lid until it subsides or you'll have popcorn flying all over the place. Then, when the popping is more or less done, get the popcorn out of the skillet as quickly as you can to avoid the bits on the bottom getting too dark.

The best way to clean out any caramelized sugar left in the skillet is to simply melt it out. Add 1 to 2 cups (235 to 475 ml) of water and bring it to a boil—that's all there is to it.

// *Yield: about 2½ quarts (2.4 L) or 2 servings*

- **RECOMMENDED SKILLET:** 10¼ inch (26 cm) with lid
- **COOKING METHOD:** Pan-Frying

⅓ cup (53 g) popcorn kernels
3 tablespoons (39 g) sugar
¼ teaspoon kosher salt

Generous pinch of cayenne pepper,
  or to taste
3 tablespoons (45 ml) canola oil

Combine the popcorn kernels, sugar, salt, and cayenne in a medium bowl. Preheat a large cast iron skillet over medium heat. Add the oil and swirl to coat the inside of the skillet. Add the popcorn kernel mixture in more or less a single layer, cover the skillet, and cook, shaking constantly, for about 2 minutes. Remove the skillet from the heat and let the popping subside for about 1 minute. Immediately transfer to a bowl and serve warm.

Candied Nuts with Warm Spices

These sweet and savory nuts are delicious eaten out of hand or used as a topping for salad or dessert. They are especially delightful sprinkled over ice cream.

Nuts can go from perfect to burned very quickly, so start checking on them as soon as you begin to notice a toasted aroma. When they come out of the oven, the nuts will be coated with molten sugar, which will harden into a crispy candy coating as they cool.

Store in a tightly sealed container in the pantry for a week or more. // *Yield: about 3 cups (435 g) or 8 to 12 servings*

■ **RECOMMENDED SKILLET:** 12 inch (30 cm)

■ **COOKING METHOD:** Toasting

2 tablespoons (40 g) honey
½ ounce (1 tablespoon, or 14 g) unsalted butter
½ teaspoon ground cinnamon
Generous pinch of cayenne pepper
½ teaspoon kosher salt

½ teaspoon pure vanilla extract
½ cup (50 g) pecan halves
½ cup (50 g) walnut halves
½ cup (73 g) almonds
½ cup (62 g) unshelled pistachios
3 tablespoons (45 g) packed brown sugar

Preheat the oven to 350°F (180°C, or gas mark 4).

Place the honey and butter into a large cast iron skillet and melt over low heat. Add the cinnamon, cayenne, salt, and vanilla and stir through. Add the pecans, walnuts, almonds, pistachios, and brown sugar and stir through. Transfer the skillet to the oven and bake, stirring occasionally, until the nuts are dark golden brown and the bubbling subsides, 25 to 30 minutes.

Give the nuts one final stir and, working quickly, spread in a single layer on a parchment paper–lined sheet tray. Let cool to room temperature. Transfer to a bowl, breaking up clumps as desired, and serve.

Furikake Potato Chips

Furikake is a Japanese seasoning blend of nori, sugar, salt, MSG, and sometimes sesame seeds and bonito flakes. It is usually sprinkled on rice, and it happens to be great on potato chips too. I think of furikake as an umami bomb, and the MSG serves to heighten the savory flavor. Both nori flakes and MSG can be found at Asian markets. If you would rather avoid MSG, simply omit it from the recipe.

Potato slices that are not perfectly even are impossible to fry properly, and even the slightest difference in thickness matters. Unevenly sliced potatoes will turn out crispy on one side and flaccid on the other or else crispy on one side and burned on the other. So use a mandolin or possibly a food processor to make very thin and even slices.

Homemade chips are best enjoyed within hours of being made. // *Yield: 4 servings*

- **RECOMMENDED SKILLET:** Deep 10¼ inch (26 cm)*
- **COOKING METHOD:** Deep-Frying

1 teaspoon nori flakes
¼ teaspoon monosodium glutamate (MSG), optional
⅛ teaspoon sugar
1½ quarts (1.4 L) canola oil (enough to come to a depth of 1½ inches [3.5 cm])

2 medium russet potatoes (about 1¾ pounds [795 g] total), peeled, cut into ¹⁄₁₆-inch (2-mm) slices, rinsed until the water runs clear, drained, and dried thoroughly on paper towels
Kosher salt

Mix together the nori, MSG, if desired, and sugar in a small bowl.

Pour the oil into a deep cast iron skillet and preheat over medium-high heat, starting over medium heat, until it registers 350°F (180°C) on a candy/jelly/deep-fry thermometer. Add about one-quarter of the potatoes and fry at a lively sizzle, stirring occasionally, until floating, golden brown, and crispy, 4 to 5 minutes. Using a wire skimmer, remove the potato chips to a paper towel–lined sheet tray, let drain for a moment, and season with salt. Transfer the potatoes to a large bowl, sprinkle with about one-quarter of the nori mixture, toss to coat, and season to taste with salt. Reheat the oil and fry and season the remaining potatoes in 3 more batches in the same manner. Let cool completely before serving.

*This can also be made in a deep 12-inch (30-cm) cast iron skillet.

Baked Cheddar & Chorizo Jalapeño & Fresno Poppers

Pepper poppers, the popular bar snack, are usually filled with cream cheese and breaded and deep-fried. This version is filled with a mixture of cheddar, Monterey Jack, and chorizo and baked in the oven. It's easier to make, not quite as heavy, and the flavor of the chile comes through better. As much as I love all things fried, I daresay these are better!

Fresno chiles are similar to jalapeños, but they're red and have pointy ends and thinner flesh. If you cannot find them, simply use all jalapeños. Store-bought chorizo may be substituted for homemade.

It's a good idea to use gloves when seeding and stuffing the chiles to keep the capsaicin from getting on your skin and burning you. // *Yield: 6 to 8 servings*

■ **RECOMMENDED SKILLET:** 12 inch (30 cm)

■ **COOKING METHOD:** Baking

12 ounces (340 g) Homemade Mexican Chorizo (page 58), broken up and cooked

4 ounces (115 g) shredded sharp cheddar (about 1 cup)

4 ounces (115 g) shredded Monterey Jack (about 1 cup)

3 tablespoons (3 g) minced cilantro

¼ teaspoon ground cumin

8 jalapeños, stems left intact, halved, and seeded

8 Fresno chiles, stems left intact, halved, and seeded

Preheat the oven to 400°F (200°C, or gas mark 6).

Mix together the chorizo, cheddar, Monterey Jack, cilantro, and cumin in a large bowl. Stuff the chile halves with the cheese mixture, heaping it and packing it firmly. Arrange the poppers filling-side up in a tight single layer in a cast iron skillet and bake until the cheese is bubbling and the chiles begin to soften, 15 to 20 minutes.

Charred Lemon Caesar Salad with Radicchio, Hearts of Romaine & Garlic Croutes

Caesar salad is something I could eat every single day. I never tire of the classic, but I also like to do variations on the theme. This colorful version with radicchio, which is made crispy and juicy and sweet from an ice water soak, has become part of the regular rotation at my house. Charring the lemons for the dressing gives them a complexity of flavor with subtle caramelized, bitter, and floral notes.

We pair this salad most often with Pork Coppa Steaks with Aleppo Pepper & Oregano (page 112). It's also great as a main course topped with Perfect Seared Sea Scallops (page 126) or Blackened Salmon with Garlic Butter (page 139).

Use a vegetable peeler to shave the Parmigiano-Reggiano. // *Yield: 4 to 6 servings*

- **RECOMMENDED SKILLETS:** 10¼ inch (26 cm) plus 12 inch (30 cm)
- **COOKING METHOD:** Charring

1 head of radicchio (12 ounces, or 340 g), cut into bite-size pieces

½ cup (120 ml) plus 2 tablespoons (30 ml) extra virgin olive oil

3 large cloves of garlic, grated on a Microplane

½ of an artisan-style baguette, cut into ½-inch (1-cm) thick slices

Kosher salt

2 lemons, halved

2 egg yolks

2 teaspoons Dijon mustard

3 anchovy fillets, minced

⅛ teaspoon Worcestershire sauce

½ teaspoon freshly ground coarse black pepper, plus more to taste

2 hearts of romaine, cut into 1-inch (2.5-cm) strips

3 ounces (85 g) shaved Parmigiano-Reggiano (about 1 cup)

Preheat the oven to 400°F (200°C, or gas mark 6).

Soak the radicchio in a large bowl of ice water until the bitterness is drawn out, 40 to 50 minutes.

Meanwhile, whisk together 2 tablespoons (30 ml) of the olive oil and about one-quarter of the garlic in a small bowl. Using a pastry brush, brush the baguette slices lightly on both sides with the oil mixture and season with salt. Arrange in a single layer in a cast iron skillet, standing up a few slices along the edges of the skillet if necessary to make them fit. Bake, flipping once, until golden brown and crispy, 28 to 32 minutes. Let cool to room temperature.

Drain the radicchio and, using a salad spinner, dry thoroughly. Refrigerate until ready to use.

Preheat a cast iron skillet over medium-high heat, starting over medium heat. Add the lemons cut-side down and cook without disturbing until dark golden brown, 3 to 4 minutes. Transfer the lemons to a bowl and let cool slightly. Juice the lemons, add the juiced lemon halves to the juice cut-side down, and let them infuse until the juice is dark brown, 15 to 20 minutes. Remove the lemon halves, giving them a firm squeeze, and discard. Strain the juice through a coarse sieve to remove the seeds but not the pulp to yield about ¼ cup (60 ml).

Whisk together the egg yolks, Dijon mustard, anchovies, and the remaining three-quarters of the garlic in a medium bowl. Whisk in the remaining ½ cup (120 ml) of olive oil in a thin stream. Add the charred lemon juice, Worcestershire sauce, and black pepper and whisk until combined. Season to taste with salt.

Place the radicchio and romaine in a large bowl. Pour the dressing over top and toss to coat. Add the garlic croutes and toss through. Divide the salad among individual plates, top with the Parmigiano-Reggiano, and then sprinkle generously with pepper. Serve immediately.

Broiled Oysters with Chipotle & Lime

If you like raw oysters on the half shell, you will love these zesty broiled oysters. Their briny flavor is enhanced as they barely warm through while the buttered bread crumbs brown under the broiler.

Select larger oysters for this recipe if you have the option and cook them within a day or two of purchase. To store oysters, keep them covered with a moist towel in a colander of ice in a bowl in the refrigerator. // **Yield: 3 to 4 servings**

- **RECOMMENDED SKILLET:** 12 inch (30 cm)
- **COOKING METHOD:** Broiling

½ cup (25 g) panko bread crumbs
1 ounce (2 tablespoons, or 28 g)
    unsalted butter, melted
Kosher salt
12 oysters

1 cup (240 g) coarse salt
1 tablespoon (15 g) Chipotle Dipping Sauce
    (page 255)
Microplane-grated zest of 1 lime

Preheat the broiler.

Mix together the panko, butter, and a generous pinch of kosher salt in a medium bowl until thoroughly combined.

Spread the coarse salt evenly in a cast iron skillet. Shuck the oysters, being careful not to spill their juices, and nestle each one into the salt in the skillet as it's shucked to keep it level. Divide the Chipotle Dipping Sauce and then the lime zest among the oysters and then top with the panko mixture. Broil until the panko is golden brown, 3 to 4 minutes. Serve immediately.

Frisee aux Lardons

Frisee aux Lardons is a classic French salad of frisee with bacon and eggs. The bacon is fried until crispy and then the dressing is made right in the skillet with the drippings.

Traditionally, the eggs are poached. I've opted for softly fried sunny-side up eggs in this version since we're cooking in cast iron here!

Diced bacon may be substituted for Andrew's Insta-Lardons (page 54).

A fresh baguette is the perfect accompaniment for this salad. // **_Yield: 4 servings_**

- **RECOMMENDED SKILLET:** 10¼ inch (26 cm)
- **COOKING METHOD:** Pan-Frying

2 small heads of frisee (about 8 ounces, or 225 g total), torn into bite-size pieces
4 ounces (115 g) uncooked Andrew's Insta-Lardons (page 54)
1 shallot, minced
3 tablespoons (45 ml) extra virgin olive oil, divided

2 tablespoons (30 ml) red wine vinegar
1 teaspoon Dijon mustard
Kosher salt
Freshly ground black pepper
4 eggs
Flaky sea salt, such as fleur de sel or Maldon

Place the frisee in a large bowl and set aside.

Preheat a cast iron skillet over medium-low heat. Add the lardons and fry, stirring occasionally, until golden brown, crispy, and rendered, 8 to 10 minutes. Using a slotted spoon, remove the lardons to a bowl. Add the shallot to the skillet and sauté until it begins to soften, about 1 minute. Remove the skillet from the heat, add 2 tablespoons (30 ml) of the olive oil, the red wine vinegar, Dijon mustard, and a generous pinch of kosher salt and pepper, and whisk until combined. Pour the dressing over the frisee, add the lardons, and toss to coat.

Return the skillet to medium-low heat, add the remaining 1 tablespoon (15 ml) of olive oil, and swirl to coat the inside of the skillet. Add the eggs one at a time and fry until the whites are nearly set and the yolks are still runny, 2 to 3 minutes.

Divide the salad among individual plates, top with the fried eggs, and then sprinkle generously with sea salt and pepper. Serve immediately.

Hot Wings

These are true spicy and vinegary unbreaded Buffalo wings, complete with celery sticks and homemade blue cheese dressing for dipping.

Serve with Fresh Herb Ranch Dipping Sauce (page 254) for those w███████ke blue cheese. // *Yield: 4 servings*

- **RECOMMENDED SKILLET:** Deep 10¼ inch (26 cm)*
- **COOKING METHOD:** Deep-Frying

½ cup (115 g) sour cream
¼ cup (60 ml) buttermilk
2 ounces (55 g) blue cheese crumbles
(about ½ cup)
1 tablespoon (3 g) minced fresh chives
Kosher salt
Freshly ground black pepper
¼ cup (60 ml) Frank's RedHot sauce,
Tabasco sauce, or other hot sauce

1½ ounces (3 tablespoons, or 42 g)
unsalted butter, melted
1½ quarts (1.4 L) canola oil (enough to
come to a depth of 1½ inches [3.5 cm])
24 chicken wing flat and drumette pieces
(2 to 2¼ pounds, or 900 g to 1 kg total)
Kosher salt
Celery sticks, for serving

Whisk together the sour cream, buttermilk, blue cheese, and chives in a medium bowl. Season to taste with salt and pepper and set aside.

Whisk together the hot sauce and butter in a large bowl.

Pour the oil into a deep cast iron skillet and preheat over medium-high heat, starting over medium heat, until it registers 375°F (190°C) on a candy/jelly/deep-fry thermometer. Add 8 of the chicken wing pieces and fry at a lively sizzle, stirring occasionally, until floating, golden brown, crispy, and the meat shrinks away from the bones, 8 to 10 minutes. Using a wire skimmer, remove the chicken wings to a paper towel–lined sheet tray, let drain for a moment, and season with salt. Reheat the oil and fry the remaining chicken wings in 2 more batches of 8 in the same manner.

Add the chicken wings to the hot sauce mixture and toss to coat. Serve immediately with the celery sticks and blue cheese dipping sauce.

*This can also be made in a deep 12-inch (30-cm) cast iron skillet.

Scotch Eggs

Scotch eggs made with hard-cooked eggs can become dry when deep-fried. I think it's much more appealing to break one open and find a tender soft-cooked egg with a runny yolk. Of course, soft cooked-eggs are also quite a bit more challenging to enclose in sausage, so be gentle and take your time when preparing them.

If you prefer, moist hard-cooked eggs may be used instead of soft-boiled, and store-bought sausage may be substituted for homemade.

Serve with grainy mustard, Creamy Horseradish Sauce (page 253), Fresh Herb Ranch Dipping Sauce (page 254), or Buffalo Mayo (page 254). // *Yield: 6 Scotch Eggs or 6 servings*

- **RECOMMENDED SKILLET:** Deep 10¼ inch (26 cm)

- **COOKING METHOD:** Deep-Frying

6 eggs
2 tablespoons (16 g) all-purpose flour
⅔ cup (75 g) panko bread crumbs

1½ pounds (680 g) uncooked Homemade Sage Breakfast Sausage (page 56)
1½ quarts (1.4 L) canola oil (enough to come to a depth of 1½ inches [3.5 cm])

Pour enough water into a small sauce pot to come to a depth of 2 inches (5 cm) and bring to a boil. Gently add the eggs and cook at a bare simmer for 7 minutes for soft-cooked. Remove the eggs to a large bowl of ice water and let cool completely. Carefully peel the eggs.

Place the flour into a medium bowl and place the panko into another medium bowl. Divide the sausage into 6 (4-ounce [115 g]) portions and gently form each portion into a ball.

Using your fingertips, gently press 1 ball of the sausage into a broad cup shape. Roll 1 egg in the flour and, shaking off any excess, place the egg into the middle of the sausage. Gently form the sausage into an ovoid around the egg, making sure that it is completely enclosed. Roll the ovoid in the panko, patting so that it adheres. Place the Scotch egg onto a plate. Make 5 more Scotch eggs with the remaining eggs, flour, sausage, and panko in the same manner.

Pour the oil into a deep cast iron skillet and preheat over medium-high heat, starting over medium heat, until it registers 360°F (182°C) on a candy/jelly/deep-fry thermometer. Add 3 of the Scotch eggs and fry at a lively sizzle, stirring occasionally, until floating, golden brown, and the sausage is cooked through, 6 to 7 minutes. Using a wire skimmer, remove the Scotch eggs to a paper towel–lined sheet tray and let drain. Reheat the oil and fry the remaining Scotch eggs in 1 more batch of 3 in the same manner. Serve hot or at room temperature.

Seared Speck-Wrapped Soft Ripened Cheese

If you are a fan of baked Brie, chances are you'll like this take on cheese cooked until warm and oozy even better. Because crispy cured pork makes everything better!

Any soft ripened cheese, whether cow's, goat's, or sheep's milk, can be used, and prosciutto or Jamón Serrano can stand in for the speck. You can opt for petit wheels of cheese if you'd like to make individual portions, and to feed a crowd, simply use a larger wheel, adjusting the amount of ham as necessary. Fat from the pork will render as it cooks, making additional oil unnecessary.

Serve as an appetizer or first course with a baguette and a salad with an acidic vinaigrette.

// *Yield: 4 to 6 servings*

- **RECOMMENDED SKILLET:** 9 inch (23 cm)
- **COOKING METHOD:** Searing

2 ounces (55 g) paper-thin slices of speck

1 wheel (5.3 ounces, or 148 g) soft ripened cheese such as Brie or Camembert, at room temperature

Wrap the speck around the cheese, making sure the cheese is swaddled neatly and not peeking through anywhere.

Preheat a cast iron skillet over medium heat. Add the wrapped cheese and cook without disturbing until the speck is golden brown and rendered, 1 to 2 minutes. Using a spatula, flip the cheese and cook until the speck is golden brown and crispy, 1 to 2 minutes. Remove to a cutting board, cut into wedges and serve immediately.

Mozzarella-Stuffed Arancini

These deep-fried Italian rice fritters are so delicious, they're reason enough to cook up a big batch of Risotto Milanese with Peas & Prosciutto (page 220). To cool freshly cooked rice quickly and safely, spread it in a thin layer on a sheet tray and refrigerate after the steam has come off of it. Transfer it to a container and cover only after it is thoroughly chilled.

If you like, you can substitute regular mozzarella for the fresh. Serve with your choice of warm Charred Tomato Sauce (page 257) or traditional marinara sauce for dipping. // *Yield: 12 arancini or 6 servings*

- **RECOMMENDED SKILLET:** Deep 10¼ inch (26 cm)
- **COOKING METHOD:** Deep-Frying

3 cups (660 g) Risotto Milanese with Peas & Prosciutto, cold (page 220)
2 eggs
1½ cups (168 g) panko bread crumbs
1 ball (4 ounces, or 115 g) fresh mozzarella, cut into 12 equal sticks and drained thoroughly on paper towels

1½ quarts (1.4 L) canola oil (enough to come to a depth of 1½ inches [3.5 cm])
Kosher salt

Mix together the Risotto Milanese with Peas & Prosciutto and eggs in a large bowl. Place the panko into a medium bowl. Scoop out ¼ cup (55 g) of the risotto mixture, press 1 piece of the mozzarella into the middle of it, and gently form the risotto into an ovoid around the mozzarella, making sure that it is completely enclosed. Roll the ovoid in the panko, patting so that it adheres. Place the arancino onto a plate. Make more arancini with the remaining risotto mixture, mozzarella, and panko in the same manner.

Pour the oil into a deep cast iron skillet and preheat over medium heat until it registers 375°F (190°C) on a candy/jelly/deep-fry thermometer. Add 4 of the arancini and fry at a lively sizzle, stirring occasionally, until floating and golden brown, 4 to 5 minutes. Using a wire skimmer, remove the arancini to a paper towel–lined sheet tray, let drain for a moment, and season with salt. Reheat the oil and fry the remaining arancini in 2 more batches of 4 in the same manner. Serve hot.

Calamari with Charred Tomato Sauce

Calamari may be dredged in all-purpose flour, cornstarch, cornmeal, rice flour, or any number of other flours or meals. Personally, I like coarse-textured semolina, which is used to make most dried extruded pasta and couscous, for its rich flavor and the nice crunch it gives.

For the best results, dredge the squid just moments before the oil reaches frying temperature.

// *Yield: 4 servings*

- **RECOMMENDED SKILLET:** Deep 10¼ inch (26 cm)*
- **COOKING METHOD:** Deep-Frying

½ cup (38 g) semolina
⅓ cup (42 g) all-purpose flour
¾ teaspoon granulated garlic
Generous pinch of cayenne pepper
Kosher salt
Freshly ground black pepper
1½ quarts (1.4 L) canola oil (enough to come to a depth of 1½ inches [3.5 cm])

1 pound (455 g) squid tubes and tentacles, rinsed, drained, dried thoroughly on paper towels, and tubes cut crosswise into ½-inch (1-cm) pieces
Warm Charred Tomato Sauce, for serving (page 257)
1 lemon, cut into 8 wedges

Whisk together the semolina, flour, granulated garlic, cayenne, and several generous pinches of salt and pepper in a large bowl.

Pour the oil into a deep cast iron skillet and preheat over medium-high heat, starting over medium heat, until it registers 375°F (190°C) on a candy/jelly/deep-fry thermometer. Just before the oil comes to temperature, add about one-third of the squid to the seasoned flour and toss to coat, separating any pieces that stick together. Shake off any excess flour, add the dredged squid to the skillet, and fry at a lively sizzle, stirring occasionally, until floating, golden brown, and crispy, 1 to 2 minutes. Using a wire skimmer, remove the squid to a paper towel–lined sheet tray and let drain for a moment. Season to taste with salt. Reheat the oil and dredge and fry the remaining squid in 2 more batches in the same manner. Serve hot with the Charred Tomato Sauce and lemon wedges.

*This can also be made in a deep 12-inch (30-cm) cast iron skillet.

Fried Squash Blossoms

Zucchini squash blossoms have a delicate taste and texture and are absolutely delectable lightly battered and fried. And they're even better if they're stuffed with a morsel of cheese first.

If you've harvesting blossoms from your own garden, pick only the male blossoms, which have straight, slender stems, for cooking. Let the female blossoms, which have fatter, bulging stems, continue to grow and develop fruit. Use squash blossoms as soon as possible, preferably the same day they are harvested or purchased, as they are extremely perishable.

Since squash blossoms are so light and there's almost nothing to them, they float on the surface of the oil from the moment they are added to the skillet and they hardly make the temperature fall. So keep a close eye on the thermometer as you cook and decrease the heat if necessary. // *Yield: 4 to 6 servings*

- **RECOMMENDED SKILLET:** Deep 10¼ inch (26 cm)*
- **COOKING METHOD:** Deep-Frying

20 zucchini blossoms (about 6 ounces, or 170 g)
1 cup (125 g) all-purpose flour
Kosher salt
1 egg

¾ cup (175 ml) plus 1 tablespoon (15 ml) soda water
1½ quarts (1.4 L) canola oil (enough to come to a depth of 1½ inches [3.5 cm])

Trim the stems on the zucchini blossoms to about ½ inch (1 cm). Gently open the petals of each flower and reach inside and remove and discard the stamen.

Whisk together the flour and several generous pinches of salt in a medium bowl. Whisk together the egg and soda water in another medium bowl. Add the egg mixture to the flour mixture and whisk until smooth.

Pour the oil into a deep cast iron skillet and preheat over medium-high heat, starting over medium heat, until it registers 375°F (190°C) on a candy/jelly/deep-fry thermometer. Just before the oil comes to temperature and, working quickly, pick up 1 blossom by the stem, dip it into the batter to coat, gently drag it along the rim of the bowl to remove any excess, add it to the skillet, and repeat with 4 more zucchini blossoms for a batch of 5. Fry at a lively sizzle, flipping once or twice, until light golden brown and crispy, 3 to 4 minutes. Using a wire skimmer, remove the zucchini blossoms to a paper towel–lined sheet tray, let drain for a moment, and season with salt. Reheat the oil and batter and fry the remaining zucchini blossoms in 3 more batches of 5 in the same manner. Serve hot.

*This can also be made in a deep 12-inch (30-cm) cast iron skillet.

Mozzarella Stuffed Variation: Cut 5 ounces (140 g) of mozzarella cheese into 1 x ½ x ½-inch (2.5 x 1 x 1-cm) sticks. After removing each stamen, tuck 1 piece of the mozzarella all the way inside the blossom and gently twist the ends of the petals together to secure it.

Blistered Padron Peppers

If you've ever been to a Spanish restaurant, you've probably been introduced to this simple snack. It often appears alongside other tapas staples such as Jamón Serrano, Manchego cheese, pan con tomate, and patatas bravas. I like it as a first course with Mussels & Spanish Chorizo in Saffron Broth (page 160) or Fried Potatoes with Pulpo, Chistorra, Green Olives, Sunny-Side Up Eggs & Pimentón Mayo (page 162).

Padrones are a relatively mild variety of chile, but there's bound to be a spicy one hiding in every batch. They're increasing in popularity and therefore becoming easier to find. Look for them during their late summer/early fall season at farmers' markets and gourmet grocers. Milder Japanese shishito peppers may be given this blistering treatment as well. // *Yield: 4 servings*

- **RECOMMENDED SKILLET:** 10¼ inch (26 cm)
- **COOKING METHOD:** Searing

2 tablespoons (30 ml) extra virgin olive oil
6 ounces (170 g) padron peppers
(about 1 dry pint)

Flaky sea salt, such as fleur de sel
or Maldon

Preheat a cast iron skillet over medium heat. Add the olive oil and swirl to coat the inside of the skillet. Add the padrones and cook, stirring occasionally (about 3 times), until blistered and brown in spots and noticeably puffed, 4 to 5 minutes. Season generously with salt, transfer to a bowl, and serve immediately.

Potato Latkes

Latkes are a type of potato pancake traditionally served during Hanukkah, bu___ ___ a treat any time of year.

The best latkes are made from shredded potatoes that are just barely bou___ ___er. The irregular edges become extra crispy as they fry.

Latkes are often topped with sour cream and applesauce, but they also g___ ___ eggs, lox, or anything else you'd serve with hash browns or rösti. // *Yield: 24 latkes or 4 to 8 servings*

- **RECOMMENDED SKILLET:** 12 inch (30 cm)
- **COOKING METHOD:** Pan-Frying

3 large russet potatoes (about 2¼ pounds, or 1 kg total), peeled and shredded
1 yellow onion, julienned
2 eggs

¼ cup (31 g) all-purpose flour
2 teaspoons kosher salt, plus more to taste
½ cup (120 ml) canola oil

Place the shredded potatoes in the center of a clean kitchen towel. Gather the corners of the towel together over the potatoes and squeeze firmly to expel excess liquid. Transfer the potatoes to a large bowl. Add the onion and eggs and stir through. Add the flour and 2 teaspoons of salt and stir through.

Pour the oil into a cast iron skillet and preheat over medium heat until a shred of potato sizzles immediately when added. Scoop the potato mixture into the skillet by the loosely packed ¼ cup (55 g), spacing the latkes 2 inches (5 cm) apart and pressing them lightly with the bottom of the measuring cup to flatten slightly. Fry the latkes until golden brown, 5 to 6 minutes. Using a slotted spatula, flip the latkes and fry until golden brown and cooked through, 4 to 5 minutes. Remove the latkes to a paper towel–lined sheet tray, let drain for a moment, season with salt, and stack to keep warm. Fry the remaining potato mixture in the same manner, tipping the bowl as you scoop to avoid any accumulated liquid at the bottom.

Serve the latkes hot.

Falafel with Lemon-Yogurt Dipping Sauce

This is a highly flavored falafel that's crispy on the outside and light and fluffy within. Falafel must be fried until it is quite dark and the bubbling of the oil subsides or it will be too dense and heavy in the center.

Serve as a mezze or tuck inside warm pita bread along with chopped lettuce, tomatoes, cucumbers, and red onion. // *Yield: 12 falafel or 4 to 6 servings*

- **RECOMMENDED SKILLET:** Deep 10¼ inch (26 cm)*
- **COOKING METHOD:** Deep-Frying

1¼ cups (250 g) chickpeas, picked over, soaked in enough water to cover by 7 inches (18 cm) overnight, and drained
½ of a red onion, coarsely diced
4 cloves of garlic, sliced
¾ cup (12 g) packed coarsely chopped cilantro
½ cup (30 g) packed coarsely chopped Italian parsley
2 teaspoons ground cumin
1 teaspoon ground coriander

½ teaspoon cayenne pepper
1½ teaspoons kosher salt, plus more to taste
¼ cup (31 g) plus 2 tablespoons (16 g) all-purpose flour
1¼ teaspoons baking powder
1½ quarts (1.4 L) canola oil (enough to come to a depth of 1½ inches [3.5 cm])
Lemon-Yogurt Dipping Sauce (page 255), for serving

Combine the chickpeas, onion, garlic, cilantro, parsley, cumin, coriander, cayenne, and salt in a food processor and process until coarsely pureed. Add the flour and baking powder and process until thoroughly combined. Let rest for 20 to 30 minutes to allow the flour to hydrate.

Scoop the chickpea mixture by the scant ¼ cup (55 g), gently patting each scoop to flatten slightly into a patty, and place the falafel onto a sheet tray.

Pour the oil into a deep cast iron skillet and preheat over medium-high heat until it registers 350°F (180°C) on a candy/jelly/deep-fry thermometer. Add 6 of the falafel and fry at a lively sizzle, stirring occasionally, until floating and dark golden brown, 7 to 8 minutes. Using a wire skimmer, remove the falafel to a paper towel–lined sheet tray, let drain for a moment, and season with salt. Reheat the oil and fry the remaining falafel in 1 more batch of 6 in the same manner. Serve hot with the dipping sauce.

*This can also be made in a deep 12-inch (30-cm) cast iron skillet.

Potstickers with Spicy Soy Dipping Sauce

If you're a sucker for dumplings like I am, then it doesn't get any better than homemade pot-stickers with wrappers from scratch. Homemade noodle wrappers are toothsome and delicious and night and day better than store-bought ones. Making them does take a bit of time, but the firm noodle dough is easy to work with and super fun to roll out into circles. And it's quite satisfying to learn to wrap the potstickers and watch how your pleating and sealing technique improves with every single one that you make.

After they are filled and formed, potstickers are cooked by a quick multistep process in which they are pan-fried until golden brown, then steamed with a small amount of water, and finally after the water is reduced out completely, the bottoms are fried for a few moments longer to become crispy again.

Potstickers may be made in quantity and then frozen, uncooked, for future use. Place them in the freezer on a parchment paper–lined sheet tray and transfer them to a large zip-top bag after they are frozen solid. When you'd like to cook a few, there's no need to thaw them but you may have to increase the cooking time by a couple of minutes. // *Yield: 20 potstickers or 4 to 6 servings*

- **RECOMMENDED SKILLET:** 12 inch (30 cm) plus lid

- **COOKING METHOD:** Pan-Frying/Steaming

⅓ cup (80 ml) plus 1 tablespoon (15 ml)
   soy sauce, divided
1 tablespoon (15 ml) unseasoned
   rice vinegar
½ teaspoon dark sesame oil, divided
1 jalapeño, sliced
Kosher salt
8 ounces (225 g) napa cabbage, thinly sliced
   (about ½ small head)
8 ounces (225 g) 20% fat ground pork
4 ounces (115 g) large (26 to 30 count)
   shrimp, peeled, deveined, and minced

2 large cloves of garlic, minced
2 teaspoons minced ginger
1 green onion, thinly sliced
1½ teaspoons cornstarch, plus more
   for dusting
¼ teaspoon sugar
Pinch of freshly ground white pepper
1⅔ (208 g) cups all-purpose flour,
   plus more for dusting
3 tablespoons (45 ml) canola oil

Mix together ⅓ cup (80 ml) of the soy sauce, rice vinegar, ¼ teaspoon of the sesame oil, and jalapeño in a small bowl.

(continued)

Pour about 3 quarts (2.8 L) of water into a large saucepot, bring to a boil, and add several generous pinches of salt. Add the cabbage and boil until tender, 3 to 4 minutes. Drain the cabbage, transfer to a large bowl of ice water to stop the cooking, and let cool completely. Drain the cabbage and transfer to a clean kitchen towel. Gather the corners of the towel together over the cabbage and squeeze firmly to expel excess water.

Mix together the cabbage, ground pork, shrimp, garlic, ginger, green onion, cornstarch, sugar, remaining 1 tablespoon (15 ml) soy sauce, remaining ¼ teaspoon sesame oil, and white pepper in a large bowl until thoroughly combined. Cover and refrigerate until ready to use.

Whisk together the flour and a pinch of salt in a medium bowl. Add ¼ cup (60 ml) plus 1 tablespoon (15 ml) boiling water and, using chopsticks, stir through. Add 3 table-spoons (45 ml) room-temperature water and mix until all of the flour is moistened and the dough is cool enough to handle. Then, knead for a minute or two until smooth and elastic. The dough will be quite firm. Cover and let rest for 10 to 15 minutes.

Cut the dough in half. Keeping the remaining dough covered as you work, roll 1 portion of dough into a 1-inch (2.5-cm) thick rope. Cut the rope into 10 equal pieces. Place 1 piece of the dough cut-side up onto a lightly floured surface and, with the palm of your hand, press flat. Using a small rolling pin, roll the dough to a 3¼-inch (8-cm) wide circle that's slightly thicker in the center and thinner around the edges. Dust the circle lightly with cornstarch. Make more circles with the remaining dough in the same man-ner. As you work, stack the wrappers neatly to keep them from drying out.

Place 1 heaping tablespoon (15 g) of the pork mixture into the center of 1 of the wrap-pers. Using a fingertip, lightly moisten the edges of the wrapper with water. Fold the wrapper in half over the filling, forming a half circle. Firmly pinch the edges together to seal, making 6 to 7 pleats in 1 side of the wrapper and pressing to eliminate any air pockets as you go. Make more potstickers with the remaining wrappers and pork mix-ture in the same manner. As you work, place the potstickers seam-side up on a clean kitchen towel–lined sheet tray.

Preheat a cast iron skillet over medium heat. Add the canola oil and swirl to coat the inside of the skillet. Add the potstickers seam-side up and cook without disturbing until golden brown and crispy, 3 to 4 minutes. Add ½ cup (120 ml) of water, bring to a boil, cover the skillet, and simmer until cooked through, 3 to 4 minutes. The potsticker filling will feel firm to the touch when they are cooked through. Adjust the heat to medium-low and cook until dry and the bottoms re-crisp, 1 to 2 minutes. Serve immediately with the dipping sauce.

Chinese Flaky Green Onion Pancakes

This dim sum favorite may be known as a pancake but in truth it's more akin to a flatbread. It's made with a hot-water dough and a rolling process that results in many thin layers of dough and oil sandwiched together. The result is at once flaky, crispy, chewy, and absolutely irresistible, addictive even.

If all that sounds complicated, don't be fooled. This is in fact one of my favorite snacks to whip up on a whim. All of the steps in the procedure are quick and easy and fun to do once you get the hang of it. As long as you know that the ratio is 2 parts flour and 1 part boiling water by volume, you don't even have to measure any of the ingredients except for the flour and water for the dough. Just take care to slice the green onion very thinly, as chunky pieces will tear through the dough. // *Yield: 6 pancakes or 4 servings*

- **RECOMMENDED SKILLET:** 9 inch (23 cm)

- **COOKING METHOD:** Pan-Frying

1 cup (125 g) plus ½ teaspoon all-purpose
   flour, divided, plus more for dusting
Kosher salt
½ cup (60 ml) boiling water

1 tablespoon (15 ml) dark sesame oil
2 large green onions, thinly sliced
¼ cup (60 ml) canola oil
Soy sauce, for serving

Whisk together 1 cup (125 ml) of the flour and a pinch of salt in a medium bowl. Add boiling water and, using the chopsticks, mix until all of the flour is moistened and the dough is cool enough to handle. Then, knead for a minute or two until smooth and elastic. The dough will be somewhat sticky. Cover and let rest for 10 to 15 minutes.

Meanwhile, mix together the sesame oil and ½ teaspoon of the flour in a small bowl.

Cut the dough into sixths and form each portion into a ball. Using a small rolling pin, roll out 1 ball of dough to a 6- to 7-inch (15- to 18-cm) wide circle on a lightly floured surface. Stir the sesame oil mixture to recombine, drizzle about ½ teaspoon over the dough circle, and spread it evenly with the back of a spoon, leaving a ¼-inch (6-mm) border at the edge. Sprinkle over about one-sixth of the green onion. Roll up the dough circle like a jelly roll. Then, coil up the roll like a snake. Tuck the outer end of the roll under the coil to secure it and then press down on the coil lightly with the palm of your hand to create a disc. Make more discs with the remaining dough, sesame oil mixture, and green onions in the same manner.

Roll the discs out in the same order as you made them: Using a small rolling pin, roll out each disc to a 6- to 7-inch (15- to 18-cm) wide pancake on a lightly floured surface. As you work, stack the pancakes, shaking off any excess flour, on a plate between sheets of parchment paper to keep them from sticking to each other.

Fry the pancakes in the same order as you rolled them: Preheat a cast iron skillet over medium-low heat. Add about 2 teaspoons of the canola oil and swirl to coat the inside of the skillet. Add 1 pancake and fry without disturbing until golden brown, about 1 minute. Using a spatula, flip the pancake and fry, pressing down on it lightly with the back of the spatula, until golden brown and crispy, about 1 minute. Remove the pancake to a cutting board and tent loosely with foil to keep warm. Fry the remaining pancakes with the remaining oil in the same manner.

Cut the pancakes into wedges and serve immediately with soy sauce for dipping.

Green Onion-Cilantro Variation: Substitute 2 tablespoons (2 g) chopped cilantro leaves for one of the green onions. Mix the cilantro and green onion together.

3

MAINS

Inside-Out Grilled Cheese Sandwiches

Who doesn't love the puddle of cheese that oozes out from between the slices of bread, hits the pan, and gets all crunchy and brown? Some say that is actually the best part. Well, this sandwich, which is a sort of mash-up between the fried cheese chips known as frico and a regular grilled cheese, is all about those crunchy cheese bits.

Building these sandwiches directly in the hot skillet seems to be the easiest way to keep the cheese from getting all over the place, just be careful not to burn your knuckles as you do it.

// *Yield: 2 servings*

- **RECOMMENDED SKILLET:** 10¼ inch (26 cm)
- **COOKING METHOD:** Pan-Frying

4 slices of artisan-style white bread
2 ounces (4 tablespoons, or 55 g) butter, softened

1½ ounces (42 g) shredded Parmigiano-Reggiano (about ¼ cup plus 2 tablespoons)
4 ounces (115 g) shredded sharp cheddar (about 1 cup)

Spread 1 side of each of the slices of bread with the butter. Place the Parmigiano-Reggiano into a shallow dish and press each of the buttered slices of bread into it buttered-side down, patting so that it adheres.

Preheat a cast iron skillet over medium-low heat. Add 2 slices of the Parmigiano-Reggiano–coated bread, cheese-side down. Divide the cheddar among them and then top with the remaining 2 slices of Parmigiano-Reggiano–coated bread, cheese-side up. Fry until golden brown, 3 to 4 minutes. Flip the sandwiches and fry until golden brown and the cheese is melted, 2 to 3 minutes. Serve immediately.

Cotswold Variation: Substitute Cotswold for the cheddar.

Cacio e Pepe Variation: Substitute Pecorino Romano for half of the Parmigiano-Reggiano and add ½ teaspoon of freshly ground coarse black pepper. Mix together the Parmigiano-Reggiano, Pecorino Romano, and pepper. Substitute 2 ounces (55 g) of sharp provolone plus 2 ounces (55 g) of mozzarella for the cheddar.

Garlic-Rubbed Heirloom Tomato Melts

These are not your average tomato melts. Using the very best tomatoes along with a combination of sharp provolone and cheddar and rubbing the bread with raw garlic once it's toasted elevates the classic sandwich to new heights. This is my personal favorite quick hot lunch in the summertime, and perhaps it will become yours too. // *Yield: 2 servings*

- **RECOMMENDED SKILLET:** 10¼ inch (26 cm)

- **COOKING METHOD:** Pan-Frying

4 slices of artisan-style white bread
1 ounce (2 tablespoons, or 28 g) butter, softened
2½ ounces (70 g) sliced sharp provolone

1 large (about 5 ounces, or 140 g) heirloom tomato, sliced
2½ ounces (70 g) sliced sharp cheddar
1 clove of garlic

Spread 1 side of each of the slices of bread with the butter. Place 2 slices of the bread buttered-side down. Divide the provolone, then the tomatoes, and then the cheddar among them. Top with the remaining 2 slices of bread, buttered-side up.

Preheat a cast iron skillet over medium-low heat. Add the sandwiches and fry until golden brown, 4 to 5 minutes. Flip the sandwiches and fry until golden brown and the cheese is melted, 2 to 3 minutes. Remove the sandwiches from the skillet and rub all over with the garlic clove. Serve immediately.

Lucy's Ultimate Five-Cheese Stovetop Mac & Cheese

When I imagine my perfect homemade comfort food macaroni and cheese, the kid in me thinks of a boldly flavored cheese sauce that's both velvety and melty, gooey, and stringy. The adult in me thinks of an effortless recipe that's a cinch to throw together on a whim with ingredients that are always on hand.

Unfortunately, most recipes don't live up to these expectations. Macaroni and cheese made with roux-based béchamel doesn't quite do it for me because it tastes more like the white sauce than the cheese, no matter how fine the ingredients and expert the execution. It doesn't have the right creaminess either. Besides all that, why should a dish so humble require at least 45 minutes, the use of both the stovetop and the oven, and the dirtying of two pots, a colander, and a baking dish?

I got to thinking . . . Why drain the cooked pasta, losing all its precious starch, just to use a different starch to thicken the sauce? Why not take advantage of the pasta's own starch for thickening the sauce? And why not cook macaroni and cheese in a broad skillet more like it was risotto, adding only as much liquid as the pasta will absorb?

Thus, my ultimate macaroni and cheese was born. The texture and flavor are exactly what I crave, and it requires little more time or effort than the boxed stuff. Using the pasta's own starch rather than a béchamel to thicken the cheese sauce means that this mac and cheese can be done with just one skillet and that there's no roux to mask the flavor of the cheese. Oh, and leftovers, should there be any, reheat nicely in the microwave. I think you'll agree it really is the ultimate.

Constant stirring ensures a creamy sauce and evenly cooked pasta. By the end of the cooking time there should be enough sauce in the skillet to just cover the macaroni—cook over higher heat if there seems to be too much sauce or stir in a bit more water if there seems to be too little, keeping in mind that the cheese will thicken the sauce considerably.

The quality of the macaroni itself makes a big difference in the texture and taste of this dish.

If possible, select a good pasta imported from Italy. Cheap shiny and translucent pasta is extruded quickly and dried at relatively high temperatures, which practically precooks the starch in the pasta and results in a thin sauce. I have had good luck with Whole Foods 365 Everyday Value macaroni.

Packaged pre-shredded cheeses cost a premium and contain anti-caking agents such as cellulose, so shred the cheeses yourself. If you don't have the time or inclination for shredding, you can also use deli sliced cheese, which will melt into the sauce nearly as well as shredded. I often use this shortcut myself. Incorporate the cheese off the heat. Do not boil the mixture once the cheese has been added, or it will have a grainy texture. Feel free to experiment with other good melting cheeses, including blue or feta, or keep it simple and use all cheddar.

Top this macaroni and cheese with toasted buttered bread crumbs or some such crunchy thing if you must, but I prefer to appreciate the creaminess unspoiled. // *Yield: 6 servings*

(continued)

- **RECOMMENDED SKILLET:** 12 inch (30 cm)
- **COOKING METHOD:** Simmering

1 pound (455 g) elbow macaroni
1 quart (946 ml) m▉▉▉
2 ounces (4 tables▉▉▉▉▉ 5 g)
    unsalted butte▉
¼ teaspoon must▉
Generous pinch o▉▉▉▉d garlic
Generous pinch of cayenne pepper
6 ounces (170 g) shredded sharp
    yellow cheddar (about 1½ cups)
2 ounces (55 g) shredded sharp provolone
    (about ⅔ cup)

2 ounces (55 g) shredded mozzarella
    (about ⅔ cup)
2 ounces (55 g) shredded sharp Swiss
    (about ⅔ cup)
2 ounces (55 g) shredded Parmigiano-
    Reggiano (about ½ cup)
½ teaspoon Worcestershire sauce
1½ teaspoons Tabasco sauce
Kosher salt
Freshly ground black pepper

Combine the macaroni, milk, butter, mustard powder, granulated garlic, cayenne, and 3 cups (700 ml) of water in a cast iron skillet. Bring to a boil, stirring constantly. Cook at a lively simmer, stirring constantly, until the sauce is thickened and the macaroni is nearly al dente, 7 to 8 minutes. Remove the skillet from the heat and let the bubbling subside. Add the cheddar, provolone, mozzarella, Swiss, Parmigiano-Reggiano, Worcestershire sauce, and Tabasco and stir through. Season to taste with salt and pepper and serve immediately.

Skillet-Roasted Chicken Breasts with Sherry Sauce

Banish dry white meat forever by using bone-in, skin-on chicken breasts and this technique. Starting them on the stovetop yields crispy, golden-brown skin, while finishing them in the oven results in juicy and succulent flesh. Then, deglazing the skillet with sherry builds a simple yet rich and flavorful sauce.

    I recommend using a digital probe thermometer inserted into the thickest part of the chicken breasts to allow you to monitor the internal temperature throughout the cooking process. It's the best way to guarantee the perfect doneness every single time. // *Yield: 4 to 8 servings*

- **RECOMMENDED SKILLET:** 12 inch (30 cm)
- **COOKING METHOD:** Pan-Roasting/Deglazing

6 large bone-in, skin-on chicken breasts
    (about 4 pounds, or 1.8 kg total)
Kosher salt
Freshly ground black pepper
3 tablespoons (45 ml) extra virgin olive oil
4 large cloves of garlic
4 sprigs of rosemary

4 sprigs of thyme
⅓ cup (80 ml) dry sherry
1 cup (235 ml) chicken stock
2 ounces (4 tablespoons, or 55 g)
    unsalted butter, cut into 1-tablespoon
    (14-g) pieces
1½ teaspoons sherry vinegar

Season the chicken breasts generously with salt and pepper and set aside at room temperature for about an hour.

Preheat the oven to 450°F (230°C, or gas mark 8).

Preheat a cast iron skillet over medium-high heat, starting over medium heat. Add the olive oil and swirl to coat the inside of the skillet. Add the chicken breasts skin-side down and cook without disturbing until golden brown and crispy, 8 to 10 minutes. Flip the chicken breasts and add the garlic, rosemary, and thyme all around them. Transfer the skillet to the oven and bake until the chicken breasts are nearly cooked through, 30 to 35 minutes. The chicken breasts will feel firm to the touch and a meat thermometer will register 160°F (71°C) when they are nearly cooked through. Remove the chicken breasts and garlic to a platter and tent loosely with foil to carry over to 165°F (74°C). Pour off all of the accumulated fat from the skillet.

Transfer the skillet back to the stovetop. Add the sherry, bring to a boil, and simmer, scraping up the browned bits from the bottom of the skillet with a heatproof spatula, until thickened slightly, about 2 minutes. Add the chicken stock and simmer until thickened slightly, 6 to 7 minutes. Remove the skillet from the heat and let the bubbling subside. Add the butter, sherry vinegar, and any accumulated chicken juices and whisk until smooth. Season to taste with salt and pepper and strain through a fine-mesh sieve.

Carve the chicken breasts against the grain as desired and serve immediately with the sauce and garlic.

Chicken-Fried Chicken Biscuit Sandwiches

Fried chicken on a biscuit has been all the rage in restaurants lately but going out for them often means an hour-long line to get seated for brunch. Here's a recipe so that you can get your fix whenever you want without the wait. Serve these biscuit sandwiches for any meal of the day and vary them as you like. Feel free to skip the pickles, lettuce, tomato, and mayo in favor of a drizzle of warm honey or a smear of Jalapeño-Maple Butter (page 47). Or, go all out and top them with a sunny-side up egg and Sausage Gravy (page 60). If you prefer dark meat chicken, go ahead and substitute boneless, skinless thighs for the breasts.

For the best results, dredge the chicken just moments before the oil reaches frying temperature.

// *Yield: 6 servings*

- **RECOMMENDED SKILLET:** Deep 10¼ inch (26 cm)
- **COOKING METHOD:** Deep-Frying

3 boneless, skinless chicken breasts
    (10 to 12 ounces, or 280 to 340 g)
¾ cup (175 ml) buttermilk
1 teaspoon granulated garlic
¼ teaspoon cayenne pepper
Kosher salt
1¼ cups (156 g) all-purpose flour

1½ quarts (1.4 L) canola oil (enough to
    come to a depth of 1½ inches [3.5 cm])
6 warm Buttermilk Biscuits (page 228)
Buffalo Mayo (page 254), for serving
Sliced tomatoes, for serving
Sliced pickles, for serving
Iceberg lettuce leaves, for serving

Gently pound out the chicken breasts to an even thickness of ¾ inch (2 cm) with a flat meat pounder and cut each breast into 2 equal portions.

Mix together the buttermilk, granulated garlic, cayenne, and a generous pinch of salt in a 1-gallon (3.8-L) zip-top bag. Add the chicken and turn to coat. Seal the bag, letting out all the air. Marinate 4 to 6 hours in the refrigerator.

Whisk together the flour and several generous pinches of salt in a shallow dish. Drizzle 1 to 2 teaspoons of the buttermilk marinade into the flour and stir through.

Pour the oil into a deep cast iron skillet and preheat over medium-high heat, starting over medium heat, until it registers 375°F (190°C) on a candy/jelly/deep-fry thermometer. Just before the oil comes to temperature and, working quickly, shake off any excess buttermilk from 1 piece of chicken and roll it in the seasoned flour to coat, patting so that it adheres. Shake off any excess flour, add the dredged chicken to the skillet, and repeat with 2 more of the chicken pieces for a batch of 3. Fry at a lively sizzle, stirring occasionally, until the chicken begins to float and is dark golden brown, crispy, and cooked through, 8 to 10 minutes. Using a wire skimmer, remove the chicken to a paper towel–lined sheet tray, let drain for a moment, and season with salt. Reheat the oil and dredge and fry the remaining chicken pieces in 1 more batch of 3 in the same manner.

Using a serrated knife, cut the biscuits in half horizontally. Arrange the biscuit bottoms cut-side up on individual plates. Divide the Buffalo Mayo, chicken, tomatoes, pickles, and lettuce among them and then top with the biscuit tops cut-side down. Serve immediately.

Chicken & Wild Mushroom Potpie with Biscuit Topping

Here's a potpie with plenty of tender biscuit topping to sop up the saucy filling. Make it with torn chanterelle, hedgehog, maitake, or oyster mushrooms in the fall or use morels cut into wedges in the springtime. You can even substitute sliced shiitake, button, or cremini mushrooms from the grocery store when wild mushrooms are unavailable. // *Yield: 4 servings*

- **RECOMMENDED SKILLET:** 10¼ inch (26 cm)
- **COOKING METHOD:** Simmering/Baking

2 ounces (4 tablespoons, or 55 g) unsalted butter, cut into 1-tablespoon (14-g) pieces, plus 4 ounces (1 stick, or 115 g), cold, divided

8 ounces (225 g) wild mushrooms, torn or cut into bite-size pieces depending on the mushroom

3 shallots, sliced

1 clove of garlic, minced

2 cups (250 g) plus 2 tablespoons (16 g) all-purpose flour, divided

1⅔ cups (395 ml) chicken stock

2 tablespoons (30 ml) dry sherry

2 tablespoons (30 ml) cream

3 sprigs of thyme

12 ounces (340 g) shredded cooked chicken (about 3 cups packed)

½ cup (65 g) frozen peas, thawed

Kosher salt

Freshly ground black pepper

1 tablespoon (14 g) baking powder

1¼ cups (295 ml) buttermilk, cold

(continued)

Preheat a cast iron skillet over medium-high heat, starting over medium heat. Add 1 ounce (2 tablespoons, or 28 g) of the butter, swirl to coat the inside of the skillet, and heat until the butter is melted and the foam subsides. Add the mushrooms and cook, stirring once or twice, until golden brown and soft, 5 to 6 minutes. Add the shallots and cook until they begin to soften, about 1 minute. Add the garlic and stir through. Decrease the heat to medium-low, add 1 ounce (2 tablespoons, or 28 g) of the butter, and stir through. Add 2 tablespoons (16 g) of the flour and slowly stir through until no dry flour remains. Add the chicken stock, sherry, cream, and thyme and bring to a boil, stirring constantly and scraping up the browned bits from the bottom of the skillet with a heatproof spatula. Simmer, stirring frequently, until thickened slightly, 6 to 7 minutes. Remove the skillet from the heat and remove and discard the thyme. Add the chicken and peas and stir through. Season to taste with salt and pepper and spread evenly in the skillet.

Preheat the oven to 425°F (220°C, or gas mark 7).

Whisk together the remaining 2 cups (250 g) of flour, baking powder, and ¾ teaspoon kosher salt in a large bowl.

Working quickly and with a light touch to prevent the butter from melting, shred the 4 ounces (1 stick, or 115 g) of cold butter into the flour mixture. Stir through and, using your fingertips, rub the butter into the flour until the mixture resembles coarse crumbs. Add the buttermilk and, using a spoon, stir just until a sticky dough forms and all of the ingredients are moistened. Scoop the dough onto the filling in the skillet by the heaping tablespoon (15 g), spacing it evenly. Bake until the filling is bubbling around the edges and the biscuit topping is light golden brown, 25 to 30 minutes. Serve hot.

Chicken Thighs with Lemon & Green Olives

This saucy and boldly flavored dish is delicious served on a bed of pastina—orzo is a favorite choice at my house.

Castelvetrano olives, which are plump and meaty with a buttery flavor and available from the olive bar at many grocers, are an excellent choice here, as are Meyer lemons when they're in season. // *Yield: 6 servings*

- **RECOMMENDED SKILLET:** 12 inch (30 cm)
- **COOKING METHOD:** Braising

6 large bone-in, skin-on chicken thighs
   (about 3 pounds, or 1.3 kg total)
Kosher salt
Freshly ground black pepper
2 tablespoons (30 ml) extra virgin olive oil
2 large shallots, sliced
⅔ cup (160 ml) chicken stock

½ cup (50 g) pitted and quartered
   green olives
2 sprigs of rosemary
½ large lemon, cut into 6 thin slices
   and seeds removed
2 tablespoons (8 g) minced Italian parsley
Freshly squeezed juice of ½ of a large lemon

Season the chicken thighs generously with salt and pepper and set aside at room temperature for about an hour.

Preheat a cast iron skillet over medium-high heat, starting over medium heat. Add the olive oil and swirl to coat the inside of the skillet. Add the chicken thighs skin-side down and cook without disturbing until golden brown and crispy, 8 to 10 minutes. Flip the chicken thighs, add the shallots all around them, and cook until the shallots begin to soften, about 1 minute. Add the chicken stock, olives, and rosemary all around the chicken thighs and bring to a boil. Top each chicken thigh with a slice of the lemon, cover the skillet, and simmer until the chicken is cooked through and tender, 14 to 18 minutes. A paring knife inserted in the center of a chicken thigh will meet no resistance when it is done. Remove the chicken thighs to a platter and tent loosely with foil to keep warm.

Simmer the sauce until thickened slightly, 6 to 8 minutes. Remove and discard the rosemary. Add the parsley, lemon juice, and any accumulated chicken juices and stir through and season to taste with salt and pepper. Serve the chicken thighs immediately with the sauce.

(continued)

Tangerine & Black Olive Variation: Substitute Kalamata olives for the green olives, tangerine slices for the lemon slices, and the juice of 1 small tangerine for the lemon juice.

▶ Pitting Olives

You don't need a special tool to pit olives. Smash each whole olive with the side of a knife just enough to loosen the flesh from around the pit. Then, simply pop out the pit. It's easy, and it doesn't take much time to pit 1 to 2 cups of olives (100 to 200 g) in this manner for a recipe.

Spicy Game Hen Under a Brick with Tomato-Garlic Hot Sauce

Pounding a spatchcocked game hen flat and then cooking it under a press maximizes the surface area of the bird in contact with the cast iron skillet and therefore the amount of golden-brown and delicious skin when it's done.

To spatchcock a game hen, place the bird in a "seated position" on a cutting board and, using a sharp boning knife, cut down on either side of the backbone to remove it, reserving it to make stock. Then, simply lay the bird flat.

If you don't have a press, use an 8- or 9-inch (20- to 23-cm) cast iron skillet or a clean brick or heavy rock wrapped in several layers of foil. // *Yield: 2 servings*

- **RECOMMENDED SKILLET:** 12 inch (30 cm) with press
- **COOKING METHOD:** Searing

½ cup (125 g) Charred Tomato Sauce (page 257) or 4 ounces (55 g) of tomato sauce
1¼ teaspoons cayenne pepper, divided
1¼ teaspoons freshly ground black pepper, divided
Kosher salt

1 game hen (1½ pounds, or 680 g), spatchcocked and patted dry
10 cloves of garlic, sliced, plus 2 cloves, minced
¼ cup (60 ml) canola oil
2 tablespoons (2 g) minced cilantro

(continued)

Combine the tomato sauce, ¼ teaspoon of the cayenne, and ¼ teaspoon of the pepper in a small saucepan. Bring to a boil, remove the saucepan from the heat, and add the minced garlic and stir through. Season to taste with salt and let cool completely.

Meanwhile, mix together the remaining 1 teaspoon of cayenne and 1 teaspoon of pepper in a small bowl. Pound out the game hen, flattening the joints, to an even thickness of 1¼ inches [3 cm] with a flat meat pounder. Season generously with salt and sprinkle evenly with the cayenne mixture on both sides. Transfer the game hen to a 1-gallon (3.8-L) zip-top bag and scatter the sliced garlic over both sides of the game hen. Seal the bag, letting out all the air. Marinate the game hen in the refrigerator and refrigerate the tomato sauce for the flavors to come together 8 hours to overnight.

Remove and discard the garlic from the game hen and set the game hen aside at room temperature for about an hour.

Preheat a cast iron skillet over medium-low heat. Add the oil and swirl to coat the inside of the skillet. Add the game hen skin-side down, top it with a heavy press, and cook without disturbing until dark golden brown, crispy, and nearly cooked through, 12 to 14 minutes. Flip the game hen and cook until cooked through, 4 to 5 minutes. The breasts will feel firm to the touch and the meat of the drumsticks will pull away from the knuckles when the game hen is cooked through. Remove the game hen to a platter, tent loosely with foil to keep warm, and let rest for 5 to 10 minutes.

Meanwhile, bring the tomato sauce to a boil, remove the saucepan from the heat, and add the cilantro and stir through.

Cut the game hen in half and serve immediately with the sauce.

Seared Duck Breasts with Honey-Balsamic Glaze

Searing duck breasts is a bit like cooking bacon—cook them until the skin's crispy, golden brown, and nicely rendered. Happily, when the skin is perfect, the flesh, which is best when a rosy medium-rare, will be too.

Choose a quality balsamic vinegar containing only one ingredient: cooked grape must. It's available at better gourmet markets.

Kale & Butternut Squash with Bacon & Toasted Garlic (page 202) would be excellent on the side. // *Yield: 2 to 4 servings*

- **RECOMMENDED SKILLET:** 10¼ inch (26 cm)
- **COOKING METHOD:** Searing/Deglazing

2 Muscovy duck breasts (8 ounces,
    or 225 g each)
Kosher salt
Freshly ground black pepper
1 shallot, sliced

¼ cup (60 ml) balsamic vinegar
2 tablespoons (40 g) honey, preferably
    citrus blossom or wildflower
1 sprig of thyme

With a sharp knife, score the skin of each duck breast in a diamond pattern, being careful not to pierce the flesh. Season generously with salt and pepper and set aside at room temperature for about an hour.

Preheat a cast iron skillet over medium-low heat. Add the duck breasts skin-side down and cook without disturbing until golden brown, crispy, and rendered, 6 to 7 minutes. Flip the duck breasts and cook until golden brown and medium-rare, 3 to 4 minutes. The duck breasts will just begin to feel firm to the touch when they are medium-rare. Remove the duck breasts to a platter, tent loosely with foil to keep warm, and let rest for about 10 minutes. Pour off nearly all of the accumulated fat from the skillet, strain through a fine-mesh sieve, and reserve for another use.

Add the shallot to the skillet and sauté until it begins to soften, about 1 minute. Add the balsamic vinegar, honey, and thyme, bring to a boil, and simmer until thickened slightly, 1 to 2 minutes. Remove and discard the thyme, add any accumulated duck juices and stir through, and season to taste with salt and pepper.

Carve the duck breasts against the grain into thin slices and serve immediately with the sauce.

Bacon-Wrapped Pork Filets Mignons with Onions & Roasted Poblanos

Bacon-wrapped filet of beef is usually considered a special-occasion dish, but here's a take using pork tenderloin that's affordable enough to be enjoyed on any weeknight. I decided to add roasted poblanos, with their campfire flavor, to further bring out the smokiness of the bacon. It's a simple recipe, but it's sure to please even the harshest critics—like my husband, who actually proclaimed it to be "righteous."

Speedy Refried Pinto Beans (page 213) and either Masa Cornbread (page 226) or Flour Tortillas (page 216) are perfect on the side. // **Yield: 4 servings**

- ■ **RECOMMENDED SKILLET:** 12 inch (30 cm)

- ■ **COOKING METHOD:** Searing/Sautéing

1 pork tenderloin (1¼ pounds, or 570 g), trimmed of silverskin and cut into 1¼-inch (3-cm) filets
Kosher salt
Freshly ground black pepper

10 to 12 thick-cut bacon strips, par-cooked
3 tablespoons (45 ml) canola oil
1 medium yellow onion, julienned
1 poblano, roasted, peeled, seeded, and julienned

Season the filets generously with salt and pepper. Wrap 1 to 2 slices of par-cooked bacon around the circumference of each filet and secure them with toothpicks or butcher twine.

Preheat a cast iron skillet over medium heat. Add the oil and swirl to coat the inside of the skillet. Add the wrapped filets and cook without disturbing until golden brown, 5 to 6 minutes. Flip the filets, add the onion all around them, and cook until the onion begins to soften, 4 to 5 minutes. Add the poblano to the onion and continue to cook until the filets are medium and the onion is soft, 1 to 2 minutes. Moisture will begin to pool on the surface of the filets and a meat thermometer will register 140°F (60°C) when they are medium. Season the onion mixture to taste with salt and pepper. Remove and discard the toothpicks or butcher twine and serve immediately.

MAINS

Pork Coppa Steaks with Aleppo Pepper & Oregano

The coppa steak is the eye of the Boston butt, or pork shoulder, and comes from the neck area. It is a well-marbled cut that cooks up exceptionally succulent with great flavor and pleasant chew. Any artisan butcher should be able to cut coppa steaks, and as they increase in popularity, nicer grocery stores are starting to market them as well. Substitute boneless pork rib chops if you cannot find coppa steaks.

Aleppo pepper, which comes from Syria, infuses this dish with a striking red color and mild spiciness. It is available at Mediterranean and Middle Eastern markets, spice shops, and at most gourmet grocers. If you can find it, sweet Calabrian chile powder is equally good in this dish.

I like to serve this dish with Charred Lemon Caesar Salad with Radicchio, Hearts of Romaine & Garlic Croutes (page 74). // *Yield: 4 servings*

- **RECOMMENDED SKILLET:** 12 inch (30 cm)
- **COOKING METHOD:** Searing

4 coppa steaks (6 ounces, or 170 g each),
   ¾ inch (2 cm) thick
Kosher salt
2 teaspoons Aleppo pepper
1 teaspoon granulated garlic

½ teaspoon oregano
½ teaspoon freshly ground coarse
   black pepper
2 tablespoons (30 ml) extra virgin olive oil

Season the steaks generously with kosher salt and set aside at room temperature for about an hour.

Whisk together the Aleppo pepper, granulated garlic, oregano, and black pepper in a small bowl.

Preheat a cast iron skillet over medium heat. Add the olive oil and swirl to coat the inside of the skillet. Add the steaks and cook without disturbing until golden brown, 2 to 3 minutes. Flip the steaks, sprinkle with half of the Aleppo pepper mixture, and cook until golden brown and nearly medium, 2 to 3 minutes. Moisture will begin to pool on the surface of the steaks when they are nearly medium. Working quickly, flip the steaks again, sprinkle the second side with the remaining half of the Aleppo pepper mixture, and flip the steaks a final time. Cook until the spices are toasted and aromatic, about 30 seconds. Remove the steaks to a platter and pour the spiced oil over top. Serve immediately.

MAINS

Egg-Battered Pork Chops

Eating these is like having both an omelet and a pork chop at the same time! It's easy and delicious and you can have it on the table inside of 15 minutes. // *Yield: 4 servings*

- **RECOMMENDED SKILLET:** 12 inch (30 cm)
- **COOKING METHOD:** Pan-Frying

1 cup (115 g) panko bread crumbs
Kosher salt
Freshly ground black pepper
4 eggs
3 cloves of garlic, minced

4 bone-in pork loin chops (5 to 6 ounces, or 140 to 170 g each), ½ inch (1 cm) thick
¼ teaspoon cayenne pepper
⅓ cup (80 ml) canola oil

Mix together the panko and a generous pinch of salt and pepper in a shallow dish. Whisk together the eggs, garlic, and a generous pinch of salt and pepper in another shallow dish.

Season the chops generously with salt and pepper and sprinkle evenly with the cayenne on both sides.

Preheat a cast iron skillet over medium heat. Add the oil and swirl to coat the inside of the skillet. Working quickly, roll 1 chop in the seasoned panko, patting so that it adheres. Dip the chop into the egg mixture to coat. Add the battered chop to the skillet, repeat with the remaining chops, and then pour any remaining egg mixture over the chops. Cook without disturbing until golden brown, 4 to 5 minutes. Flip the chops and cook until golden brown and medium, 3 to 4 minutes. The chops will begin to feel firm to the touch and a meat thermometer will register 140°F (60°C) when they are medium. Serve immediately.

MAINS

Mushroom & Herb–Stuffed Pork Chops

This dish is a showstopper. Make it for friends and family, and you'll have them convinced you've been moonlighting as a chef.

Despite all appearances, the recipe is not difficult to execute. Just take your time cutting a broad pocket inside of each pork chop, keeping the slit in the side relatively narrow to stop the stuffing from falling out as the chops cook. Adding bread crumbs to the skillet with the mushrooms soaks up the butter they were cooked in for a moist and delicious stuffing.

// *Yield: 4 servings*

- **RECOMMENDED SKILLET:** 12 inch (30 cm)
- **COOKING METHOD:** Pan-Roasting/Deglazing

3½ ounces (7 tablespoons, or 100 g) unsalted butter, cut into 1-tablespoon (14-g) pieces, divided
8 ounces (225 g) button or cremini mushrooms, diced (about 3 cups)
3 cloves of garlic, minced
1½ teaspoons minced fresh sage
1 teaspoon minced fresh rosemary
½ teaspoon minced fresh thyme

¼ teaspoon Worcestershire sauce
¾ cup (90 g) panko bread crumbs
Kosher salt
Freshly ground black pepper
4 bone-in pork loin chops (10 ounces, or 280 g each), 1 to 1¼ inches (2.5 to 3 cm) thick
2 tablespoons (30 ml) extra virgin olive oil
⅔ cup (160 ml) dry marsala

Preheat a cast iron skillet over medium heat. Add 2 ounces (4 tablespoons, or 55 g) of the butter, swirl to coat the inside of the skillet, and heat until the butter is melted and the foam subsides. Add the mushrooms and cook, stirring once or twice, until golden brown and soft, 4 to 5 minutes. Add the garlic and stir through. Add the sage, rosemary, thyme, and Worcestershire and stir through. Remove the skillet from the heat and add the panko and stir until thoroughly combined. Season to taste with salt and pepper, remove from the skillet, and let cool to room temperature. Wipe out the skillet.

Preheat the oven to 450°F (230°C, or gas mark 8).

Using a sharp boning or paring knife, carefully cut a 1½-inch (3.5-cm) slit in the fat-cap side of each chop and carefully widen it into a pocket that runs to the bone and through the entire length of the meat. Divide the mushroom mixture among the pockets, packing it firmly. Press each chop gently to flatten. Season generously with salt and pepper.

Preheat the skillet over medium-high heat, starting over medium heat. Add the olive oil and swirl to coat the inside of the skillet. Add the chops and cook without disturbing until light golden brown, 2 to 3 minutes. Flip the chops, transfer the skillet to the oven, and bake until medium, 8 to 10 minutes. Moisture will begin to pool on the surface of the chops and a meat thermometer will register 140°F (60°C) when they are medium. Remove the chops to a platter and tent loosely with foil to keep warm.

Transfer the skillet back to the stovetop. Add the marsala, bring to a boil, stirring constantly and scraping up the browned bits from the bottom of the skillet with a heatproof spatula, and simmer until thickened slightly, 6 to 7 minutes. Remove the skillet from the heat and let the bubbling subside. Add the remaining 1½ ounces (3 tablespoons, or 42 g) of butter to the sauce, whisk until smooth, and season to taste with salt and pepper. Serve the chops immediately with the sauce.

Smash Burgers

Throw balls of ground beef into a smoking-hot cast iron skillet and smash them flat right in the pan and you've got smash burgers. The idea is to maximize the contact between the ground beef and the skillet and create a substantial dark golden-brown crust. The result is delicious burgers that are as fun to make as they are to eat.

This recipe makes 4 burgers (⅓ pound, or 150 g each), but if you're feeding big eaters, you can, of course, double up on the ground beef, Lucy's Seasoned Salt, and cheese and make twice as many patties to stack for double burgers. And feel free to add bacon! // *Yield: 4 servings*

- **RECOMMENDED SKILLET:** 12 inch (30 cm)
- **COOKING METHOD:** Searing

4 artisan-style hamburger buns, split
1½ ounces (3 tablespoons, or 42 g)
   unsalted butter, softened
1⅓ pounds (600 g) 15% fat ground beef
2 tablespoons (30 ml) canola oil
Lucy's Seasoned Salt (page 249)
4 slices of American or cheddar cheese

Mayonnaise, for serving
Yellow mustard, for serving
Sliced tomatoes, for serving
Sliced red onions, for serving
Sliced pickles, for serving
Iceberg lettuce leaves, for serving

(continued)

Spread the cut sides of the buns with the butter.

Divide the ground beef into 4 equal portions and gently form each portion into a ball.

Preheat a cast iron skillet over medium-high heat, starting over medium heat. Add the oil and swirl to coat the inside of the skillet. Add 2 of the balls of beef and, using the back of a sturdy spatula, smash them into ½-inch (1-cm) thick patties. Sprinkle each patty generously with Lucy's Seasoned Salt and cook without disturbing until golden brown, 3 to 4 minutes. Flip the patties, sprinkle each one generously with Lucy's Seasoned Salt, top each one with a slice of the cheese, and cook until golden brown and just cooked through, 2 to 3 minutes. They will feel firm to the touch when they are just cooked through. Remove the burgers to a platter and tent loosely with foil to keep warm. Cook and season the remaining balls of beef and top with the remaining cheese in the same manner. Pour off all of the accumulated fat from the skillet.

Decrease the heat to medium-low and add 2 of the buns to the skillet, cut-side down. Toast until golden brown, about 2 minutes. Remove the buns to a plate and toast the remaining 2 buns in the same manner.

Arrange the bun bottoms cut-side up on individual plates. Divide the mayonnaise, mustard, burgers, tomatoes, onions, pickles, and lettuce among them and then top with the bun tops cut-side down. Serve immediately.

Hamburger Steaks with Mushroom & Onion Gravy

Save the binders and mix-ins for your meatballs and meatloaf because bread crumbs and eggs have no place in these hearty hamburger steaks. These are full of bold, beefy flavor and require a knife and fork, like any steak should.

This recipe makes plenty of lightly thickened gravy for topping your rice or mashed potatoes. If you prefer a thick gravy, decrease the amount of stock to 2½ cups (570 ml). // *Yield: 4 servings*

- **RECOMMENDED SKILLET:** 12 inch (30 cm)

- **COOKING METHOD:** Braising

1½ pounds (680 g) 15% fat ground beef
Lucy's Seasoned Salt (page 249)
Freshly ground black pepper
3 tablespoons (45 ml) canola oil
1 yellow onion, julienned
6 ounces (170 g) button or cremini
    mushrooms, sliced (about 3 cups)

3 tablespoons (24 g) all-purpose flour
3 cups (700 ml) beef stock
1 bay leaf
1 sprig of thyme
Several drops of Worcestershire sauce
Kosher salt

Divide the ground beef into 4 equal portions and gently form each portion into a ball. Gently pat each ball into a 3 x 5-inch (7.5 x 13-cm) oval patty. Season the patties generously with Lucy's Seasoned Salt and pepper.

Preheat a cast iron skillet over medium heat. Add the oil and swirl to coat the inside of the skillet. Add the patties and cook without disturbing until golden brown, 3 to 4 minutes. Flip the patties and cook until golden brown, 2 to 3 minutes. Remove the patties to a platter.

Add the onion to the skillet and sauté until it begins to soften, 2 to 3 minutes. Add the mushrooms and cook, stirring once or twice, until they begin to soften, 3 to 4 minutes. Add the flour and slowly stir through until no dry flour remains. Add the beef stock and bring to a boil, stirring constantly and scraping up the browned bits from the bottom of the skillet with a heatproof spatula. Return the patties and any accumulated juices to the skillet, add the bay leaf, thyme, and Worcestershire sauce. Simmer, flipping the patties occasionally, until the sauce is thickened slightly and the patties are medium, 7 to 9 minutes. Moisture will pool on the surface of the patties and they will feel firm to the touch when they are medium with a piping hot center. Remove and discard the bay leaf and thyme, season the gravy to taste with salt and pepper, and serve immediately.

Steak, Goat Cheese & Pickled Red Onion Sandwiches

This sandwich is in the regular rotation at my house. The combination of red meat, fresh chèvre, and pungent and vinegary onions is surprisingly satisfying. We've tried adding baby greens, tomatoes, roasted red peppers, olives, and various other fillings, but we always agree that this simplest version is still the best. I will say that if you can get your hands on them during their short spring season, try substituting ramps for the onions for another winning flavor combination.

If you don't use up all of the pickled onions on the sandwich, store any leftovers in the pickling liquid in a tightly sealed container in the refrigerator. They'll keep just about indefinitely.

// *Yield: 4 servings*

- **RECOMMENDED SKILLET:** 12 inch (30 cm)

- **COOKING METHOD:** Searing

1 small red onion, thinly sliced
½ cup (120 ml) white vinegar
2 tablespoons (26 g) sugar
1 teaspoon kosher salt, plus more if needed
1 flank steak (1¼ pounds, or 570 g)

Freshly ground black pepper
¼ teaspoon granulated garlic
2 tablespoons (30 ml) canola oil
1 artisan-style baguette, warmed and split
4 ounces (115 g) chèvre, softened

Place the onion in a small jar. Combine the vinegar, sugar, salt, and ¼ cup (60 ml) of water in a small saucepan. Bring to a boil, stirring to dissolve the sugar, and pour over the onion. Top the onion with a pickling weight or zip-top bag filled with water to completely submerge it and let cool to room temperature.

Season the steak generously with kosher salt and black pepper, sprinkle evenly with the granulated garlic on both sides, and set aside at room temperature for about an hour.

MAINS

Preheat a cast iron skillet over medium-high heat, starting over medium heat. Add the oil and swirl to coat the inside of the skillet. Add the steak and cook without disturbing until golden brown, 4 to 5 minutes. Flip the steak and cook until golden brown and medium-rare, 3 to 4 minutes. Moisture will begin to appear on the surface of the steak when it is medium-rare. Remove the steak to a platter, tent loosely with foil to keep warm, and let rest for about 10 minutes.

Remove as many pickled onions as desired from the pickling liquid and blot dry on paper towels. Carve the steak against the grain into thin slices. Place the baguette bottom cut-side up on a cutting board. Spread it evenly with the chèvre and then arrange the steak slices and pickled onions over the top of it. Top with the baguette top cut-side down, cut into quarters, and serve immediately.

Constant Flip–Method Steaks with Butter, Frizzled Herbs & Garlic

When cooking instructors (including myself) teach searing technique for steaks and chops, they usually advise adding the meat to a very hot pan, leaving it alone for the most part, and flipping it once and only once. This recommendation keeps things straightforward and easy to understand and yields great results. But for what I like to think of as "advanced" searing technique, try the constant-flip method in a cast iron skillet. It may require a bit more attention and a few more minutes of attended cooking time, but it pays off in a steak with a superbly dark golden-brown crust and a perfectly even doneness in the center. Frequent flipping allows for the heat to be more evenly conducted to the center of the steak, or as my resident science guy puts it, "In effect, you have a series of heat waves running through the meat." It virtually eliminates any gradient of overcooked gray around the edges.

If the steaks have a significant fat cap, start them in the skillet fat cap–side down for a couple of minutes. That'll give it a head start rendering and crisping up. Then, lay them down and continue as directed.

Not that these steaks need any other embellishment, but you can pass a bowl of Creamy Horseradish Sauce (page 253) at the table to go with them. // *Yield: 2 to 4 servings*

- **RECOMMENDED SKILLET:** 10¼ inch (26 cm)
- **COOKING METHOD:** Searing

(continued)

2 ribeye steaks (14 to 16 ounces,
   or 390 to 455 g each), 1½ inch
   (3.5 cm) thick
Kosher salt
2 tablespoons (30 ml) canola oil
2 teaspoons Cajun Spice (page 250)
4 sprigs of rosemary

4 sprigs of thyme
1 ounce (2 tablespoons, or 28 g)
   unsalted butter, cut into 1-tablespoon
   (14-g) pieces
1 clove garlic, sliced
Flaky sea salt, such as fleur de sel
   or Maldon

Season the steaks generously with kosher salt and set aside at room temperature for about an hour.

Preheat a cast iron skillet over medium heat. Add the oil and swirl to coat the inside of the skillet. Add the steaks and cook, flipping every minute, until dark golden brown and nearly medium-rare, 8 to 9 minutes. Moisture will begin to appear on the surface of the steaks when they are nearly medium-rare. Working quickly, sprinkle the steaks with half of the Cajun Spice, flip them again, add the rosemary and thyme around them, and sprinkle the second side with the remaining half of the Cajun Spice. Flip the steaks a final time, immediately add the butter and garlic around them, and baste the steaks with the butter as it melts, cooking until the spices are toasted and aromatic, about 30 seconds. Remove the steaks, herbs, and garlic to a platter and pour over the spiced butter. Tent loosely with foil to keep warm and let rest for about 10 minutes.

Carve the steaks as desired, sprinkle with a generous pinch of sea salt, and serve immediately with the herbs, garlic, and mixture of spiced butter and any accumulated steak juices.

Seared Sous Vide Steaks

Sous vide, which is French for "under vacuum," is a moist low-heat modern cooking method. It can be used both for small, naturally tender foods and for large foods that are high in connective tissue, depending on the cooking temperature and time. Food in a vacuum-sealed pouch is placed into a temperature-controlled water bath and left there until done. An immersion circulator in the water maintains a specific temperature within a fraction of a degree for a specific length of time. The precision temperature control of sous vide makes possible previously unheard-of low cooking temperatures coupled with long cooking times and offers new and surprising flavor and texture results.

Until recently sous vide cooking was only found in commercial kitchens. Now a variety of inexpensive immersion circulators has made sous vide cooking more accessible to the home cook.

Sous vide cooking is usually followed by quick searing. So while a CI skillet would not be used for sous vide, it would be indispensable for the searing step.

These steaks are first cooked slowly in a water bath kept at 130°F (54°C) using an immersion circulator and then seared quickly in an extremely hot cast iron skillet. Steaks cooked in this manner turn out perfectly medium-rare and pink from edge to edge, without any gradient of overcooked gray and without the guesswork of determining doneness. The two-step cooking method also brings out a bold beefy flavor in the meat.

If you don't have a vacuum sealer or immersion circulator, you can still make this recipe. Use a 1-gallon (3.8-L) zip-top bag and lower it into water to allow displacement to force out all the air before sealing. Use a cooler filled with 130°F (54°C) water for the bath—the cooler will maintain the temperature for the time it takes to cook the steak.

Serve with Creamy Horseradish Sauce (page 253), if desired. // *Yield: 2 to 4 servings*

- **RECOMMENDED SKILLET:** 10¼ inch (26 cm)
- **COOKING METHOD:** Sous Vide/Searing

2 strip steaks (12 to 14 ounces, or 340 to 390 g each), 1½ inch (3.5 cm) thick
2 cloves of garlic, sliced
2 fresh bay leaves, torn in half
1 ounce (2 tablespoons, or 28 g) unsalted butter, cut into 1-tablespoon (14-g) pieces

Kosher salt
Freshly ground black pepper
2 tablespoons (30 ml) canola oil
Flaky sea salt, such as fleur de sel or Maldon

Using an immersion circulator, preheat a water bath with a rack to 130°F (54°C).

Place the steaks in a vacuum sealer bag, scatter the sliced garlic and bay leaves over both sides of the steaks, and add the butter. Vacuum seal the bag. Add the bag to the water bath and circulate for 1 to 1½ hours. Remove the bag from the water bath and let rest for 5 to 10 minutes.

Preheat a cast iron skillet over medium-high heat, starting over medium heat. Meanwhile, remove the steaks from the bag, reserving the bag with the juices. Remove and discard the garlic and bay leaves, blot the steaks dry on paper towels, and season generously with salt and pepper. Return the bag with the juices to the water bath, positioning it so that it doesn't spill, to keep warm. Add the oil to the skillet and swirl to coat the inside. Add the steaks and cook without disturbing until golden brown, 1 to 2 minutes. Flip the steaks and cook until golden brown, 1 to 2 minutes. Stand the steaks on the fat-cap side and cook until golden brown, 1 to 2 minutes. Remove the steaks to a platter. Tent loosely with foil to keep warm and let rest for 2 to 3 minutes.

Season the bag juices to taste with salt and pepper. Carve the steaks as desired, sprinkle with a generous pinch of sea salt, and serve immediately with the juices.

Seared Whole Trout

Whole trout at the fishmonger is often sold "butterflied," which means gutted, boned, and with the head, tail, and fins removed and makes for easy preparation and great eating. But bone-in, head-on trout would work just as well for this recipe, only it might take an extra minute or two to cook. Either way, take the time to scale the trout by scraping a paring knife against the skin, going from tail to head in firm strokes. The crispy skin on seared scaled trout is the best part. // *Yield: 2 to 4 servings*

- **RECOMMENDED SKILLET:** 12 inch (30 cm)
- **COOKING METHOD:** Searing

2 butterflied rainbow trout (10 ounces, or 280 g each), preferably scaled
Kosher salt
2 teaspoons Lemon Pepper (page 250)

1 ounce (2 tablespoons, or 28 g) unsalted butter, thinly sliced
8 to 10 sprigs of dill
¼ cup (60 ml) canola oil
1 lemon, cut into 8 wedges

Season the trout generously with kosher salt inside and out and sprinkle evenly with the Lemon Pepper on the inside. Set aside at room temperature for about an hour.

Tuck the dill sprigs and sliced butter inside the trout. Preheat a cast iron skillet over medium heat. Add the oil and swirl to coat the inside of the skillet. Add the trout and cook without disturbing until golden brown, 4 to 5 minutes. Flip the trout and cook until golden brown and just beginning to flake, 3 to 4 minutes. Remove the trout to a platter and, if desired, carefully open each one and cut apart the fillets. Serve immediately with the lemon wedges.

Perfect Seared Sea Scallops

Sea scallops are incredibly quick and easy to ▮▮▮▮ home. The key to success is sourcing the best quality possible and getting an excel▮▮▮▮sing a CI skillet.

They are sold by size: the smaller the numb▮▮▮▮ger the scallops. For example, U-10 indicates that there are fewer than 10 scallop▮▮▮▮nd (455 g). Select only those labeled "dry" from a reputable fishmonger. "Wet" scallops, _____ soaked in a phosphate solution to increase their weight and help preserve them, will exude liquid as soon as they hit the heat—they'll simmer in their own juices and never brown. When preparing scallops, take the time to remove the translucent, crescent-shaped bit of tissue known as the foot, which is rubbery when cooked.

Sea scallops are at their juiciest and most tender when they're cooked to medium-rare. They are done when they're brown on the surface but still feel slightly soft to the touch. Another sure sign that they're ready is when moisture appears on the surface of the scallops. The center should remain slightly translucent.

Though you could deglaze the skillet with a bit of white wine and then swirl in some cold butter and herbs off the heat, perfectly cooked sea scallops really need no sauce. Serve these over the Charred Lemon Caesar Salad with Radicchio, Hearts of Romaine & Garlic Croutes (page 74) or pair them with the Constant Flip–Method Steaks with Butter, Frizzled Herbs & Garlic (page 119) for an indulgent surf and turf meal. // *Yield: 2 to 3 servings*

- **RECOMMENDED SKILLET:** 10¼ inch (26 cm)
- **COOKING METHOD:** Searing

6 U-10 sea scallops, feet removed
Kosher salt

Freshly ground black pepper
2 tablespoons (30 ml) canola oil

Season the scallops generously with salt and pepper and set aside at room temperature for about half an hour.

Preheat a cast iron skillet over medium heat. Add the oil and swirl to coat the inside of the skillet. Add the scallops and cook without disturbing until golden brown, about 2 minutes. Flip the scallops and cook until golden brown and medium-rare, 1 to 2 minutes. Moisture will begin to appear on the surface of the scallops when they are medium-rare. Serve hot or at room temperature.

Beer-Battered Fish

Fantastically light and crunchy, homemade fried fish with homemade Tartar Sauce (page 253) is as good as it gets. If you would like an extra crispy coating, substitute 2 or 3 tablespoons (16 to 24 g) of the flour in the batter with cornstarch.

For the best results, opt for fresh fish as frozen exudes a lot of water when cooked.

// *Yield: 4 servings*

- **RECOMMENDED SKILLET:** Deep 10¼ inch (26 cm)

- **COOKING METHOD:** Deep-Frying

1½ cups (188 g) all-purpose flour, divided
Kosher salt
¾ teaspoon baking powder
1 egg
¾ cup (175 ml) beer, preferably ale
1½ quarts (1.4 L) canola oil (enough to come to a depth of 1½ inches [3.5 cm])

1½ pounds (680 g) center cut halibut, cod, or haddock fillets, skinned, boned, and cut into 12 (1-inch [2.5-cm]) wide strips
Freshly ground black pepper
½ teaspoon granulated garlic
Tartar Sauce (page 253), for serving
1 lemon, cut into 8 wedges

Whisk together ¾ cup (94 g) of the flour and several generous pinches of salt in a medium bowl. Whisk together the remaining ¾ cup (94 g) of the flour, baking powder, and a generous pinch salt in another medium bowl. Whisk together the egg and beer in another medium bowl.

Pour the oil into a deep cast iron skillet and preheat over medium-high heat, starting over medium heat, until it registers 375°F (190°C) on a candy/jelly/deep-fry thermometer. Meanwhile, blot the fish dry on paper towels, season generously with salt and pepper, and sprinkle evenly with the granulated garlic on both sides. Just before the oil comes to temperature, quickly add the egg mixture to the flour–baking powder mixture and whisk until smooth. Roll 1 strip of the fish in the seasoned flour to coat. Shake off any excess flour and dip it into the batter to coat. Shake off any excess batter, add it to the skillet, and repeat with 5 more strips of fish for a batch of 6. Fry at a lively sizzle, flipping once or twice, until golden brown and crispy, 3 to 4 minutes. Using a wire skimmer, remove the fish to a paper towel–lined sheet tray, let drain for a moment, and season with salt. Reheat the oil and batter and fry the remaining strips of fish in 1 more batch of 6 in the same manner. Serve hot with the Tartar Sauce and lemon wedges.

Dungeness Crab Cakes with Roasted Red Pepper Vinaigrette

Dungeness crab is an expensive luxury, so on the rare occasion I splurge on it, I really want crab cakes that allow the sweet flavor of the crab to shine through. Binders mask the crabmeat, so I use the bare minimum necessary for the crab cakes to just hold together and I leave any lumps of crabmeat intact. And since crab and butter is a perfect pairing, I fry them in a blend of butter and oil. The result is tender, delicate, moist, and extremely flavorful crab cakes.

A sharp and tangy vinaigrette is a nice upgrade from simple lemon wedges. If desired, serve the dish on a bed of butter lettuce. // *Yield: 8 large crab cakes or 4 servings*

- **RECOMMENDED SKILLET:** 12 inch (30 cm)
- **COOKING METHOD:** Pan-Frying

2 red bell peppers, roasted, peeled, seeded, and coarsely diced
¼ cup (60 ml) red wine vinegar
½ cup (120 ml) extra virgin olive oil
1 teaspoon Dijon mustard
3 cloves of garlic, grated on a Microplane
8 leaves basil
Generous pinch of cayenne pepper
Kosher salt
Freshly ground black pepper
1 egg
¼ cup (60 g) mayonnaise, preferably Best Foods

1 large green onion, thinly sliced
½ teaspoon Tabasco sauce
¼ teaspoon Worcestershire sauce
¾ pound (340 g) Dungeness crabmeat, picked over
1¼ cups (140 g) panko bread crumbs, divided
3 tablespoons (45 ml) canola oil
1½ ounces (3 tablespoons, or 42 g) unsalted butter, cut into 1-tablespoon (14-g) pieces

Combine the roasted red bell peppers, red wine vinegar, olive oil, Dijon mustard, about one-third of the garlic, basil, and cayenne in a blender and blend until pureed. Season to taste with salt and pepper.

Mix together the egg, mayonnaise, green onion, remaining two-thirds of garlic, Tabasco, and Worcestershire in a large bowl. Add the crabmeat and ¾ cup (84 g) of the panko and stir through. Season with a generous pinch of salt and pepper. Scoop the crab mixture by the packed ¼ cup (55 g), gently patting each scoop to flatten slightly into a patty, and place the crab cakes onto a sheet tray. Place the remaining ½ cup (56 g) of panko into a medium bowl, roll each crab cake in the panko, patting so that it adheres, and place the crab cakes onto a sheet tray.

(continued)

Pour the canola oil into a cast iron skillet, add the butter, and preheat over medium heat until a pinch of panko sizzles immediately when added. Add the crab cakes and cook without disturbing until golden brown, 3 to 4 minutes. Flip the crab cakes and cook until golden brown and heated through, 2 to 3 minutes. Serve immediately with the Roasted Red Pepper Vinaigrette.

Fried Razor Clam Strips

Razor clams are often breaded with panko or cracker crumbs and pan-fried whole, but as far as I'm concerned, deep-frying strips with a flour and cornstarch dredge makes for better eating. The thinner, lighter coating allows the clam flavor to better shine through and completely submerging the clams in hot oil rather than frying one side at a time minimizes the cooking time and keeps them more tender.

For the best results, dredge the clams just moments before the oil reaches frying temperature.

Serve with your choice of Tartar Sauce (page 253), Fresh Herb Ranch Dipping Sauce (page 254), Buffalo Mayo (page 254), or Chipotle Dipping Sauce (page 255) on the side.

// *Yield: 4 servings*

- **RECOMMENDED SKILLET:** Deep 10¼ inch (26 cm)*
- **COOKING METHOD:** Deep-Frying

1 cup (125 g) all-purpose flour
¼ cup (33 g) cornstarch
Lucy's Seasoned Salt (page 249)
1½ quarts (1.4 L) canola oil (enough to come to a depth of 1½ inches [3.5 cm])

1 pound (455 g) cleaned razor clams (6 to 8), rinsed, drained, dried thoroughly on paper towels, and cut crosswise into ½-inch (1-cm) wide strips
Kosher salt

Whisk together the flour, cornstarch, and several generous pinches of Lucy's Seasoned Salt in a large bowl.

Pour the oil into a deep cast iron skillet and preheat over medium-high heat, starting over medium heat, until it registers 375°F (190°C) on a candy/jelly/deep-fry thermometer. Just before the oil comes to temperature, add about one-third of the clams to the seasoned flour and toss to coat, separating any pieces that stick together. Shake off any excess flour, add the dredged clams to the skillet, and fry at a lively sizzle, stirring occasionally, until floating, golden brown, and crispy, about 1 minute. Using a wire skimmer, remove the clams to a paper towel–lined sheet tray and let drain for a moment. Season to taste with salt. Reheat the oil and dredge and fry the remaining clams in 2 more batches in the same manner. Serve hot.

*This can also be made in a deep 12-inch (30-cm) cast iron skillet.

Seared Beef Tongue on Rye with Creamy Horseradish Sauce

Tongue is a rich, boldly flavored and silky textured cut of meat. If you've never had it and you like beef, you're missing out. Definitely give it a try—in my experience, most people love it at first bite.

Tongue must be simmered for a relatively long time to become tender, and then it can be sliced and either served cold or browned quickly in a hot cast iron skillet and served hot, as in these sandwiches. // **Yield: 4 servings**

- **RECOMMENDED SKILLET:** 12 inch (30 cm)
- **COOKING METHOD:** Simmering/Searing

1 beef tongue (3¼ pounds, or 1.5 kg)
6 cloves of garlic, smashed
10 allspice berries
2 bay leaves
1 teaspoon black peppercorns
Kosher salt
8 slices of artisan-style rye bread

2 ounces (4 tablespoons, or 55 g)
   unsalted butter, softened
3 tablespoons (45 ml) canola oil
Creamy Horseradish Sauce (page 253),
   for serving
Thinly sliced red onions, for serving
Sliced pickles, for serving

(continued)

Combine the beef tongue, garlic, allspice, bay leaves, peppercorns, and several generous pinches of salt in a large pot and add enough water to cover by 7 inches (18 cm). Bring to a boil, cover the pot, and simmer until the tongue is very tender, 3½ to 4 hours. Transfer to a large bowl of ice water until cool enough to handle, reserving the broth for another use. Drain the tongue and blot dry on paper towels. Transfer to a cutting board and peel off the skin. Let cool completely and then refrigerate until chilled, about 4 hours, before slicing.

Cut the tongue crosswise into ½-inch (1-cm) thick slices and trim off and discard the fat and glands from both sides of the base, if desired. Season generously with salt.

Spread 1 side of each slice of bread with the butter.

Preheat a cast iron skillet over medium-high heat, starting over medium heat. Add the oil and swirl to coat the inside of the skillet. Add the slices of tongue and cook without disturbing until golden brown, about 2 minutes. Flip the tongue and cook until golden brown and heated through, about 2 minutes. Remove the tongue to a platter and tent loosely with foil to keep warm. Pour off all of the accumulated fat from the skillet.

Decrease the heat to medium-low and add 2 of the slices of bread to the skillet, buttered-side down. Toast until light golden brown, about 1 minute. Remove the bread to a plate and toast the remaining 6 slices of bread in the same manner.

Arrange 4 of the slices of bread, toasted-side down, on individual plates. Divide the Creamy Horseradish Sauce, tongue, onions, and pickles among them and then top with the remaining 4 slices of bread, toasted-side up. Serve immediately.

Philly Cheesesteaks

There's a lot of spirited debate about what makes a proper cheesesteak sandwich. Having never been to Philadelphia myself, I can't claim I know what's the most authentic—but I can certainly say what's delicious. And that is ribeye steak and provolone cheese.

In a restaurant, beef for cheesesteak sandwiches is cut very thin on a deli slicer. To re-create this texture at home as easily as possible, partially freeze the meat until it begins to firm up before cutting it into very thin slices using a sharp knife.

Feel free to add condiments such as mayo, but rest assured that this sandwich is plenty juicy as is and needs no other embellishment. // *Yield: 4 servings*

- **RECOMMENDED SKILLET:** 12 inch (30 cm)
- **COOKING METHOD:** Sautéing

2 ribeye steaks (12 to 14 ounces, 340 to 390 g each), 1 to 1¼ inches (2.5 to 3 cm) thick
¼ cup (60 ml) canola oil
1 yellow onion, julienned
1 green bell pepper, julienned
1 clove of garlic, minced, optional
Kosher salt
Freshly ground black pepper
8 slices of sharp provolone
4 artisan-style hoagie rolls, warmed and split three-quarters of the way

Cut the steaks into quarters and freeze in a single layer until it just begins to solidify, 30 to 35 minutes. Transfer the steak pieces to a cutting board and, using a sharp chef knife, cut into ⅛- to 3/16-inch (3- to 5-mm) slices. Set aside at room temperature for about an hour.

Preheat a cast iron skillet over medium heat. Add the oil and swirl to coat the inside. Add the onion and sauté until it begins to soften, about 2 minutes. Add the bell pepper and cook, stirring frequently, until nearly soft and golden brown in spots, 7 to 8 minutes. Add the garlic, if desired, and stir through. Season to taste with salt and pepper and, using a slotted spoon, remove the onion mixture to a bowl.

Increase the heat to medium-high, add the steak to the skillet, and cook, stirring frequently, until nearly cooked through, 3 to 4 minutes. Season to taste with salt and pepper. Divide the steak into 4 stacks. Divide the onion mixture among them and then top with the provolone. Cook without disturbing until the steak begins to brown and the provolone is melted, 2 to 3 minutes.

Arrange the hoagie rolls on individual plates. Divide the filling among them and serve immediately.

Smothered Beef Tips

This is a saucy, long-simmering, rich stew, meant to be served over mashed potatoes or steamed rice.

"Beef tips" is a nebulous marketing term that can refer to any number of cuts of beef cut into little pieces and sold at a premium. Sometimes, it's used for cuts from the sirloin; other times, it's used for stew meat. Whatever the case, I prefer to buy the exact whole piece of meat I need for the recipe and cut it up myself so that I don't pay a premium for some sort of mystery cut that's possibly had time to oxidize. In the case of this particular recipe, the best cut of meat would be from the chuck, which becomes succulent and meltingly tender once braised. Boneless short ribs would be an excellent alternative. If you do select precut beef tips, just make sure they come from a cut that's suitable for stewing. // **Yield: 6 servings**

- **RECOMMENDED SKILLET:** 12 inch (30 cm)

- **COOKING METHOD:** Braising

2 pounds (900 g) boneless beef chuck roast, cut into 1 x ¾ x 2-inch (2.5 x 2 x 5-cm) strips
Kosher salt
Freshly ground black pepper
¼ cup (60 ml) canola oil, divided
1 yellow onion, julienned
2 stalks of celery, julienned
1 large carrot, julienned

4 cloves of garlic, minced
2 tablespoons (32 g) tomato paste
¼ cup (31 g) all-purpose flour
3 cups (700 ml) beef stock
1 bay leaf
3 sprigs of thyme
3 stems of Italian parsley
1 tablespoon (15 ml) red wine vinegar
3 tablespoons (12 g) minced Italian parsley

Season the beef generously with salt and pepper.

Preheat a cast iron skillet over medium-high heat, starting over medium heat. Add 2 tablespoons (30 ml) of the oil and swirl to coat the inside. Add about one-half of the beef and cook, stirring occasionally, until golden brown, 5 to 6 minutes. Using a slotted spoon, remove the beef to a bowl. Sear the remaining beef in the same manner.

Decrease the heat to medium-low, add the remaining 2 tablespoons (30 ml) of oil to the skillet, and swirl to coat the inside. Add the onion and sauté until it begins to soften, 2 to 3 minutes. Add the celery and carrot and sauté until soft, 4 to 5 minutes. Add the garlic and stir through and then add the tomato paste and stir through. Add the flour and slowly stir through until no dry flour remains. Add the beef stock and bring to a boil, stirring constantly and scraping up the browned bits from the bottom of the skillet with a heatproof spatula. Return the beef and any accumulated juices to the skillet and add the bay leaf, thyme, and parsley stems. Cover the skillet and simmer, stirring occasionally, until the sauce is thickened and the beef is tender, 2¼ hours to 2½ hours. Remove and discard the bay leaf, thyme, and parsley stems. Add the red wine vinegar and minced parsley and stir through. Season to taste with salt and pepper. Serve hot.

Perfect Chicken-Fried Steak Fingers with Peppered Gravy

Chicken-fried steak is often pan-fried, but in my opinion, deep-frying yields far better results. Completely submerging the steak in hot oil rather than frying one side at a time minimizes the cooking time and keeps it tender while creating a crispier crust. And cutting the steak into strips adds surface area to maximize that crust! Deep-frying does mean making the gravy in a separate pan but toasting the black pepper in the roux before adding the milk gives it a boost of flavor. // *Yield: 4 servings*

- **RECOMMENDED SKILLET:** Deep 10¼ inch (26 cm)*
- **COOKING METHOD:** Deep-Frying

1 pound (455 g) cube steak
Lucy's Seasoned Salt (page 249)
2¾ cups (344 g) all-purpose flour, divided
1 teaspoon paprika
1 teaspoon granulated garlic
½ teaspoon granulated onion
Kosher salt
Freshly ground black pepper

1 cup (235 ml) buttermilk
1 egg
1½ ounces (3 tablespoons, or 42 g) unsalted butter, cut into 1-tablespoon (14-g) pieces
2 cups (475 ml) milk
1½ quarts (1.4 L) canola oil (enough to come to a depth of 1½ inches [3.5 cm])

(continued)

Season the steak generously with Lucy's Seasoned Salt, cut into 1¼- to 1½-inch (3- to 3.5-cm) wide strips, and set aside at room temperature for about an hour.

Meanwhile, whisk together 2½ cups (313 g) of the flour, paprika, granulated garlic, granulated onion, and several generous pinches of salt and pepper in a large bowl. Transfer about one-third of the flour mixture to a medium bowl. Whisk together the buttermilk, egg, and a generous pinch of salt and pepper in another medium bowl. Drizzle about 1 tablespoon (15 ml) of the buttermilk mixture into the large bowl of flour and stir through.

Place the butter into a small saucepan and melt over medium heat. Add the remaining ¼ cup (31 g) of flour and whisk until smooth. Add ¾ teaspoon of pepper and whisk until combined. Add the milk and bring to a boil, whisking constantly. Simmer, whisking frequently, until thickened, 7 to 9 minutes. Season to taste with salt. Cover and keep warm.

Pour the oil into a deep cast iron skillet and preheat over medium-high heat, starting over medium heat, until it registers 375°F (190°C) on a candy/jelly/deep-fry thermometer. Just before the oil comes to temperature, add about one-half of the steak strips to the smaller bowl of seasoned flour and toss to coat. Shake off any excess flour, transfer the steak to the buttermilk mixture, and stir to coat. Shake off any excess liquid, transfer the steak to the large bowl of seasoned flour, and toss to coat, separating any pieces that stick together. Shake off any excess flour, add the dredged steak to the skillet, and fry at a lively sizzle, stirring occasionally, until floating, golden brown, and crispy, 4 to 5 minutes. Using a wire skimmer, remove the steak to a paper towel–lined sheet tray and let drain for a moment. Season to taste with salt. Reheat the oil and dredge and fry the remaining steak in 1 more batch in the same manner. Serve hot with the gravy.

*This can also be made in a deep 12-inch (30-cm) cast iron skillet.

Southern-Fried Chicken Gizzards

Whenever my mother or grandmother made chicken soup, the gizzard, which was picked out of the little bag of giblets and affectionately referred to in Russian as the "belly button," always went into the pot to be served as a treat before the meal to one lucky family member. And when I was little, the lucky one was usually me.

To this day I still love gizzards, with their chewy, sometimes crunchy, texture and their bold dark meat flavor. But rather than boil them, I prefer to confit them or fry them like this.

For the best results, dredge the gizzards just moments before the oil reaches the frying temperature.

Serve with Peppered Gravy (page 135) or Buffalo Mayo (page 254) for dipping. // **Yield: 4 servings**

- **RECOMMENDED SKILLET:** Deep 10¼ inch (26 cm)*
- **COOKING METHOD:** Deep-Frying

1 cup (235 ml) buttermilk
1 teaspoon granulated garlic
1 teaspoon paprika
½ teaspoon granulated onion
¼ teaspoon cayenne pepper
⅛ teaspoon celery seeds, ground
Kosher salt

Freshly ground black pepper
1 pound (455 g) chicken gizzards, trimmed
of large areas of connective tissue
and cut into bite-size pieces
1½ cups (188 g) all-purpose flour
1½ quarts (1.4 L) canola oil (enough to
come to a depth of 1½ inches [3.5 cm])

Mix together the buttermilk, granulated garlic, paprika, granulated onion, cayenne, celery seeds, and a generous pinch of salt and pepper in a 1-gallon (3.8-L) zip-top bag. Add the gizzards and turn to coat. Seal the bag, letting out all the air. Marinate 4 to 6 hours in the refrigerator.

Whisk together the flour and several generous pinches of salt and pepper in a large bowl. Drizzle about 2 teaspoons of the buttermilk marinade into the flour and stir through.

Pour the oil into a deep cast iron skillet and preheat over medium-high heat, starting over medium heat, until it registers 375°F (190°C) on a candy/jelly/deep-fry thermometer. Just before the oil comes to temperature, shake off any excess buttermilk from about one-half of the gizzards, transfer to the seasoned flour, and toss to coat, separating any pieces that stick together. Shake off any excess flour, add the dredged gizzards to the skillet, and fry at a lively sizzle, stirring occasionally, until floating, golden brown, and crispy, 2 to 3 minutes. Using a wire skimmer, remove the gizzards to a paper towel–lined sheet tray and let drain for a moment. Season to taste with salt. Reheat the oil and dredge and fry the remaining gizzards in 1 more batch in the same manner. Serve hot.

*This can also be made in a deep 12-inch (30-cm) cast iron skillet.

Cornmeal-Crusted Catfish

This catfish makes a satisfying main course served with Tartar Sauce (page 253) and Southern-Fried Okra (page 212) and Creamed Corn with Basil (page 202) on the side. It's also fantastic tucked into split French bread along with lettuce, tomatoes, pickles, and Buffalo Mayo (page 254), po-boy style.

You can certainly deep-fry the catfish if you prefer. The cooking time will be a couple of minutes shorter. // *Yield: 4 servings*

- **RECOMMENDED SKILLET:** 12 inch (cm)
- **COOKING METHOD:** Pan-Frying

1 teaspoon granulated garlic
1 teaspoon paprika
¼ teaspoon cayenne pepper
⅔ cup (93 g) fine cornmeal
Kosher salt

Freshly ground black pepper
4 catfish fillets (8 ounces, or 85 g each)
¾ cup (175 ml) canola oil
1 lemon, cut into 8 wedges

Mix together the granulated garlic, paprika, and cayenne in a small bowl. Whisk together the cornmeal and a generous pinch of salt and pepper in a shallow dish.

Season the catfish generously with salt and pepper and sprinkle evenly with the paprika mixture on both sides.

Pour the oil into a cast iron skillet and preheat over medium heat until a pinch of the cornmeal sizzles immediately when added. Just before the oil comes to temperature, quickly roll 1 fillet in the seasoned cornmeal to coat, shake off any excess cornmeal, add it to the skillet, and repeat with 1 more fillet. Cook without disturbing until golden brown, 4 to 5 minutes. Flip the fillets and cook until they are golden brown and just begin to flake, 3 to 4 minutes. Remove the fillets to a paper towel–lined sheet tray, let drain, and season with salt. Reheat the oil and dredge and fry the remaining 2 catfish fillets in 1 more batch in the same manner. Serve hot with the lemon wedges.

Blackened Salmon with Garlic Butter

Out of all of the countless ways fish can be prepared, blackened is my personal favorite. I just cannot resist the spicy and smoky, crispy crust. In fact, the desire to learn how to make it myself was the impetus for me to acquire my first cast iron skillet.

Redfish is, of course, the classic choice for blackening, but salmon is excellent too. If at all possible, opt for fresh fish as frozen exudes a lot of water when cooked.

Blackening is the hottest of all of the cooking methods, and the skillet must be preheated until it is visibly smoking. And as you might imagine, quite a bit of smoke is generated throughout the blackening process. Turn on the range hood to vent it away or even consider cooking outdoors.

Serve with a warm baguette to sop up the melted garlic butter and Almond Green Beans (page 197) on the side. It's also perfect atop Charred Lemon Caesar Salad with Radicchio, Hearts of Romaine & Garlic Croutes (page 74). // **Yield: 4 servings**

- **RECOMMENDED SKILLET:** 12 inch (30 cm)

- **COOKING METHOD:** Blackening

4 center cut salmon fillets (6 ounces, or 170 g each), skinned and boned
Kosher salt
2 ounces (4 tablespoons, or 55 g) unsalted butter, softened, plus 3 ounces (6 tablespoons, or 85 g), melted, divided

1 large clove of garlic, grated on a Microplane
1 tablespoon (9 g) plus 1 teaspoon Cajun Spice (page 250)
1 lemon, cut into 8 wedges

Season the salmon fillets generously with kosher salt and set aside at room temperature for about an hour.

Mix together the softened butter, garlic, and ¼ teaspoon salt in a small bowl.

Preheat a cast iron skillet over high heat, starting over medium heat. Meanwhile, place 3 tablespoons (42 g) of the melted butter into a shallow dish. Add the fillets and turn to coat. Sprinkle evenly with the Cajun Spice on both sides. Add the fillets to the skillet skinned-side up, drizzle each one with 1 teaspoon of the melted butter, and cook without disturbing until charred, 3 to 4 minutes. Flip the fillets, drizzle each one with 1 teaspoon of the melted butter, and cook until the fillets are charred and just begin to flake, 2 to 3 minutes. Serve immediately with the garlic butter and lemon wedges.

Shrimp Etouffee

Like so many dishes of Cajun and Creole cuisine, this dish utilizes a dark oil-and-flour roux, the holy trinity of onion, green bell pepper, and celery, and plenty of garlic and Cajun Spice. A simple stock made from the shrimp shells imparts a rich seafood flavor. *Etouffee* means "smother," so this recipe yields a generous amount of sauce to smother both the shrimp and the rice it's served with.

You can add oysters, crabmeat, and/or crawfish tails if you're feeling flush. // ***Yield: 4 servings***

- **RECOMMENDED SKILLET:** 12 inch (30 cm)

- **COOKING METHOD:** Simmering

20 jumbo (16 to 20 count) shrimp
⅔ cup (160 ml) canola oil
¾ cup (94 g) all-purpose flour
1 yellow onion, diced
1 green bell pepper, diced
2 stalks of celery, diced
Kosher salt
4 cloves of garlic, minced
1 tablespoon (9 g) Cajun Spice (page 250)

½ teaspoon cayenne pepper
1 can (14½ ounces, or 410 g) of diced
    tomatoes in juice
1 bay leaf
Freshly squeezed juice of 1 small lemon
2 large green onions, sliced
2 tablespoons (8 g) minced Italian parsley
Hot white rice, for serving
Tabasco sauce, for serving

Peel and devein the shrimp, reserving the shells. Combine the shells and water in a saucepot. Bring to a boil and simmer until flavorful, 15 to 20 minutes. Strain through a fine-mesh sieve.

Preheat a cast iron skillet over medium heat. Add the oil and flour. Whisk until smooth. Cook, whisking constantly, until the color of peanut butter, 4 to 5 minutes. Add the onion, bell pepper, celery, and a generous pinch of salt and cook, stirring frequently, until soft, 12 to 14 minutes. Add the garlic and stir through. Add the Cajun Spice and cayenne and stir through. Add the shrimp stock, canned tomatoes along with their juice, and bay leaf and bring to a boil, stirring constantly and scraping up the browned bits from the bottom of the skillet with a heatproof spatula. Simmer, stirring occasionally, until thickened, 20 to 25 minutes. Add the shrimp, stir through, and simmer until they are pink and just cooked through, 3 to 4 minutes. The shrimp will curl head to tail into a letter C when they are just cooked through; do not wait until they curl into a letter O or they will be overcooked. Remove the skillet from the heat and remove and discard the bay leaf. Add the lemon juice and stir through. Season to taste with salt. Sprinkle with the green onions and parsley. Serve immediately over the rice with the Tabasco sauce.

▶ Sourcing Shrimp

Opt for gulf shrimp or shrimp that's labeled "Product of the USA" whenever possible. It has a nice, firm texture and sweet, fresh flavor. Farm-raised shrimp from Southeast Asia may be cheaper, but it inevitably has a mushier texture and muddy flavor.

Southwestern Patty Melts

This spiced-up version of the classic American diner sandwich has a double dose of chiles: sliced pickled jalapeños in the topping and chipotles in the spread. I'd say it's a solid medium in terms of heat. If you like the flavor of chiles but prefer something a little milder, try the variation using a mild New Mexico green chile. // *Yield: 4 servings*

- **RECOMMENDED SKILLET:** 12 inch (30 cm)
- **COOKING METHOD:** Searing

(continued)

8 slices of artisan-style sourdough bread

2 ounces (4 tablespoons, or 55 g) unsalted butter, softened

1⅓ pounds (600 g) 15% fat ground beef

Kosher salt

Freshly ground black pepper

¼ cup (60 ml) canola oil, divided

1 yellow onion, julienned

⅓ cup (35 g) drained sliced pickled jalapeños

4 thin slices of sharp cheddar

4 thin slices of Monterey Jack

Chipotle Dipping Sauce (page 255)

Spread 1 side of each of the slices of bread with the butter.

Divide the ground beef into 4 equal portions and gently form each portion into a ball. Gently pat each ball into a 4¼-inch (10.5-cm) patty that's slightly thinner in the center and thicker around the edges. Season the patties generously with salt and pepper.

Preheat a cast iron skillet over medium-high heat, starting over medium heat. Add 2 tablespoons (30 ml) of the oil and swirl to coat the inside. Add the onion and cook, stirring frequently, until nearly soft and golden brown in spots, 4 to 5 minutes. Season to taste with salt and, using a slotted spoon, remove the onion to a bowl.

Add the remaining 2 tablespoons (30 ml) of oil to the skillet and swirl to coat the inside. Add the patties and cook without disturbing until golden brown, 3 to 4 minutes. Working quickly, flip the patties, divide the onion and then the jalapeños among them, then top each one with a slice of the cheddar and Monterey Jack, and cook until the cheese begins to melt and the patties are golden brown and medium, 2 to 3 minutes. The patties will feel firm to the touch when they are medium with a piping hot center. Remove the patties to a platter and tent loosely with foil to keep warm and finish melting the cheese. Pour off all of the accumulated fat from the skillet.

Decrease the heat to medium-low and add 2 to 3 of the slices of the bread to the skillet, buttered-side down. Toast until light golden brown, about 1 minute. Remove the toast to a plate and toast the remaining slices of bread in the same manner.

Arrange 4 slices of the toast, toasted-side down, on individual plates. Divide the Chipotle Dipping Sauce and topped patties among them and then top with the remaining 4 slices of toast, toasted-side up. Serve immediately.

New Mexico Green Chile Variation: Add 1 roasted, peeled, seeded, and julienned New Mexico green chile to the onion just before it's nearly soft and stir through. Omit the sliced pickled jalapeños and, if desired, substitute mayonnaise for the Chipotle Dipping Sauce.

Chicken with Peppers & Mexican Chorizo

This recipe was inspired by a great little taqueria I used to go to back when I lived in Austin, Texas, nearly twenty years ago. One of the tastiest and most satisfying things on the menu was a dish of chicken, chorizo, peppers, and onions, all smothered in cheese and salsa, and I like to re-create it at home often. Serve with Charred Tomatillo Salsa (page 256), Speedy Refried Pinto Beans (page 213), and Flour Tortillas (page 216). And, of course, margaritas are the other requisite accompaniments.

Store-bought chorizo and salsa may be substituted for homemade. Look for pure guajillo chile powder, which is mildly spicy, at Mexican markets or order it online. // **Yield: 6 servings**

■ **RECOMMENDED SKILLET:** 12 inch (30 cm)

■ **COOKING METHOD:** Pan-Frying/Broiling

¼ cup (60 ml) canola oil, divided
Freshly squeezed juice of 1 large lime
2 cloves of garlic, grated on a Microplane
½ teaspoon ground cumin
Generous pinch of cayenne pepper
Kosher salt
1½ pounds (680 g) boneless, skinless chicken thighs, cut into 1½-inch (3.5-cm) pieces
1 red onion, julienned
1 red bell pepper, julienned

1 poblano, julienned
1 pound (455 g) uncooked Homemade Mexican Chorizo (page 58), broken up
1 teaspoon guajillo chile powder
4 ounces (115 g) shredded sharp cheddar (about 1 cup)
4 ounces (115 g) shredded Monterey Jack (about 1 cup)
⅓ cup (5 g) minced cilantro
1 large avocado, diced
1 lime, cut into 6 wedges

Mix together 2 tablespoons (30 ml) of the oil, lime juice, garlic, cumin, cayenne, and a generous pinch of salt in a 1-gallon (3.8-L) zip-top bag. Add the chicken and turn to coat. Seal the bag, letting out all the air. Marinate 4 to 6 hours in the refrigerator.

Preheat the broiler.

Preheat a cast iron skillet over medium heat. Add the remaining 2 tablespoons (30 ml) of oil and swirl to coat the inside. Add the onion and sauté until it begins to soften, about 2 minutes. Add the bell pepper and poblano and sauté until they begin to soften, 5 to 6 minutes. Using a slotted spoon, remove the onion mixture to a bowl.

(continued)

Add the chorizo to the skillet and cook, stirring occasionally, until golden brown and cooked through, 8 to 9 minutes. Using a slotted spoon, remove the chorizo to another bowl. Add the chicken to the skillet and cook, stirring occasionally, until golden brown and cooked through, 16 to 18 minutes.

Add the guajillo chile powder and stir through. Return the onion mixture to the skillet and stir through. Season to taste with salt. Sprinkle with the chorizo and then the cheddar and Monterey Jack.

Broil until the cheese is melted and golden brown, 2 to 3 minutes. Sprinkle with the cilantro and then the avocado. Serve immediately with the lime wedges.

Pork Carnitas

The best pork carnitas are golden brown and crispy and still moist. They should have plenty of big succulent chunks as well as little shredded bits. The trick to cooking such carnitas is starting with a relatively fatty cut of pork from the shoulder, simmering it until it's almost tender, then letting the water reduce out completely, and finally browning it in its own rendered fat. The process takes a little bit of time, but it's quite easy to do.

Dried de arbol chiles are available at Mexican markets. Tien Tsin chiles, or Szechuan chiles, may be substituted if de arbols are not available.

To make authentic taqueria-style tacos, fold these carnitas, along with diced onion and minced cilantro, inside corn or Flour Tortillas (page 216). Top with Charred Tomatillo Salsa (page 256) and serve with Speedy Refried Pinto Beans (page 213) on the side. // *Yield: 6 servings*

- **RECOMMENDED SKILLET:** 12 inch (30 cm) plus lid
- **COOKING METHOD:** Reverse Braising

2 pounds (900 g) boneless pork butt, cut
    into 1½-inch (3.5-cm) pieces
½ of a yellow onion
3 cloves of garlic, smashed
2 whole dried de arbol chiles

1 bay leaf
8 black peppercorns
3 allspice berries
Kosher salt

Combine the pork, onion, garlic, chiles, bay leaf, peppercorns, allspice, a generous pinch of salt, and 1½ cups (355 ml) of water in a cast iron skillet. Bring to a boil, cover the skillet, and simmer, stirring occasionally, until the pork is nearly tender, 45 to 50 minutes. Uncover and simmer, stirring occasionally, until all of the water evaporates, 30 to 35 minutes. Remove and discard the onion, garlic, chiles, bay leaf, peppercorns, and allspice. Adjust the heat to medium-low and cook, stirring occasionally, until the pork is golden brown all over, 12 to 16 minutes. Using a spoon, break up the pieces of pork until there's a nice mix of large chunks and little shredded pieces and cook, stirring frequently, until the little shredded pieces are golden brown and crispy, 4 to 6 minutes. Season to taste with salt and serve hot.

French Lentils with Smoked Sausage

French green lentils, also known as *lentils du Puy*, retain their shape once cooked and have a firm texture and earthy flavor that goes perfectly with smoked sausage. They should be picked over for any stones and then rinsed before cooking, but they do not require presoaking. // *Yield: 4 to 6 servings*

- **RECOMMENDED SKILLET:** 12 inch (30 cm) with lid
- **COOKING METHOD:** Simmering

2 tablespoons (30 ml) extra virgin olive oil
1 yellow onion, diced
2 stalks of celery, diced
1 carrot, diced
3 cloves of garlic, minced
2 cups (384 g) French green lentils,
    picked over and rinsed

12 ounces (340 g) kielbasa or smoked
    sausage, cut into ½-inch (1-cm)
    thick slices
1 bay leaf
3 sprigs of fresh thyme
Kosher salt
Freshly ground black pepper
3 tablespoons (12 g) minced Italian parsley

Preheat a cast iron skillet over medium-low heat. Add the olive oil and swirl to coat the inside. Add the onion and sauté until it begins to soften, 5 to 6 minutes. Add the celery and carrot and sauté until they begin to soften, 5 to 6 minutes. Add the garlic and stir through. Add the lentils, kielbasa, bay leaf, thyme, and 1 quart (946 ml) of water. Bring to a boil, cover the skillet, and simmer, stirring occasionally, until the lentils are tender but toothsome, 45 to 50 minutes. Remove and discard the bay leaf and thyme. Add the parsley and stir through, season to taste with salt and pepper, and serve hot.

Spaghetti Frittata

A frittata is basically an Italian omelet, and just like an American omelet it's often filled with cooked meat and/or vegetables. But ironically, the simplest and seemingly most obvious filling is often overlooked: spaghetti! Pasta in a cast iron frittata crisps up around the edges even better than it does in a lasagna or baked penne, and who doesn't love the crispy edges? Make this frittata and you won't have to fight over the corner pieces!

Note that 8 ounces (225 g) of uncooked spaghetti will yield about 3½ cups (490 g) cooked. You can also use other long cut pastas, such as linguini or fettuccini, instead of spaghetti.

// *Yield: 6 servings*

- **RECOMMENDED SKILLET:** 10¼ inch (26 cm)
- **COOKING METHOD:** Pan-Frying/Baking

8 eggs
⅓ cup (80 ml) milk
2 ounces (55 g) shredded Parmigiano-Reggiano (about ½ cup)
2 tablespoons (5 g) minced fresh basil

1 clove of garlic, grated on a Microplane
½ teaspoon kosher salt, plus more as needed
Freshly ground black pepper
¼ cup (60 ml) extra virgin olive oil
3½ cups (490 g) cooked spaghetti, cold

Preheat the oven to 400°F (200°C, or gas mark 6).

Whisk together the eggs, milk, Parmigiano-Reggiano, basil, garlic, ½ teaspoon of salt, and a generous pinch of pepper in a medium bowl.

Preheat a cast iron skillet over medium heat. Add the olive oil and swirl to coat the inside of the skillet. Add the spaghetti and cook without disturbing until it begins to brown, 5 to 6 minutes. Add the egg mixture and fry until the edges puff and begin to set, 3 to 4 minutes. Transfer the skillet to the oven and bake until golden brown around the edges and set in the center, 10 to 15 minutes. Season with salt, cut into wedges, and serve hot or at room temperature.

Carbonara Variation: Omit the basil. After preheating the skillet, add 4 ounces (115 g) of guanciale, pancetta, or bacon, cut into thin strips, and sauté until golden brown, crispy, and rendered. Add enough olive oil to total about ¼ cup (60 ml) of fat in the skillet. Add the spaghetti and stir through before browning.

Cacio e Pepe Variation: Omit the basil, increase the black pepper to 1 teaspoon, and substitute Pecorino Romano for the Parmigiano-Reggiano.

MAINS

Fried Bologna Sandwiches

Did you know that the now ubiquitous pink lunchmeat baloney originated in a small town in Italy called Bologna? It's the original distinctly porky version, known as *mortadella*, that stars in this indulgent version of the ordinarily humble sandwich. Seek out mortadella imported from Italy as it has superior flavor and texture. // **Yield: 2 servings**

- **RECOMMENDED SKILLET:** 10¼ inch (26 cm) with lid
- **COOKING METHOD:** Pan-Frying

8 ounces (225 g) thinly sliced mortadella
1 tablespoon (15 ml) extra virgin olive oil
2 ounces (55 g) sliced pickled peppers
    (about ¼ cup), such as Mama Lil's
    or pepperoncini

3 ounces (85 g) sliced sharp provolone
2 artisan-style ciabatta rolls, warmed
    and split
1 tablespoon (11 g) Dijon mustard

Make 2 stacks of the mortadella, letting the slices fold and drape randomly as if they were falling off a deli slicer.

Preheat a cast iron skillet over medium heat. Add the olive oil and swirl to coat the inside of the skillet. Add the stacks of mortadella and fry until golden brown and crispy, about 2 minutes. Flip the stacks, divide the pickled peppers and then the provolone among them, cover the skillet, and fry until the provolone is melted and the mortadella is golden brown, crispy, and heated through, about 2 minutes.

Arrange the ciabatta bottoms cut-side up on individual plates. Divide the Dijon mustard and then the mortadella among them and then top with the ciabatta tops, cut-side down. Serve immediately.

Skizza Margherita

If there's one recipe that proves the versatility of the 12-inch (30-cm) cast iron skillet, it's this one in which you turn your skillet upside down and use the bottom as a pizza stone! It works like a charm, resulting in pizza crust that's crispy all the way to the center.

In addition to using the skillet in an unorthodox manner, I employ another cheat: I like to use parchment paper rather than semolina to peel the pizzas in and out of the oven. This method is foolproof even if you don't have pro peeling skills, and it keeps down the mess too!

For more flavorful pizza crust, mix and ferment the dough one day and after dividing and rounding each portion, seal each ball in a separate zip-top bag and keep them in the refrigerator overnight. The next day, let the dough come to room temperature before you make and bake the pizzas. You can of course vary the pizza toppings to your heart's content. Be careful not to overload the crusts with toppings, or you may end up with soggy pizza. // *Yield: 4 servings*

- **RECOMMENDED SKILLET:** 12 inch (30 cm)
- **COOKING METHOD:** Baking

Extra virgin olive oil, for greasing the bowl
3½ cups (438 g) all-purpose flour,
    plus more for dusting
2¼ teaspoons kosher salt
1¼ teaspoons instant yeast
1⅓ cups (327 g) Charred Tomato Sauce
    (page 257)

½ teaspoon oregano
8 ounces (225 g) fresh mozzarella, sliced
    and drained thoroughly on paper towels
2 ounces (55 g) shredded Parmigiano-
    Reggiano (about ½ cup)
12 basil leaves

Oil a large bowl.

Mix together the flour and salt in a stand mixer bowl. Add the yeast and stir through. Add 1¼ cups (295 ml) plus 3 tablespoons (45 ml) of tepid (85°F [29°C]) water and stir until a shaggy dough begins to form. Fit onto the mixer with the dough hook attachment and mix on low speed until a smooth and elastic dough forms, 8 to 10 minutes. The dough will be quite sticky. Using oiled hands, form the dough into a ball with a tight skin by tucking all of the edges into the bottom, transfer to the oiled bowl seam-side down, and cover the bowl with plastic wrap. Let the dough ferment at room temperature for about 2½ hours. After about 30 minutes, 1 hour, and 1½ hours of fermentation, and working with the dough directly in the bowl, gently stretch the dough from the center to double its length and fold it like a tri-fold letter, turn it 90 degrees and stretch and fold again, turn it seam-side down, and re-cover the bowl with plastic wrap.

(continued)

Place a cast iron skillet upside down on a rack in the center of the oven and preheat the oven to 500°F (250°C, or gas mark 10).

Working with a light touch to prevent it from deflating too much, gently tip the dough out onto a lightly floured surface. Cut the dough into quarters and form each portion into a ball by tucking all of the edges into the bottom. Place seam-side down, cover with a clean kitchen towel, and let rest for 20 to 30 minutes.

Stretch one ball of dough to an 8½- to 9-inch (21- to 23-cm) wide crust that's slightly thicker around the edges and place it onto a 10-inch (25.5-cm) parchment circle on a pizza peel. Scoop about ⅓ cup (82 g) of the Charred Tomato Sauce onto the crust and spread it evenly with the back of a spoon, leaving a border at the edge. Sprinkle about one-quarter of the oregano over the tomato sauce. Arrange about one-quarter of the mozzarella, tearing it into pieces, over the top of the tomato sauce. Sprinkle about one-quarter of the Parmigiano-Reggiano over the mozzarella. Carefully slide the pizza on the parchment circle to the bottom of the skillet in the oven and bake until the crust is golden brown around the edges and on the bottom and the cheese is bubbling, 10 to 12 minutes. Transfer to a cutting board. Tear 3 leaves of basil into pieces and sprinkle over the pizza. Cut the pizza into wedges and serve hot.

Make and bake more pizzas with the remaining dough, Charred Tomato Sauce, oregano, mozzarella, Parmigiano-Reggiano, and basil in the same manner.

Pepperoni Variation: Arrange 1 to 1½ ounces (28 to 42 g) of sliced pepperoni over the top of the cheese on each pizza before baking.

Tartufo Variation: Omit the Charred Tomato Sauce, oregano, and basil. Top each pizza with 1 ounce (28 g) of sliced sharp provolone, torn into pieces, after the mozzarella. Sprinkle with a generous pinch of freshly ground coarse black pepper and then arrange 1 sliced large button or cremini mushroom over the top of the cheese before baking. Drizzle each pizza with ½ teaspoon of truffle oil immediately after baking.

Chicken Parmesan

Chicken parm has been one of my favorites since I was a little girl, so I make it on a regular basis. And I'm always striving to perfect my approach. As a result of all my experimentation, I've determined that aside from starting with the best-quality ingredients, the secret to the most fantastic chicken parm is creating and, perhaps even more importantly, maintaining a crunchy crust. Doing the Three-Step Breading Procedure (page 21) and pan-frying like a pro is all for nothing if the breading winds up getting soggy when the chicken is topped with the tomato sauce and cheese. So, I have found that using a relatively thick sauce like my Charred Tomato Sauce (page 257) and then keeping the chicken elevated on a rack out of any moisture that might accumulate beneath it during the broiling step keeps the breading perfectly crisp. I'll even go out on a limb and say it makes for the best chicken parm ever!

Serve this chicken with a side of pasta with additional Charred Tomato Sauce. It also makes a great sandwich. // **Yield: 4 servings**

- **RECOMMENDED SKILLET:** 12 inch (30 cm)

- **COOKING METHOD:** Pan-Frying/Broiling

⅓ cup (42 g) all-purpose flour
Kosher salt
Freshly ground black pepper
1 egg
1 cup (115 g) panko bread crumbs
1⅓ ounces (38 g) shredded Parmigiano-
   Reggiano (about ⅓ cup)
1 teaspoon oregano

2 boneless, skinless chicken breasts
   (10 to 12 ounces, 280 to 340 g each)
½ cup (120 ml) canola oil
1 cup (245 g) warm Charred Tomato Sauce
   (page 257)
4 ounces (115 g) sliced mozzarella
   or sharp provolone

Whisk together the flour and a generous pinch of salt and pepper in a shallow dish. Whisk together the egg, 2 tablespoons (30 ml) of water, and a generous pinch of salt and pepper in another shallow dish. Mix together the panko, Parmigiano-Reggiano, oregano, and a generous pinch of salt and pepper in another shallow dish bowl.

Gently pound out the chicken breasts to an even thickness of ¾ inch (2 cm) with a flat meat pounder and cut each breast into 2 equal portions. Season generously with salt and pepper.

(continued)

Roll each portion of chicken in the seasoned flour to coat. Shake off any excess flour and dip each portion of chicken into the egg mixture to coat. Shake off any excess egg and roll each portion of chicken in the panko mixture, patting so that it adheres. Place the chicken portion onto a rack on a sheet tray and set aside for 15 to 20 minutes to allow the breading to set.

Preheat the broiler.

Pour the oil into a cast iron skillet and preheat over medium heat until a pinch of panko sizzles immediately when added. Add the chicken and cook without disturbing until golden brown, 6 to 7 minutes. Flip the chicken and cook until golden brown and cooked through, 5 to 6 minutes. The chicken will feel firm to the touch when it is cooked through. Transfer the chicken to a rack on a sheet tray. Divide the Charred Tomato Sauce among the chicken portions and then top with the cheese. Broil until the cheese is melted and golden brown, 2 to 3 minutes. Serve immediately.

Chicken Piccata

Piccata sauce, with its wine, lemon juice, and capers, is rather acidic and tends to strip off a bit of the skillet's seasoning. This is not a big deal as long as you make it in a skillet with a well-established seasoning layer. Just be sure to oil the skillet and heat it on the stovetop until it smokes after washing it (page 34).

Serve on a bed of pasta.

Turkey, pork, or veal cutlets may be substituted for the chicken. // *Yield: 4 servings*

- **RECOMMENDED SKILLET:** 12 inch (30 cm)
- **COOKING METHOD:** Sautéing

⅓ cup (42 g) all-purpose flour
Kosher salt
Freshly ground black pepper
2 boneless, skinless chicken breasts
   (10 to 12 ounces, or 280 to 340 g each)
2 tablespoons (30 ml) extra virgin olive oil
2 ounces (4 tablespoons, or 55 g)
   unsalted butter, cut into 1-tablespoon
   (14-g) pieces, divided

¾ cup (175 ml) white wine
3 tablespoons (45 ml) freshly squeezed
   lemon juice
¼ cup (34 g) drained capers
3 tablespoons (12 g) minced Italian parsley

Whisk together the flour and a generous pinch of salt and pepper in a shallow dish.

Gently pound out the chicken breasts to an even thickness of ¾ inch (2 cm) with a flat meat pounder and cut each breast into 2 equal portions. Season generously with salt and pepper.

Preheat a cast iron skillet over medium heat. Add the olive oil and ½ ounce (1 tablespoon, or 14 g) of the butter, swirl to coat the inside of the skillet, and heat until the butter is melted and the foam subsides. Just before the oil and butter come to temperature, quickly roll 1 portion of chicken in the seasoned flour to coat, shake off any excess flour, add it to the skillet, and repeat with the remaining 3 portions. Cook without disturbing until golden brown, about 4 to 5 minutes. Flip the chicken and cook until golden brown, 3 to 4 minutes. Remove the chicken to a platter.

Add the wine, lemon juice, and capers to the skillet, bring to a boil, stirring constantly and scraping up the browned bits from the bottom of the skillet with a heatproof spatula. Simmer until thickened slightly, 2 to 3 minutes. Return the chicken and any accumulated juices to the skillet and simmer, flipping the chicken occasionally, until the sauce is thickened and the chicken is cooked through, 5 to 6 minutes. The chicken will feel firm to the touch when it is cooked through. Remove the skillet from the heat and let the bubbling subside. Add the parsley and remaining 1½ ounces (3 tablespoons, or 42 g) butter to the sauce and stir until smooth. Season the sauce to taste with salt and pepper and serve immediately.

Homemade Spicy Italian Sausage

Here's another recipe that's a significant upgrade over store-bought. The bulk sausage can be stuffed into casings, but why bother? I find that patties work in pretty much any recipe that would ordinarily be made with links.

Add browned crumbles to tomato sauce for pasta or use as a topping for Skizza Margherita (page 149). Tuck cooked patties inside split hoagie rolls along with some sautéed peppers and onions, top with Charred Tomato Sauce (page 257) and then mozzarella or sharp provolone, and heat in a hot oven until the cheese is melted.

Wild fennel seed, which is usually imported from Italy, has a lovely sweet quality and can be found online.

When making fresh sausage, do not try to use ground pork with a lower fat content. Keep all equipment and ingredients well chilled and mix until thoroughly blended and visibly sticky to ensure proper emulsification. Stickiness is a sign that the proteins have bound with the liquid in the meat and the emulsion is set. The result when cooked is juicy sausage that holds together because fat won't render as readily.

Using a gram scale is certainly preferred. But since not everybody has one, I have included the amount of each ingredient in both weight and approximate volume measurements to use for 2 pounds (900 grams) of ground pork.

You can cook the sausage as soon as it is mixed, but the flavor benefits from being refrigerated overnight. Raw sausage may be kept tightly sealed in the refrigerator for 3 to 4 days or in the freezer for several weeks. Portion bulk sausage into zip-top or vacuum sealer bags and flatten to a thickness of no more than ¾ inch (2 cm) before sealing for speedy freezing and thawing.

// *Yield: about 2 pounds (900 grams)*

- **RECOMMENDED SKILLET:** 12 inch (30 cm)
- **COOKING METHOD:** Pan-Frying

PERCENTAGE	AMOUNT FOR 2 POUNDS (900 G) OF GROUND PORK	
100%	900 grams/2.00 pounds	20 to 30% fat ground pork, broken up
1.75%	15.9 grams/0.56 ounces/2 tablespoons plus 1 teaspoon	kosher salt
0.5%	4.5 grams/0.16 ounces/2 teaspoons	fennel seeds, preferably wild
0.4%	3.6 grams/0.13 ounces/1 tablespoon	red chile flakes
0.1%	0.91 grams/0.03 ounces/½ teaspoon	freshly ground black pepper
1%	9.1 grams/0.32 ounces/1 tablespoon plus 1 teaspoon	minced garlic
1.5%	13.6 grams/0.48 ounces/1 tablespoon	red wine
0.5%	4.5 grams/0.16 ounces/1 teaspoon	red wine vinegar

TO COOK:
2 tablespoons (30 ml) extra virgin olive oil

Whisk together the salt, fennel, red chile flakes, and pepper in a small bowl.

Place the pork into a stand mixer bowl, sprinkle with the salt mixture, garlic, red wine, and red wine vinegar, fit onto the mixer with the paddle attachment, and mix on low speed until thoroughly blended and visibly sticky, about 2 minutes.

To cook crumbles, break the raw sausage into small bits.

Preheat a cast iron skillet over medium-low to medium heat. Add the olive oil and swirl to coat the inside of the skillet. Add 12 to 16 ounces (340 to 455 g) of broken up sausage at a time and cook, stirring occasionally, until golden brown, 4 to 6 minutes for partially cooked and 6 to 10 minutes for completely cooked through, depending on the final use.

To cook patties, divide the raw sausage into 3-ounce (85-g) portions and gently form each portion into a ball. Gently pat each ball into a 3¼-inch (8-cm) patty that's slightly thinner in the center and thicker around the edges; doing this prevents the patty from cooking up into a ball shape.

Preheat a cast iron skillet over medium-low heat. Add the olive oil and swirl to coat the inside of the skillet. Add 5 to 6 patties at a time and cook without disturbing until golden brown, 5 to 6 minutes. Flip the patties and cook until golden brown and just cooked through, 4 to 5 minutes. Moisture will pool on the surface of the patties and they will feel firm to the touch when they are just cooked through. Serve hot.

Pork Cutlet Marsala

The deep, rich flavor of this dish makes it difficult to believe that it takes less than half an hour to make from start to finish. Pounded chicken breasts or veal cutlets may be substituted for the pork. Serve this saucy dish over pasta. // *Yield: 4 servings*

- **RECOMMENDED SKILLET:** 12 inch (30 cm)
- **COOKING METHOD:** Sautéing

⅓ cup (42 g) all-purpose flour
Kosher salt
Freshly ground black pepper
4 boneless pork rib chops, center cut loin
   chops, or sirloin chops (4 ounces,
   or 115 g each), ¾ inch (2 cm) thick
2 tablespoons (30 ml) extra virgin olive oil

2 ounces (4 tablespoons, or 55 g)
   unsalted butter, cut into 1-tablespoon
   (14-g) pieces, divided
8 ounces (225 g) button or cremini
   mushrooms, sliced (about 1 quart)
1 shallot, minced
1 cup (235 ml) dry marsala
½ cup (120 ml) chicken stock

Whisk together the flour and a generous pinch of salt and pepper in a shallow dish. Gently pound out the pork chops to an even thickness of ⅜ inch (1 cm) with a flat meat pounder and season generously with salt and pepper.

Preheat a cast iron skillet over medium heat. Add the olive oil and 1 ounce (2 tablespoons, or 28 g) of the butter, swirl to coat the inside of the skillet, and heat until the butter is melted and the foam subsides. Just before the oil and butter come to temperature, quickly roll 1 cutlet in the seasoned flour to coat, shake off any excess flour, add it to the skillet, and repeat with the remaining 3 cutlets. Cook without disturbing until light golden brown, about 2 minutes. Flip the cutlets and cook until light golden brown, 1 to 2 minutes. Remove the cutlets to a platter.

Add the mushrooms to the skillet and cook, stirring once or twice, until golden brown and soft, 5 to 6 minutes. Add the shallot and sauté until it begins to soften, about 1 minute. Add the marsala, bring to a boil, stirring constantly and scraping up the browned bits from the bottom of the skillet with a heatproof spatula, and simmer until thickened slightly, 2 to 3 minutes. Add the chicken stock and simmer until thickened slightly, 4 to 5 minutes. Return the cutlets and any accumulated juices to the skillet and simmer, flipping the cutlets occasionally, until the sauce is thickened and the cutlets are heated through, about 2 minutes. Remove the skillet from the heat and let the bubbling subside. Add the remaining 1 ounce (2 tablespoons, or 28 g) of butter to the sauce and stir until smooth. Season the sauce to taste with salt and pepper and serve immediately.

Meatballs with Charred Tomato Sauce

Making this recipe is not an all-day affair, but it sure tastes like it is. The relatively short simmer time is enough to infuse the tomato sauce with loads of meaty flavor.

If you like to make meatballs with a combination of different meats, feel free to substitute pork and/or veal for a portion of the beef. And if you like your tomato sauce a bit on the sweeter side, feel free to throw in some diced onion after browning the meatballs and let it cook a couple of minutes until it begins to soften before adding the sauce.

Serve over spaghetti or tuck inside split hoagie rolls, top with mozzarella or sharp provolone, and heat in a hot oven until the cheese is melted. // *Yield: 4 servings*

- **RECOMMENDED SKILLET:** 12 inch (30 cm) plus lid
- **COOKING METHOD:** Braising

1 egg
1 tablespoon (16 g) tomato paste
3 tablespoons (12 g) minced Italian parsley
3 cloves of garlic, minced
¼ teaspoon red chile flakes
Kosher salt
Freshly ground black pepper

1¼ pounds (570 g) 15% fat ground beef
1 cup (115 g) panko bread crumbs
2 ounces (55 g) shredded Parmigiano-Reggiano (about ½ cup)
3 tablespoons (45 ml) extra virgin olive oil
2½ cups (613 g) Charred Tomato Sauce (page 257)

Mix together the egg, tomato paste, parsley, garlic, red chile flakes, and several generous pinches of salt and pepper in a large bowl. Add the ground beef, panko, and Parmigiano-Reggiano and mix just until thoroughly combined. Pinch off golf ball–size pieces of the beef mixture and gently form each portion into a ball to make 16 (1¾-inch [4.5-cm]) meatballs.

Preheat a cast iron skillet over medium heat. Add the olive oil and swirl to coat the inside of the skillet. Add the meatballs and cook, flipping occasionally, until golden brown all over, 8 to 10 minutes. Add the Charred Tomato Sauce and bring to a boil. Cover the skillet and simmer until the meatballs are tender, 55 to 60 minutes. Season the sauce to taste with salt and pepper. Serve hot.

Veal Saltimbocca

With little more than veal, sage, and prosciutto, this recipe is saltimbocca in its most essential form. Other versions call for dredging the scaloppini in flour or making a pan sauce, but to my mind, those steps are superfluous and detract from the golden-brown, crispy, and rendered prosciutto.

The recipe takes perhaps 5 minutes to prepare and literally only 2 minutes to cook. This means it's even faster than takeout and significantly more healthy and delicious.

Pounded chicken breasts or pork or turkey cutlets may be substituted for the veal.

// *Yield: 4 servings*

- **RECOMMENDED SKILLET:** 12 inch (30 cm)
- **COOKING METHOD:** Searing

4 veal scaloppini (3 ounces, or 85 g each),
   ¼ inch (6 mm) thick
Kosher salt
Freshly ground black pepper
12 sage leaves

2½ ounces (70 g) paper-thin slices
   prosciutto
2 tablespoons (30 ml) extra virgin olive oil
1 lemon, cut into 8 wedges, optional

Season the scaloppini generously with kosher salt and pepper. Arrange 3 sage leaves on each scaloppini and then drape the prosciutto over them, pressing so that it adheres.

Preheat a cast iron skillet over medium-high heat, starting over medium heat. Add the olive oil and swirl to coat the inside of the skillet. Add the scaloppini prosciutto-side down and cook without disturbing until the prosciutto is golden brown, about 1 minute. Flip the scaloppini and cook until golden brown, about 1 minute. Serve immediately with the lemon wedges, if desired.

Skillet-Roasted Fish Fillets with Olives, Capers, Tomatoes & Parmigiano-Reggiano Bread Crumbs

This dish, which is loosely inspired by the flavors of Italy, can be made with any variety of thick, firm-fleshed fish fillets. If the fishmonger doesn't have fresh salmon or halibut, by all means substitute whatever looks best that day. Tuna, swordfish, mahi, haddock, and many others would work. Just opt for fresh fish as frozen exudes a lot of water when cooked.

Serve on a bed of orzo or other pasta or polenta. // *Yield: 4 servings*

- **RECOMMENDED SKILLET:** 12 inch (30 cm)

- **COOKING METHOD:** Pan-Roasting

4 center cut salmon or halibut fillets
   (6 ounces, or 170 g each), skinned
   and boned
Kosher salt
Freshly ground black pepper
⅔ cup (75 g) panko bread crumbs
2 ounces (55 g) shredded Parmigiano-
   Reggiano (about ½ cup)
¼ cup (60 ml) plus 2 tablespoons (30 ml)
   extra virgin olive oil, divided

12 ounces (340 g) cherry or grape tomatoes,
   halved (about 2 cups)
¼ cup (25 g) pitted and quartered
   Kalamata olives
2 tablespoons (17 g) drained capers
2 cloves of garlic, minced
3 tablespoons (12 g) minced Italian parsley
1 teaspoon oregano

Season the fillets generously with kosher salt and pepper and set aside at room temperature for about an hour.

Preheat the oven to 450°F (230°C, or gas mark 8).

Mix together the panko, Parmigiano-Reggiano, 2 tablespoons (30 ml) of the olive oil, and a generous pinch of salt and pepper in a medium bowl. Mix together the tomatoes, olives, capers, garlic, parsley, oregano, 2 tablespoons (30 ml) of the olive oil, and a generous pinch of salt and pepper in another medium bowl.

Preheat a cast iron skillet over medium-high heat, starting over medium heat. Add the remaining 2 tablespoons (30 ml) of olive oil and swirl to coat the inside of the skillet. Add the fillets skinned-side up and cook without disturbing until light golden brown, 2 to 3 minutes. Working quickly, flip the fillets, add the tomato mixture all around them, and top with the panko mixture. Transfer the skillet to the oven and bake until the panko mixture is light golden brown, the tomato mixture is bubbling, and the fillets just begin to flake, 4 to 6 minutes. Serve immediately.

Mussels & Spanish Chorizo in Saffron Broth

Live mussels are highly perishable and should be cooked the same day they are purchased. To prepare mussels, pick through them and discard those with broken shells and any that stay open after being jostled as they are no longer alive. Scrub them with a stiff bristled brush under cool running water and tear off the little tuft of fibers known as the beard. Discard any mussels that remain tightly shut after being cooked.

Serve these mussels with a baguette for dipping into the broth and a salad with an acidic vinaigrette. // **Yield: 2 to 4 servings**

- **RECOMMENDED SKILLET:** Deep 10¼ inch (26 cm) with lid
- **COOKING METHOD:** Steaming

2 tablespoons (30 ml) extra virgin olive oil
6 ounces (170 g) Spanish chorizo, cut into ³⁄₁₆-inch (5-mm) thick slices
3 large cloves of garlic, minced
¼ teaspoon red chile flakes
1 quart (946 ml) chicken stock
Generous pinch of saffron
1 can (14.5 ounces, or 410 g) of diced tomatoes in juice, drained

1 red bell pepper, roasted, peeled, seeded, and diced
2 pounds (908 g) mussels, scrubbed and debearded
3 tablespoons minced (12 g) Italian parsley
2 ounces (4 tablespoons, or 55 g) unsalted butter, cut into 1-tablespoon (14-g) pieces
Kosher salt
Freshly ground black pepper

Preheat a deep cast iron skillet over medium heat. Add the olive oil and swirl to coat the inside of the skillet. Add the chorizo and sauté until golden brown, about 2 minutes. Add the garlic and red chile flakes and stir through. Add the chicken stock, saffron, tomatoes, and bell pepper and bring to a boil. Add the mussels, cover the skillet, and simmer just until the mussels open, 3 to 4 minutes. Remove the skillet from the heat. Using a wire skimmer, divide the mussels and chorizo among individual bowls, discarding any mussels that did not open. Add the parsley and butter to the skillet and whisk until smooth. Season the broth to taste with salt and pepper, divide among the individual bowls, and serve immediately.

MAINS

Fried Potatoes with Pulpo, Chistorra, Green Olives, Sunny-Side Up Eggs & Pimentón Mayo

The popular Spanish dish patatas bravas inspired me to create this recipe. With a few tasty additions, I turned the popular tapa into a substantial main course.

Pulpo is Spanish for "octopus." I recommend Matiz brand oil-packed canned octopus, but you can choose to omit it from this dish if you're not a fan of strongly flavored seafood. Chistorra is a partially cured smoky Spanish cooking sausage that's often served with eggs. If you cannot fine it, use Spanish chorizo, which is more widely available. Choose sweet Spanish paprika, or pimentón dulce, as opposed to hot, or picante, for this dish. All of these ingredients can be found at gourmet markets and online. // *Yield: 4 servings*

- **RECOMMENDED SKILLETS:** 10¼ inch (26 cm) and 12 inch (30 cm)

- **COOKING METHOD:** Pan-Frying

½ cup (115 g) mayonnaise, preferably
    Best Foods
Freshly squeezed juice of 1 small lemon
2 cloves of garlic, grated on a Microplane
2 teaspoons sweet Spanish paprika
Kosher salt
½ cup (120 ml) plus 2 tablespoons
    (30 ml) olive oil, divided
8 ounces (225 g) chistorra sausage,
    cut into ½-inch (1-cm) pieces

4 medium (about 2½ pounds, or 1.1 kg total)
    russet potatoes, peeled, cut into ½-inch
    (1-cm) cubes, rinsed until the water runs
    clear, drained, and dried thoroughly on
    paper towels
⅓ cup (33 g) pitted and quartered
    green olives
2 (4-ounce [115-g]) cans of oil-packed
    octopus, drained
Freshly ground black pepper
4 eggs

Whisk together the mayonnaise, lemon juice, garlic, and Spanish paprika in a medium bowl and season to taste with salt. Cover and set aside.

Preheat a cast iron skillet over medium heat. Add ½ cup (120 ml) of the olive oil and swirl to coat the inside of the skillet. Add the chistorra and sauté until golden brown, 2 to 3 minutes. Using a slotted spoon, remove the chistorra to a bowl. Add the potatoes to the skillet and fry, stirring every 5 minutes or so, until dark golden brown, crispy, and nearly tender, 28 to 32 minutes. Return the chistorra to the skillet and fry, stirring occasionally, until the potatoes are tender and the chistorra is heated through, about 2 minutes. Remove the skillet from the heat and add the olives and octopus and stir through. Season to taste with salt and pepper and set aside to keep warm.

Preheat another cast iron skillet over medium heat. Add the remaining 2 tablespoons (30 ml) of olive oil and swirl to coat the inside of the skillet. Add the eggs one at a time, decrease the heat to medium-low, and fry until the whites are nearly set and the yolks are still runny, 2 to 3 minutes. Season with salt and pepper.

Top the potatoes with the fried eggs and serve immediately with the Pimentón Mayo.

Beer-Braised Bratwurst & Cabbage

When you need a quick, easy, and hearty dinner that everyone's sure to love, look no further. Serve grainy mustard for dipping and some sort of fried potatoes on the side. // *Yield: 4 servings*

- **RECOMMENDED SKILLET:** 12 inch (30 cm) with lid
- **COOKING METHOD:** Braising

2 tablespoons (30 ml) canola oil
4 links of fresh bratwurst (about 1¼ pounds, or 570 g total)
½ of a small sweet onion, sliced
¼ teaspoon caraway seeds
½ of a large green cabbage (about 1¾ pounds, or 795 g), cut through the core end into 4 equal wedges

1 cup (235 ml) pilsner beer
1 clove of garlic, grated on a Microplane
1 ounce (2 tablespoons, or 28 g) unsalted butter, cut into 1-tablespoon (14-g) pieces
Kosher salt
Freshly ground black pepper

Preheat a cast iron skillet over medium heat. Add the oil and swirl to coat the inside of the skillet. Add the bratwurst and fry until golden brown, about 2 minutes. Flip the bratwurst, add the onion all around them, and fry until the bratwurst are golden brown, 1 to 2 minutes. Add the caraway seeds and stir through. Nestle in the cabbage wedges. Add the beer, garlic, and butter and bring to a boil. Cover the skillet and simmer, flipping the cabbage occasionally, until the bratwurst are cooked through and the cabbage is tender, 15 to 20 minutes. Season to taste with salt and pepper and serve immediately.

MAINS

Turkey Cordon Bleu

Cordon bleu is French for "blue ribbon," and this preparation of ham and cheese sandwiched inside turkey breast cutlets and then pan-fried until golden brown and crispy is indeed worthy of a prize.

Some cooks use toothpicks to secure the stuffed cutlets, but as long as you're careful to keep all the layers together, there's no need. Also, I find that toothpicks just get in the way during the Three-Step Breading Procedure (page 21).

Cordon bleu is often prepared with chicken, and chicken breasts can of course be substituted for the turkey. You can also use pork or veal cutlets. // **Yield: 4 to 6 servings**

- **RECOMMENDED SKILLET:** 12 inch (30 cm)
- **COOKING METHOD:** Pan-Frying

⅓ cup (42 g) all-purpose flour
Kosher salt
Freshly ground black pepper
1 egg
1¼ cups (140 g) panko bread crumbs
4 turkey breast cutlets (7 ounces,
   or 200 g each)
2 teaspoons Dijon mustard

2 ounces (55 g) sliced Jarlsberg
   or Swiss cheese
2 ounces (55 g) thinly sliced
   Black Forest ham
¾ cup (175 ml) canola oil
2 ounces (4 tablespoons, or 55 g)
   unsalted butter, cut into 1-tablespoon
   (14-g) pieces

Whisk together the flour and a generous pinch of salt and pepper in a shallow dish. Whisk together the egg, 2 tablespoons (30 ml) of water, and a generous pinch of salt and pepper in another shallow dish. Mix together the panko and a generous pinch of salt and pepper in another shallow dish bowl.

Gently pound the cutlets to an even thickness of ½ inch (1 cm) with a flat meat pounder. Season generously with salt and pepper. Spread the Dijon mustard over one-half of each cutlet, leaving a ¼- to ½-inch (6-mm to 1-cm) border at the edge, and then layer the Jarlsberg or Swiss and Black Forest ham over the top of the mustard. Fold each cutlet in half over the filling and press firmly to seal.

Being careful to keep the stuffed cutlets intact, roll each one in the seasoned flour to coat. Shake off any excess flour and dip each cutlet into the egg mixture to coat. Shake off any excess egg and roll each cutlet in the panko mixture, patting so that it adheres. Place the cutlets onto a rack on a sheet tray and set aside for 15 to 20 minutes to allow the breading to set.

MAINS

Pour the oil into a cast iron skillet, add the butter, and preheat over medium heat until a pinch of panko sizzles immediately when added. Add the cutlets and cook without disturbing until golden brown, 7 to 8 minutes. Flip the cutlets and cook, decreasing the heat a bit if they seem to be browning too quickly, until golden brown and cooked through, 6 to 7 minutes. The cutlets will feel firm to the touch when they are cooked through. Remove the cutlets to a platter, tent loosely with foil to keep warm, and let rest for 5 to 10 minutes.

Carve the cutlets against the grain as desired and serve immediately.

Rösti Potatoes with Lox, Sour Cream & Chives

Rösti is a Swiss dish and basically hash browns by another name. Of course, they may be served simply with fried eggs, but here they're fancied up with cured salmon and fresh chives.

Potatoes for rösti and hash browns are often shredded, but taking the time to julienne them into ⅛-inch (3-mm) thick matchstick pieces, either with a knife or mandoline, yields far superior results. That's because potatoes cut with a sharp knife exude significantly less starchy liquid than shredded potatoes, and so they brown less and wind up with a more desirable texture. Par-cooking the potatoes in the microwave cuts down on the cooking time and the sticking as well. If you find the skillet too heavy to pick up and easily slide the rösti out, simply use two large spatulas and lift it out. // *Yield: 2 to 4 servings*

- **RECOMMENDED SKILLET:** 10¼ inch (26 cm)
- **COOKING METHOD:** Pan-Frying

¼ cup (60 g) sour cream
3 tablespoons (9 g) minced fresh chives
2 medium russet potatoes
    (about 1½ pounds, or 680 g total),
    peeled and julienned

Kosher salt
⅓ cup (80 ml) canola oil
Freshly ground black pepper
4 ounces (115 g) sliced lox

Whisk together the sour cream and chives in a small bowl and season to taste with salt. Cover and set aside.

(continued)

Preheat a cast iron skillet over medium-low heat. Meanwhile, place the potatoes into a shallow microwave-safe dish, cover with plastic wrap, and microwave, stirring occasionally, until steamy, translucent, and tender-crisp, 3 to 4 minutes. Add the oil to the skillet and swirl to coat the inside. Add the potatoes, pressing them firmly and evenly into the skillet with the back of a spatula, and fry until golden brown and crispy, 12 to 14 minutes. Run a spatula around the edge of the skillet to loosen the potatoes and slide out of the skillet onto a plate, being careful not to spill the hot oil. Place another plate over the potatoes and invert to flip them. Slide the rösti and any accumulated oil back into the skillet, piecing any bits that may have broken back together again, and fry until golden brown, crispy, and tender, 6 to 7 minutes. Transfer to a platter and season to taste with salt and pepper.

Spread the sour cream mixture over the rösti and then arrange the lox over the top of it, cut into wedges, and serve immediately.

Beef Stroganoff

Here's a slow-cooked version of the Russian dish of beef and mushrooms in a richly flavored *smetana*, or sour cream, sauce. Serve it over hot egg noodles or rice. // **Yield: 4 servings**

- **RECOMMENDED SKILLET:** 12 inch (30 cm)
- **COOKING METHOD:** Braising

1¾ pounds (795 g) boneless beef chuck
   roast, cut into ½ x ½ x 2-inch
   (1 x 1 x 5-cm) strips
Kosher salt
Freshly ground black pepper
3 tablespoons (45 ml) canola oil

1 yellow onion, julienned
8 ounces (225 g) button or cremini
   mushrooms, sliced (about 1 quart)
¼ cup (65 g) tomato paste
1¼ cups (295 ml) beef stock
½ cup (115 g) sour cream

Season the beef generously with salt and pepper.

Preheat a cast iron skillet over medium-high heat, starting over medium heat. Add the oil and swirl to coat the inside. Add about one-half of the beef and cook, stirring occasionally, until golden brown, 5 to 6 minutes. Using a slotted spoon, remove the beef to a bowl. Sear the remaining beef in the same manner. Return the first batch of beef and any accumulated juices to the skillet.

Decrease the heat to medium-low, add the onion and a generous pinch of salt, and cook, stirring frequently, until the onion is nearly golden brown, 40 to 45 minutes. Add the mushrooms and cook, stirring frequently until they begin to soften, 8 to 10 minutes. Add the tomato paste and cook, stirring constantly, until it begins to brown, 2 to 3 minutes. Add the beef stock and bring to a boil, stirring constantly and scraping up the browned bits from the bottom of the skillet with a heatproof spatula. Cover the skillet and simmer, stirring occasionally, until the beef is tender, 1¾ hours to 2 hours. Remove the skillet from the heat and let the bubbling subside. Skim off the fat from the surface as desired. Add the sour cream and stir through. Season to taste with salt and pepper. Serve hot.

Lamb Sliders with Roasted Red Pepper & Feta Sauce

These burgers may be diminutive in size, but they have full-size taste. Grated onion, along with coriander and cumin, flavors the meat and makes the patties especially tender, juicy, and succulent. With pureed feta as its base, the brightly colored sauce adds saltiness and tang and highlights the lamb perfectly.

If you like, top the burgers with thinly sliced red onions and quartered Kalamata olives in addition to the butter lettuce and sauce. // *Yield: 4 to 6 servings*

- **RECOMMENDED SKILLET:** 12 inch (30 cm)
- **COOKING METHOD:** Searing

5 ounces (140 g) sharp feta cheese
1 red bell pepper, roasted, peeled, seeded, and coarsely diced
2 cloves of garlic, sliced
¼ cup (60 ml) extra virgin olive oil
Freshly squeezed juice of 1 large lemon
Kosher salt
Freshly ground black pepper
1½ pounds (680 g) 15% fat ground lamb

½ of a small red onion, grated
1 teaspoon ground coriander
½ teaspoon ground cumin
Generous pinch of cayenne pepper
3 tablespoons (45 ml) canola oil
12 warm artisan-style slider buns or dinner rolls, split
1 (5-ounce [140-g]) carton butter lettuce heart leaves

(continued)

MAINS

Combine the feta, roasted red bell pepper, garlic, olive oil, and lemon juice in a blender and blend until smooth. Season to taste with salt and pepper and set aside at room temperature.

Combine the lamb, onion, coriander, cumin, cayenne, and a generous pinch of salt and pepper in a large bowl and mix just until thoroughly combined. Pinch off ping pong ball–size pieces of the lamb mixture and gently form each portion into a ball. Gently pat each ball into a 3-inch (7.5-cm) patty that's slightly thinner in the center and thicker around the edges to make 12 patties. Season the patties generously with salt and pepper.

Preheat a cast iron skillet over medium heat. Add the canola oil and swirl to coat the inside of the skillet. Add 6 of the patties and cook without disturbing until golden brown, 3 to 4 minutes. Flip the patties and cook until golden brown and just cooked through, 2 to 3 minutes. Moisture will pool on the surface of the patties and they will feel firm to the touch when they are just cooked through. Remove the patties to a platter and tent loosely with foil to keep warm. Cook the remaining patties in the same manner.

Arrange the bun bottoms, cut-side up, on a platter. Divide the patties, lettuce, and sauce among them and then top with the bun tops cut-side down. Serve immediately.

Chicken & Couscous with Pine Nuts, Golden Raisins & Moroccan Spices

A heady blend of spices inspired by the cuisine of North Africa, including coriander, cumin, cinnamon, and chile, gives this couscous dish its exotic flavor. I don't claim it to be authentic, but it is absolutely delicious and perfect for when you're in the mood for something a little different.

Aleppo pepper, which comes from Syria, is a mildly hot ground chile. It is available at Mediterranean and Middle Eastern markets, spice shops, and at most gourmet grocers. // *Yield: 4 to 6 servings*

■ **RECOMMENDED SKILLET:** 12 inch (30 cm)

■ **COOKING METHOD:** Searing/Steaming

1 pound (455 g) boneless, skinless chicken
    thighs, cut into 1½-inch (3.5-cm) pieces
Kosher salt
3 tablespoons (45 ml) extra virgin olive oil
3 green onions, sliced
4 cloves of garlic, minced
1 tablespoon (6 g) minced ginger
2 teaspoons ground coriander
1½ teaspoons ground cumin
1½ teaspoons Aleppo pepper
1¼ teaspoons ground cinnamon
¼ teaspoon freshly ground black pepper
1 red bell pepper, roasted, seeded,
    and diced
2 cups (350 g) couscous
3 tablespoons (27 g) golden raisins
2 tablespoons (18 g) pine nuts, toasted
¼ cup (4 g) minced cilantro
1 lime, cut into 8 wedges

Season the chicken generously with salt.

Preheat a cast iron skillet over medium heat. Add the olive oil and swirl to coat the inside of the skillet. Add the chicken and cook, flipping occasionally, until light golden brown, 3 to 4 minutes. Add the green onions, garlic, and ginger and stir through and then add the coriander, cumin, Aleppo pepper, cinnamon, and pepper and stir through. Add 3 cups (700 ml) of water and the bell pepper, bring to a boil, and simmer until the chicken is just cooked through, about 1 minute. Season to taste with salt. The water should taste a little salty now for perfectly seasoned cooked couscous later. Add the couscous, raisins, and pine nuts and stir through. Cover the skillet, remove from the heat, and let stand until the couscous is tender and all the water is absorbed, 14 to 16 minutes. Fluff the couscous with a fork, sprinkle with the cilantro, and serve immediately with the lime wedges.

Coriander-Cumin Spiced Lamb Rib Chops

As far as I'm concerned, lamb and coriander and cumin is a match made in heaven. It's inspired by the cuisine of the Middle East and one of my very favorite flavor combinations, especially with the addition of plenty of cayenne and black pepper. The spiciness and heat of this aromatic spice rub is cooled by a yogurt-based sauce.

Serve with warm pita bread or on a bed of basmati rice. // *Yield: 4 servings*

- **RECOMMENDED SKILLET:** 12 inch (30 cm)
- **COOKING METHOD:** Searing

1 teaspoon ground coriander
1 teaspoon ground cumin
1 teaspoon granulated garlic
½ teaspoon oregano
½ teaspoon cayenne pepper
½ teaspoon freshly ground black pepper

8 bone-in lamb rib chops (3 ounces,
    or 85 g each), 1 inch (2.5 cm) thick
Kosher salt
3 tablespoons (45 ml) extra virgin olive oil
Lemon-Yogurt Dipping Sauce (page 255),
    for serving

Mix together the coriander, cumin, granulated garlic, oregano, cayenne, and pepper in a small bowl.

Season the chops generously with salt, sprinkle evenly with the coriander mixture on both sides, patting so that it adheres, and set aside at room temperature for about an hour.

Preheat a cast iron skillet over medium heat. Add the olive oil and swirl to coat the inside of the skillet. Add the chops and cook without disturbing until golden brown, 4 to 5 minutes. Flip the chops and cook until golden brown and medium-rare, 3 to 4 minutes. Moisture will begin to appear on the surface of the chops when they are nearly medium-rare. Stand the chops on the fat-cap side and cook until golden brown, 1 to 2 minutes. Serve immediately with the Lemon-Yogurt Dipping Sauce.

Lap Cheong & Shiitake Fried Rice

Unlike takeout, this fried rice is loaded with goodies. Plenty of lapchong, a sweet and salty Chinese sausage, and savory shiitake mushrooms mean every single mouthful is loaded with umami.

Make extra whenever you are cooking white rice to enjoy this recipe later. To cool freshly cooked rice quickly and safely, spread it in a thin layer on a sheet tray and refrigerate after the steam has come off of it. Transfer it to a container and cover only after it is thoroughly chilled. Note that 1½ cups (278 g) uncooked long-grain white rice will yield about 6 cups (948 g) cooked.

Lapchong and dried shiitakes are available in Asian markets. // *Yield: 4 servings*

- **RECOMMENDED SKILLET:** 12 inch (30 cm)
- **COOKING METHOD:** Stir-Frying

8 dried shiitake mushrooms
3 large eggs
¼ cup (60 ml) canola oil
3 links of lapchong (about 4 ounces, or 115 g), diced
¾ cup (98 g) frozen peas, thawed

1 large carrot, diced
2 cloves of garlic, minced
6 cups (948 g) cooked long-grain white rice, cold
2 large green onions, sliced
3 tablespoons (45 ml) soy sauce

Place the shiitakes in a medium bowl and add enough boiling water to cover. Let soak until rehydrated and pliable, 10 to 15 minutes. Drain the shiitakes and blot dry on paper towels. Transfer to a cutting board, trim off and discard the stems, and dice the caps.

Lightly beat the eggs in a medium bowl.

Preheat a cast iron skillet over medium heat. Add the oil and swirl to coat the inside of the skillet. Add the eggs and cook until scrambled but not dry, about 30 seconds. Remove the eggs to a bowl. Add the lapchong to the skillet and stir-fry until golden brown, 1 to 2 minutes. Add the peas and carrot and stir-fry until the carrot begins to soften, 1 to 2 minutes. Add the garlic and stir through. Add the rice, green onions, shiitakes, and eggs and stir-fry, breaking up any clumps of rice and eggs, until heated through, 4 to 5 minutes. Add the soy sauce and stir through. Transfer to a platter and serve immediately.

Rice Noodle, Shrimp & Broccoli Stir-Fry with Eggs

This simple stir-fry, inspired by one of my husband's favorite dishes to order when we go out for Chinese food, is a weeknight staple at our house. It's so quick and easy to throw together, it's faster than going for takeout. Sometimes, I vary it with separated baby bok choy leaves rather than broccoli, or if I can find time to swing by the local factory, I use fresh rice noodles instead of dry. // *Yield: 4 servings*

- **RECOMMENDED SKILLET:** 12 inch (30 cm)
- **COOKING METHOD:** Stir-Frying

10 ounces (280 g) dried wide rice noodles
½ cup (60 ml) canola oil, divided
4 large eggs
8 ounces (225 g) broccoli florets
    (1 to 1¼ quarts)

4 large cloves of garlic, minced
¼ teaspoon red chile flakes
1 pound (455 g) large (26 to 30 count)
    shrimp, peeled and deveined
¼ cup (60 ml) soy sauce

Place the noodles in a large bowl and add enough boiling water to cover. Let soak until rehydrated and pliable, 3 to 4 minutes. Drain the noodles and blot dry on paper towels.

Preheat a cast iron skillet over medium-high heat, starting over medium heat. Add 2 tablespoons (30 ml) of the oil and swirl to coat the inside. Add the eggs and cook until scrambled but not dry, about 30 seconds. Remove the eggs to a bowl. Add 2 tablespoons (30 ml) of the oil to the skillet and swirl to coat the inside. Add the broccoli and stir-fry until bright green, about 1 minute. Add about half of the garlic and red chile flakes and stir through. Remove the broccoli mixture to a bowl. Add 1 tablespoon (15 ml) of the oil to the skillet at swirl to coat the inside. Add the shrimp to the skillet and stir-fry until pink and nearly cooked through, 1 to 2 minutes. Add the remaining half of the garlic and red chile flakes and stir through. Remove the shrimp mixture to a bowl. Add the remaining 3 tablespoons (45 ml) of oil to the skillet and swirl to coat the inside. Add the noodles and stir-fry until golden brown in spots and nearly tender, 2 to 3 minutes. Return the eggs, broccoli, and shrimp to the skillet and add the soy sauce. Stir-fry, breaking up any clumps of noodles and eggs, until the noodles are just tender, the shrimp is just cooked through, and the broccoli is tender-crisp, 2 to 3 minutes. Transfer to a platter and serve immediately.

Pork, Shiitake & Water Chestnut Lettuce Wraps

These lettuce wraps take very little time to make and are great for when you're in the mood for a light yet flavorful meal. Water chestnuts and iceberg lettuce give the dish a refreshing crunch. Butter lettuce or romaine leaves can be substituted for the iceberg, and if you would like to make this a bit more substantial, feel free to scoop a spoonful of hot sticky rice into each lettuce cup before adding the pork mixture.

Shiitake mushrooms and Tien Tsin chiles, also known as Szechuan chiles, as well as the other ingredients are available at Asian markets. // *Yield: 12 wraps or 4 servings*

- **RECOMMENDED SKILLET:** 12 inch (30 cm)

- **COOKING METHOD:** Stir-Frying

6 dried shiitake mushrooms
2 tablespoons (30 g) hoisin sauce
1 tablespoon (15 ml) soy sauce
1 tablespoon (18 g) oyster sauce
1 tablespoon (15 ml) unseasoned rice
    vinegar
¼ teaspoon dark sesame oil
1 teaspoon sugar
1 large head of iceberg lettuce

2 tablespoons (30 ml) canola oil
Several whole dried Tien Tsin chiles
1 pound (455 g) 20% fat ground pork
3 cloves of garlic, minced
1 teaspoon minced ginger
½ of a (5-ounce, or 140-g) can of
    water chestnuts, drained and diced
2 green onions, sliced

Place the dried shiitakes in a medium bowl and add enough boiling water to cover. Let soak until rehydrated and pliable, 10 to 15 minutes. Drain the shiitakes and blot dry on paper towels. Transfer to a cutting board, trim off and discard the stems, and dice the caps.

Whisk together the hoisin, soy sauce, oyster sauce, rice vinegar, sesame oil, and sugar in a small bowl.

Cut the core out of the lettuce and cut the lettuce in half. Carefully separate the leaves, reserving the heart for another use, and, using 2 leaves per wrap, arrange cupped-side up on a platter.

Preheat a cast iron skillet over medium heat. Add the canola oil and swirl to coat the inside. Add the dried chiles and stir-fry until golden brown, about 15 seconds. Add the pork and stir-fry until golden brown, 2 to 3 minutes. Add the garlic and ginger and stir through. Add the shiitakes, water chestnuts, and green onions and stir through, and then add the hoisin mixture and stir through. Scoop about ¼ cup (55 g) of the pork mixture into each of the lettuce leaf cups and serve immediately.

MAINS

Stir-Fried Pork & Japanese Eggplant

Bright purple, long and slender Japanese eggplants have thinner, more tender skin, fewer seeds, and less bitterness compared to the common globe variety. This delicate but meaty eggplant gets the starring role in this quick and easy stir-fry.

Japanese eggplants and Tien Tsin chiles, also known as Szechuan chiles, are available at Asian markets.

Serve with plenty of hot sticky rice and, if desired, sriracha on the side. // *Yield: 4 servings*

- **RECOMMENDED SKILLET:** 12 inch (30 cm)

- **COOKING METHOD:** Stir-Frying

¾ cup (175 ml) chicken stock
3 tablespoons (45 ml) soy sauce
1 tablespoon (15 ml) unseasoned
    rice vinegar
2 tablespoons (16 g) cornstarch
¼ cup (60 ml) canola oil
Several whole dried Tien Tsin chiles

3 medium Japanese eggplants
    (about 1¼ pounds, or 570 g total),
    cut into ⅔-inch (1.7-cm) cubes
1 pound (455 g) 20% fat ground pork,
    broken up
4 cloves of garlic, minced
2 large green onions, sliced

Whisk together the chicken stock, soy sauce, rice vinegar, and cornstarch in a medium bowl.

Preheat a cast iron skillet over medium heat. Add the oil and swirl to coat the inside. Add the dried chiles and stir-fry until golden brown, about 15 seconds. Add the eggplant and stir-fry until translucent and tender, 4 to 5 minutes. Remove the eggplant and chiles to a bowl. Add the pork to the skillet and stir-fry until golden brown, 2 to 3 minutes. Add the garlic and green onions and stir through. Return the eggplant and chiles to the skillet and stir through. Give the stock mixture one final whisk to recombine, add to the skillet, and bring to a boil, stirring constantly. Simmer, stirring constantly, until the sauce is thickened, 1 to 2 minutes. Transfer to a platter and serve immediately.

Beef with Blistered Snow Peas

Cooking snow peas in an extremely hot CI skillet without any oil causes them to blister and char ever so slightly and suffuses them with a hint of a smokiness that's surprisingly delicious.

This simple stir-fry is a flash in the pan—it actually cooks in less time than it takes to preheat the skillet. There should be no more than ½ pound (225 g) of snow peas in the skillet at a time to get them to blister nicely, so if you'd like to serve more than 2, simply make batches.

Serve with plenty of hot sticky rice. // *Yield: 2 servings*

- **RECOMMENDED SKILLET:** 12 inch (30 cm)
- **COOKING METHOD:** Charring/Stir-Frying

2 tablespoons (30 ml) soy sauce
1 teaspoon sugar
¼ teaspoon dark sesame oil
8 ounces (225 g) snow peas, strings
    removed
2 tablespoons (30 ml) canola oil

10 ounces (280 g) beef sirloin, flap, tri-tip,
    or flank, cut against the grain into
    ¼-inch (6-mm) thick bite-size pieces
3 cloves of garlic, minced
¼ teaspoon red chile flakes

Whisk together the soy sauce, sugar, and sesame oil in a small bowl.

Preheat a cast iron skillet over medium-high heat, starting over medium heat. Add the snow peas and cook, stirring occasionally, until bright green and lightly charred in spots, 2 to 3 minutes. Remove the snow peas to a bowl. Add the canola oil to the skillet and swirl to coat the inside. Add the beef and stir-fry until golden brown, about 2 minutes. Add the garlic and red chile flakes and stir through. Return the snow peas to the skillet and stir through and then add the soy sauce mixture and stir through. Transfer to a platter and serve immediately.

Vietnamese Salmon Yellow Curry

This colorful dish was loosely inspired by something a friend ordered at a Vietnamese restaurant. It doesn't claim to be totally authentic, but it is hot, sour, salty, sweet, and vibrantly delicious. And it's surprisingly quick and easy to cook.

There's an ample amount of sauce to serve with plenty of hot jasmine rice or rice noodles.

// *Yield: 4 servings*

- **RECOMMENDED SKILLET:** 10¼ inch (26 cm)
- **COOKING METHOD:** Braising

1 (19-ounce [540-g]) can of coconut milk

1 small red onion, cut into 1-inch (2.5-cm) pieces

1 red bell pepper, cut into 1-inch (2.5-cm) pieces

1 jalapeño, sliced

1 large clove of garlic, sliced

2 tablespoons (12 g) Curry Powder (page 252)

1 (8-ounces [225-g]) can of sliced bamboo shoots, drained

1 pound (455 g) salmon fillet, skinned, boned, and cut into 1½-inch (3.5-cm) cubes

4 ounces (115 g) snow peas, strings removed

Freshly squeezed juice of 1 lime

2 tablespoons (30 g) packed light brown sugar

¼ cup (60 ml) fish sauce

2 green onions, sliced

⅓ cup (5 g) minced cilantro

Preheat a cast iron skillet over medium-low heat. Spoon the fat off the top of the coconut milk, add to the skillet, and swirl to coat the inside. Add the onion and sauté until it begins to soften, 3 to 4 minutes. Add the bell pepper and jalapeño and sauté until they begin to soften, 3 to 4 minutes. Add the garlic and stir through and then add the Curry Powder and stir through. Add the remaining coconut milk and bamboo shoots and bring to a boil. Add the salmon, snow peas, lime juice, sugar, and fish sauce and simmer, stirring occasionally, until the salmon just begins to flake, 5 to 6 minutes. Sprinkle with the green onions and cilantro and serve immediately.

Black & White Sesame-Crusted Tuna Chirashi Bowl

Chirashi is a type of sushi that's particularly well-suited to making at home because instead of being formed into rolls, the seasoned rice is simply served in bowls with the desired toppings. The recipe for these chirashi bowls happens to be inspired by my personal favorite of spicy tuna rolls. It includes slices of seared rare sesame-crusted tuna steaks and a spicy mayo loaded with sriracha. // *Yield: 4 servings*

- **RECOMMENDED SKILLET:** 10¼ inch (26 cm)
- **COOKING METHOD:** Searing

2 sushi-quality ahi tuna steaks (8 ounces, or 225 g each), 1¼ inch (3 cm) thick
Kosher salt
¼ cup (60 ml) unseasoned rice vinegar
¼ cup (50 g) sugar
2 tablespoons (16 g) sesame seeds
2 tablespoons (16 g) black sesame seeds
½ cup (115 g) mayonnaise, preferably Best Foods
¼ cup (60 ml) sriracha sauce
1 tablespoon (15 ml) soy sauce, plus more for serving

½ teaspoon dark sesame oil
2 cups (400 g) sticky rice, rinsed until the water runs clear and drained
2 tablespoons (30 ml) canola oil
2 Persian cucumbers, julienned
1 small carrot, julienned
1 large avocado, sliced
¼ cup (25 g) shredded nori
2 green onions, sliced
Wasabi, for serving
Pickled ginger, for serving

Season the tuna steaks generously with kosher salt and set aside at room temperature for about an hour.

Combine the rice vinegar and sugar in a small saucepan and heat over low heat, stirring occasionally, until the sugar dissolves. Mix together the sesame seeds and black sesame seeds in a shallow dish. Whisk together the mayonnaise, sriracha, soy sauce, and sesame oil in a medium bowl.

Combine the rice and 2⅔ cups (635 ml) of water in another small saucepan. Bring to a boil, season to taste with salt, and boil 1 minute. The water should taste a little salty now for perfectly seasoned cooked rice later. Cover the saucepan, decrease the heat to low, and cook until the rice is tender and all the water is absorbed, 20 minutes.

Transfer the rice to a shallow dish and, fanning constantly to drive off the steam and cool to room temperature as quickly as possible, pour over the vinegar mixture and toss to coat until glossy, or to taste.

Roll each tuna steak in the sesame seed mixture, patting so that it adheres. Preheat a cast iron skillet over medium-high heat, starting over medium heat. Add the canola oil and swirl to coat the inside of the skillet. Add the steaks and cook without disturbing until golden brown, 1 to 2 minutes. Flip the steaks and cook until golden brown and rare, about 1 minute. The steaks will feel soft to the touch when they are rare. Remove the steaks to a platter and let rest for about 5 minutes.

Carve the tuna into slices. Divide the rice among individual bowls and then arrange the cucumbers, carrot, and avocado decoratively atop the rice. Top with the tuna and nori and sprinkle with the green onions. Serve immediately with the sriracha sauce, wasabi, pickled ginger, and additional soy sauce, if desired.

Thai Fried Chicken with Sweet Red Chile Sauce

This recipe is inspired by the fried chicken sold by street vendors in Thailand. It's particularly interesting because the batter, which includes rice flour for a super-crispy crust, doubles as a marinade.

Traditionally, cilantro root is used to flavor the chicken, but since it's nearly impossible to find in stores in the United States, I use cilantro stems. Fresno chiles are similar to jalapeños, but they're red and have pointy ends and thinner flesh.

When cutting up the chicken, remove the back bone and cut each of the wings to include a bit of the breast meat.

Serve this fried chicken with hot jasmine rice. The recipe makes plenty of sauce to eat with both the chicken and the rice. // *Yield: 4 servings*

- **RECOMMENDED SKILLET:** Deep 10¼ inch (26 cm)
- **COOKING METHOD:** Deep-Frying

1 teaspoon coriander seeds, toasted
¼ teaspoon white peppercorns, toasted
3 tablespoons (3 g) minced cilantro stems
4 cloves of garlic, sliced
2 cups (320 g) rice flour
⅔ cup (160 ml) fish sauce, divided
½ teaspoon cayenne pepper

1 chicken (3¾ to 4 pounds, or 1.7 to 1.8 kg), cut into 8 pieces
1 cup (235 ml) rice vinegar
1¼ cups (250 g) sugar
5 to 6 Fresno chiles, seeded and sliced
1½ quarts (1.4 L) canola oil (enough to come to a depth of 1½ inches [3.5 cm])

(continued)

Combine the coriander and white peppercorns in a mortar and pestle and grind to a powder. Add the cilantro stems and garlic and pound to a paste. Transfer to a medium bowl, add the rice flour, ⅓ cup (80 ml) of the fish sauce, cayenne, and 1 cup (235 ml) of water, and whisk until smooth. Transfer to a 1-gallon (3.8-L) zip-top bag, add the chicken, and turn to coat. Seal the bag, letting out all the air. Marinate overnight in the refrigerator.

Set the bag of chicken aside at room temperature for about an hour.

Meanwhile, combine the rice vinegar, sugar, and Fresno chiles in a blender and blend until pureed. Transfer to a small saucepan, bring to a boil, and simmer until thickened and syrupy, 20 to 25 minutes. Remove the saucepan from the heat and let cool slightly. Add the remaining ⅓ cup (80 ml) of fish sauce and stir through. Set aside at room temperature.

Pour the oil into a deep cast iron skillet and preheat over medium-high heat, starting over medium heat, until it registers 350°F (180°C) on a candy/jelly/deep-fry thermometer. Just before the oil comes to temperature, turn the bag of chicken several times to redistribute the rice flour in the marinade. Shaking off any excess marinade, add 4 pieces of the chicken to the skillet and fry at a lively sizzle, flipping occasionally and decreasing the heat to medium if the chicken seems to be browning too quickly, until it begins to float and is golden brown, crispy, and cooked through, 14 to 16 minutes. Using a wire skimmer, remove the fried chicken to a paper towel–lined sheet tray and let drain. Reheat the oil and fry the remaining 4 pieces of chicken in 1 more batch in the same manner. Serve hot with the sauce.

Sweet Green Chile Sauce Variation: Substitute 3 to 4 jalapeños for the Fresno chiles.

Pork Belly & Kimchi Stew

Heat lovers, this chile-stained, Korean-inspired dish is for you. It's got the right level of spiciness to warm you right up on a chilly day. And in addition to the chiles, it's loaded with ingredients that take the umami quotient through the roof!

Mature spicy kimchi brings the most flavor to this dish. Korean red chile powder, which is seed-free and moderately spicy, is called *gochugaru*. *Gochujang* is Korean fermented chile paste, and *doenjang* is Korean fermented soybean paste similar to miso. All of these ingredients are available at Asian markets.

Hot sticky rice is the perfect accompaniment for this dish. // ***Yield: 4 to 6 servings***

- **RECOMMENDED SKILLET:** 12 inch (30 cm)
- **COOKING METHOD:** Braising

1 pound (455 g) ¼-inch (6-mm) thick slices skinless pork belly, cut into 2-inch (5-cm) pieces
1 small yellow onion, julienned
4 cloves of garlic, minced
1 tablespoon (6 g) minced ginger
1½ cups (360 g) kimchi with juice
1 tablespoon (5 g) gochugaru

3 tablespoons (66 g) gochujang
2 tablespoons (44 g) doenjang
1 teaspoon dark sesame oil
16 ounces (455 g) soft tofu, drained thoroughly and cut into 1-inch (2.5-cm) cubes
1 green onion, sliced

Preheat a cast iron skillet over medium-high heat, starting over medium heat. Add the pork belly and stir-fry until light golden brown, about 2 minutes. Add the onion and stir-fry until it begins to soften, about 2 minutes. Add the garlic and ginger and stir through. Add the kimchi, gochugaru, and 1½ quarts (1.4 L) of water, bring to a boil, and simmer, stirring occasionally, until the pork belly is nearly tender, 15 to 20 minutes.

Meanwhile, whisk together the gochujang, doenjang, sesame oil, and ¼ cup (60 ml) of the hot cooking liquid in a medium bowl.

Add the tofu to the skillet and simmer, stirring occasionally, until the pork belly is tender, 8 to 10 minutes. Remove the skillet from the heat and add the green onions and gochujang mixture and stir through. Serve immediately.

MAINS

CI Skillet Bibimbap

Bibimbap is a popular Korean dish of rice with seasoned meat and a variety of vegetables and garnishes. The colorful toppings are arranged in neat little piles, so it's a feast for the eyes as well as the stomach.

When it's presented in individual hot stone bowls, the dish is known as dolsot bibimbap and the rice gets irresistibly brown and crunchy on the bottom. Eight-inch (20-cm) CI skillets are perfect stand-ins for the traditional dolsot bowls. If you don't have two small skillets, bibimbap is still excellent served in regular dinner bowls.

When bringing this dish to the table, be sure to use heatproof underliners and handle holders for the hot individual CI skillets and warn your dining companion to be cautious.

Gochujang and boneless beef short ribs cut very thinly on a deli slicer and all the other ingredients are available at Asian markets. // *Yield: 2 servings*

- **RECOMMENDED SKILLETS:** 2 (8 inch [20 cm]) plus 12 inch (30 cm)

- **COOKING METHOD:** Simmering/Stir-Frying

3 dried shiitake mushrooms
3 tablespoons (66 g) gochujang
1 tablespoon (15 ml) plus 1¼ teaspoons
    dark sesame oil, divided
½ pound (225 g) thinly sliced boneless
    beef short ribs, julienned
3 tablespoons (45 ml) soy sauce
1 tablespoon (13 g) sugar
2 cloves of garlic, minced
1½ teaspoons minced ginger
1 green onion, sliced
Freshly ground black pepper
1 cup (200 g) sticky rice, rinsed until
    the water runs clear and drained

Kosher salt
3 tablespoons (45 ml) canola oil, divided
1 small carrot, julienned
1 small zucchini, halved lengthwise
    and sliced
4 ounces (115 g) mung bean sprouts
    (about 2 cups)
3 ounces (85 g) baby spinach leaves
    (about 1 quart)
2 eggs
¼ cup (25 g) shredded nori
2 teaspoons toasted sesame seeds

(continued)

Preheat the oven to 450°F (230°C, or gas mark 8). Place two cast iron skillets in the oven to preheat.

Place the shiitakes in a medium bowl and add enough boiling water to cover. Let soak until rehydrated and pliable, 10 to 15 minutes. Drain the shiitakes and blot dry on paper towels. Transfer to a cutting board, trim off and discard the stems, and slice the caps.

Whisk together the gochujang, ¼ teaspoon of the sesame oil, and 3 tablespoons (45 ml) of warm water in a small bowl and set aside at room temperature.

Mix together the short ribs, soy sauce, sugar, garlic, ginger, green onion, and a generous pinch of black pepper in a medium bowl and set aside at room temperature to marinate.

Combine the rice and 1⅓ cups (315 ml) of water in a small saucepan. Bring to a boil, season to taste with salt, and boil for 1 minute. The water should taste a little salty now for perfectly seasoned cooked rice later. Cover the saucepan, decrease the heat to low, and cook until the rice is tender and all the water is absorbed, 20 minutes.

Preheat a cast iron skillet over medium heat. Add 1 tablespoon (15 ml) of the canola oil and swirl to coat the inside. Add the carrot and stir-fry until tender-crisp, about 1 minute. Remove the carrot to a bowl. Add the zucchini to the skillet and stir-fry until just tender, about 2 minutes. Remove the zucchini to a separate bowl. Add the bean sprouts to the skillet and stir-fry until just tender, about 2 minutes. Remove the bean sprouts to a separate bowl. Add the spinach to the skillet and stir-fry until wilted, about 1 minute. Remove the spinach to a separate bowl. Add 1 tablespoon (15 ml) of the canola oil to the skillet and swirl to coat the inside. Add the short rib mixture and stir-fry until just cooked through, about 2 minutes. Remove the beef to a separate bowl. Add the remaining 1 tablespoon (15 ml) of canola oil to the skillet and swirl to coat the inside. Add the eggs one at a time and fry until the whites are nearly set and the yolks are still runny, 2 to 3 minutes.

Working quickly, divide the remaining 1 tablespoon (15 ml) plus 1 teaspoon of sesame oil among the hot 8-inch (20-cm) skillets and swirl each one to coat the inside. Divide the hot rice among the skillets, then arrange the shiitakes, carrot, zucchini, bean sprouts, spinach, and beef decoratively atop the rice, top with the fried eggs and nori, and sprinkle with the sesame seeds. Serve immediately with the gochujang sauce.

Beef Dang Myun

Dang myun is a Korean noodle made of sweet potato starch. It's crystal clear once it's cooked, and it has a wonderfully chewy and slippery texture. Dang myun's also a flavor chameleon—with no discernible taste of its own, it takes on the flavor of whatever sauce it's in. In this case, it soaks up a beefy and salty and sweet sauce redolent of garlic, ginger, and onions.

When boiling dang myun, be careful not to overcook it. Keep in mind that these noodles are still very chewy even when completely cooked through.

Dang myun and boneless beef short ribs cut very thinly on a deli slicer and all the other ingredients are available at Asian markets. Do not confuse dang myun with rice noodles or bean thread noodles. // *Yield: 4 servings*

- **RECOMMENDED SKILLET:** 12 inch (30 cm)
- **COOKING METHOD:** Boiling/Stir-Frying

¾ pound (340 g) thinly sliced boneless beef short ribs, cut into 2-inch (5-cm) pieces
¼ cup (60 ml) soy sauce
3 tablespoons (39 g) sugar
4 cloves of garlic, minced
1 tablespoon (6 g) minced ginger
Freshly ground black pepper

8 ounces (225 g) dang myun
2 tablespoons (30 ml) canola oil
1 small yellow onion, julienned
3 green onions, cut into 1-inch (2.5-cm) pieces
2 tablespoons (16 g) toasted sesame seeds
2 teaspoons dark sesame oil

Mix together the short ribs, soy sauce, sugar, garlic, ginger, and a generous pinch of black pepper in a medium bowl and set aside at room temperature to marinate.

Meanwhile, cook the dang myun in a large pot of boiling water until tender but toothsome, 6 to 7 minutes. Drain, rinse thoroughly with cold water to stop the cooking, and drain again.

Preheat a cast iron skillet over medium heat. Add the canola oil and swirl to coat the inside. Add the onion and stir-fry until it begins to soften, 2 to 3 minutes. Add the green onions and short rib mixture and stir-fry until the beef is nearly cooked through, 2 to 3 minutes. Add the dang myun and stir-fry until it takes on the color of the soy sauce and is heated through, 2 to 3 minutes. Add the sesame seeds and sesame oil and stir through. Serve immediately.

Saag Paneer

This vegetarian dish of cubed paneer cheese in a fragrant and creamy spinach sauce is an Indian restaurant favorite. It's easy to prepare at home but making this cheese does require quite a bit of unattended waiting time, so plan to start in the morning for it to be ready for dinner.

Making the paneer from scratch is a fun and rewarding project. Watching the milk separate into curds and whey is like seeing a magic trick performed, only the results are far tastier. The finished fresh cheese has a mild, milky, and somewhat tangy flavor. It's not a melting cheese, but rather it sears up nicely in a cast iron skillet and retains its shape when simmered.

You can take a shortcut and use prepared paneer, which is available at Indian markets along with mildly hot Kashmiri chile powder.

Serve as a vegetarian main course with hot basmati rice.

The whey that remains from the cheese-making process may be used for baking and in smoothies. // *Yield: 4 to 6 servings*

- **RECOMMENDED SKILLET:** 10¼ inch (26 cm)
- **COOKING METHOD:** Braising

2 quarts (1.9 L) milk
¼ cup (60 ml) freshly squeezed lemon juice
Kosher salt
2 (10-ounce [280-g]) packages
    of frozen spinach, thawed
1 cup (235 ml) cream
2 tablespoons (30 ml) canola oil
½ of a yellow onion, diced
1 jalapeño, seeded and minced

3 cloves of garlic, minced
1 tablespoon (6 g) minced ginger
1¼ teaspoons ground cumin
½ teaspoon ground turmeric
¼ to ½ teaspoon Kashmiri chile powder
1 large Roma tomato, diced
1½ teaspoons Garam Masala (page 252)
3 tablespoons (3 g) minced cilantro
Freshly squeezed juice of ½ of a lime

Pour the milk into a nonreactive saucepot and place over medium heat, stirring occasionally, until steamy, foamy, and bubbling around the edges. Add the lemon juice and stir through. Continue to heat, stirring slowly, until the milk separates into curds and whey. Pour into a cheesecloth-lined fine-mesh sieve set over a large bowl. Gather the corners of the cheesecloth together over the curds and squeeze firmly to expel excess whey. Reserve the whey for another use.

Open the cheesecloth, add ¼ teaspoon salt to the curds, and stir through. Gather the corners of the cheesecloth together over the curds and squeeze gently to compact them. Transfer the wrapped cheese to a cutting board, press to flatten slightly, and then fold the cheesecloth over neatly to lay flat. Cover loosely with plastic wrap and top with a cast iron skillet to press until solid, 2 to 3 hours.

Refrigerate the wrapped paneer until firm, 3 to 4 hours.

Cut the paneer into 1-inch (2.5-cm) pieces. Combine the spinach and cream in a food processor and process until smooth.

Preheat a cast iron skillet over medium-low heat. Add the oil and swirl to coat the inside. Add the paneer and cook without disturbing until golden brown, 2 to 3 minutes. Flip the paneer and cook until golden brown, about 2 minutes. Remove the paneer to a bowl. Add the onion to the skillet and sauté until it begins to soften, 3 to 4 minutes. Add the jalapeño, garlic, and ginger and sauté until the jalapeño begins to soften, about 2 minutes. Add the cumin, turmeric, and Kashmiri chile powder and stir through. Add the tomato, spinach mixture, and ¾ cup (175 ml) of water, bring to a boil, and simmer until thickened slightly, 12 to 15 minutes. Add the Garam Masala, cilantro, and lime juice and stir through. Return the paneer to the skillet, stir through, and simmer slowly until the flavors come together, 10 to 12 minutes. Season to taste with salt and serve immediately.

Indian Chicken Stir-Fry

If you enjoy the vibrant colors and flavors of Indian food, you'll love this quick and easy stir-fry. It's aromatic and highly seasoned like you'd expect of an Indian dish, but unlike many curries it comes together in minutes.

Serve with plenty of steaming basmati rice. // *Yield: 4 servings*

- **RECOMMENDED SKILLET:** 12 inch (30 cm)
- **COOKING METHOD:** Stir-Frying

1 pound (455 g) boneless, skinless chicken
    thighs, cut into 1½-inch (3.5-cm) pieces
2 teaspoons cornstarch
1 teaspoon ground coriander
1 teaspoon ground cumin
½ teaspoon ground turmeric
¼ teaspoon fennel seeds, ground
Kosher salt
3 tablespoons (45 ml) canola oil
½ of a red onion, cut into 1-inch
    (2.5 cm)-pieces

1 red bell pepper, cut into 1-inch
    (2.5-cm) pieces
1 poblano, cut into 1-inch (2.5-cm) pieces
3 cloves of garlic, minced
1 teaspoon minced ginger
¼ to ½ teaspoon red chile flakes
Freshly squeezed juice of 1 lime
2 tablespoons (12 g) minced fresh mint
2 tablespoons (2 g) minced cilantro

Mix together chicken, cornstarch, coriander, cumin, turmeric, fennel seeds, and a generous pinch of salt in a medium bowl and set aside at room temperature to marinate for 20 to 30 minutes.

Preheat a cast iron skillet over medium heat. Add the oil and swirl to coat the inside. Add the onion, bell pepper, and poblano and stir-fry until they begin to soften, about 2 minutes. Using a slotted spoon, remove the onion mixture to a bowl. Add the chicken mixture to the skillet and stir-fry until golden brown and nearly cooked through, 6 to 7 minutes. Add the garlic, ginger, and red chile flakes and stir through. Return the onion mixture to the skillet and stir-fry until the chicken is cooked through, 1 to 2 minutes. Remove the skillet from the heat. Add the lime juice, mint, and cilantro and stir through. Season to taste with salt and serve immediately.

Lamb Chukka

My husband and I were first introduced to spicy lamb chukka in a little South Indian restaurant in the western suburbs of Portland, Oregon. He can never get enough lamb or chile, so he loved the dish at first bite. Considering the drive to this particular restaurant is nearly an hour one way on a good traffic day, I was determined to reverse engineer the recipe.

After many "research" trips across town and much experimentation, I developed the following recipe. The distinctive flavor of the dish comes from a blend of many aromatic spices, the fennel seeds and pungent curry leaves in particular.

Mildly hot Kashmiri chile powder and glossy green curry leaves, which are unrelated to curry powder and used in a similar manner to bay leaves but edible, are available at Indian markets.

Serve with hot basmati rice or naan. // *Yield: 4 servings*

- **RECOMMENDED SKILLETS:** 10¼ inch (26 cm) plus 12 inch (30 cm) with lid
- **COOKING METHOD:** Reverse Braising

1⅔ pounds (755 g) boneless leg of lamb, cut into 1-inch (2.5-cm) pieces
1 red onion, julienned, divided
1 (14.5-ounce [410-g]) can of diced tomatoes in juice, drained
Kosher salt
2 tablespoons (30 ml) canola oil
4 cloves of garlic, minced
1 tablespoon (6 g) minced ginger
1 jalapeño, minced
1 tablespoon (6 g) ground coriander

2 teaspoons ground cumin
1 teaspoon Kashmiri chile powder
½ teaspoon ground turmeric
½ teaspoon fennel seeds, ground
½ teaspoon freshly ground black pepper
½ teaspoon Garam Masala (page 252)
¼ teaspoon cayenne pepper
16 curry leaves
Freshly squeezed juice of ½ of a lemon
2 tablespoons (2 g) minced cilantro

Combine the lamb, about one-half of the onion, tomatoes, a generous pinch of salt, and 1½ cups (355 ml) of water in a cast iron skillet. Bring to a boil, cover the skillet, and simmer, stirring occasionally, until the lamb is tender, 2 to 2¼ hours.

(continued)

Just before the lamb is tender, preheat another cast iron skillet over medium heat. Add the oil and swirl to coat the inside. Add the remaining one-half of the onion and cook, stirring frequently, until golden brown in spots, 6 to 7 minutes. Add the garlic, ginger, and jalapeño and stir through and then add the coriander, cumin, Kashmiri chile powder, turmeric, fennel seeds, pepper, Garam Masala, and cayenne and stir through. Add ½ cup (120 ml) of water and bring to a boil, scraping up the browned bits from the bottom of the skillet with a heatproof spatula. Transfer the onion mixture to the skillet with the lamb.

Uncover the skillet with the lamb, add one-half of the curry leaves, and simmer, stirring occasionally, until all of the water evaporates, 30 to 35 minutes. Adjust the heat to medium-low, add the remaining one-half of the curry leaves, and cook, stirring occasionally, until the fat begins to separate from the sauce, 12 to 16 minutes. Season to taste with salt, sprinkle with the cilantro, and serve hot.

Coconut Shrimp with Mango Salsa

Generously sized shrimp are breaded in a combination of shredded coconut and panko and then fried in this version of the ever-popular dish. The zesty fresh salsa, which provides a nice contrast to the richness of the shrimp, is only mildly spicy. You can turn up the heat by substituting serrano peppers, Thai red chiles, or if you dare, habaneros or Scotch Bonnets for the jalapeños. You can also vary the salsa by using pineapple in place of or in addition to the mango.

Cook some sticky rice using a mixture of equal parts water and coconut milk with a splash of soy sauce to serve on the side. // *Yield: 4 servings*

- **RECOMMENDED SKILLET:** Deep 10¼ inch (26 cm)*
- **COOKING METHOD:** Deep-Frying

1 large mango, diced
½ of a red onion, diced
1 jalapeño, minced
½ cup (8 g) minced cilantro
Freshly squeezed juice of 1 lime
Kosher salt
⅓ cup (42 g) all-purpose flour
1 egg
2 tablespoons (30 ml) milk

Generous pinch of cayenne pepper
¾ cup (84 g) panko bread crumbs
¾ cup (64 g) unsweetened shredded
    coconut
24 jumbo (16 to 20 count) shrimp,
    peeled and deveined
1½ quarts (1.4 L) canola oil (enough to
    come to a depth of 1½ inches [3.5 cm])

Mix together the mango, onion, jalapeño, cilantro, and lime juice in a large bowl. Season to taste with salt, and let macerate, stirring occasionally, until juicy, 15 to 20 minutes.

Whisk together the flour and a generous pinch of salt in a medium bowl. Whisk together the egg, milk, cayenne, and a generous pinch of salt in another medium bowl. Mix together the panko, coconut, and a generous pinch of salt in another medium bowl. Season the shrimp generously with salt.

Working with 4 or 6 shrimp at a time, roll each shrimp in the seasoned flour to coat. Shake off any excess flour and dip each shrimp into the egg mixture to coat. Shake off any excess egg and roll each shrimp in the panko mixture, patting so that it adheres. Place the shrimp onto a rack on a sheet tray and set aside for 15 to 20 minutes to allow the breading to set.

Pour the oil into a deep cast iron skillet and preheat over medium-high heat, starting over medium heat, until it registers 375°F (190°C) on a candy/jelly/deep-fry thermometer. Add half of the shrimp and fry at a lively sizzle, stirring occasionally, until golden brown, crispy, and just cooked through, 2 to 3 minutes. The shrimp will curl head to tail into a letter C when they are just cooked through; do not wait until they curl into a letter O or they will be overcooked. Using a wire skimmer, remove the shrimp to a paper towel–lined sheet tray and let drain for a moment. Season with salt. Reheat the oil and fry the remaining shrimp in 1 more batch in the same manner. Serve hot with the mango salsa.

*This can also be made in a deep 12-inch (30-cm) cast iron skillet.

4

SIDES

Buttered Radishes with Herbs

If you've never tried cooked radishes, this dish is sure to delight. A brief sauté maintains their crunch but tames their peppery quality just a bit. Definitely try it in the springtime, when radishes are abundant at the market.

With all the butter and tender herbs, it would be a lovely accompaniment for lightly seasoned whitefish fillets. // **Yield: 4 servings**

- **RECOMMENDED SKILLET:** 12 inch (30 cm)

- **COOKING METHOD:** Sautéing

3 tablespoons (42 g) butter, divided
2 bunches of radishes, trimmed
    and cut into ⅛-inch (3-mm) slices
2 tablespoons (6 g) minced fresh chives
1 tablespoon (4 g) minced fresh dill

1 tablespoon minced (4 g) Italian parsley
2 teaspoons minced fresh tarragon
Kosher salt
Freshly ground black pepper

Preheat a cast iron skillet over medium heat. Add 2 tablespoons (28 g) of the butter, swirl to coat the inside of the skillet, and heat until the butter is melted and the foam subsides. Add the radishes and sauté until translucent and tender-crisp, about 2 minutes. Remove the skillet from the heat. Add the chives, dill, parsley, tarragon, and the remaining 1 tablespoon (14 g) of butter and stir through. Season to taste with salt and pepper, immediately transfer to a platter, and serve.

Asparagus with Brown Butter, Orange & Herbs

A bunch of asparagus will just about fit in a single layer in a 12-inch (30-cm) cast iron skillet and cook to golden brown in no time at all. Then, loads of herbs and orange juice and zest embellish it for a lovely springtime dish. // *Yield: 4 servings*

- **RECOMMENDED SKILLET:** 12 inch (30 cm)
- **COOKING METHOD:** Sautéing

1½ ounces (3 tablespoons, or 42 g)
    unsalted butter, cut into 1-tablespoon
    (14-g) pieces
1 bunch of asparagus (about 1 pound,
    or 455 g), trimmed
¼ cup (12 g) minced fresh chives

2 tablespoons (8 g) minced Italian parsley
1 teaspoon minced fresh thyme
1 teaspoon orange zest
Freshly squeezed juice of 1 orange
Kosher salt
Freshly ground black pepper

Preheat a cast iron skillet over medium-low heat. Add the butter and cook, stirring constantly, until golden brown and nutty, about 2 minutes. Add the asparagus and sauté until golden brown and tender-crisp, 4 to 5 minutes. Add the chives, parsley, thyme, and orange zest and stir through. Add the orange juice and stir through. Season to taste with salt and pepper and serve immediately.

Creamed Swiss Chard

Creamed spinach is a steak house classic; here's a version of that dish to go with Constant Flip–Method Steaks with Butter, Frizzled Herbs & Garlic (page 119) featuring a more robust and flavorful green.

Many creamed vegetable recipes rely on béchamel, or white sauce, but I prefer simply using heavy cream and letting it reduce until thickened. While I can't claim my approach yields lighter results, it certainly does make for luscious, silky, and tender greens even a meat-and-potatoes person would happily devour.

The chard stems and ribs must be separated from the leaves, diced, and cooked longer since they are more substantial. They add a nice crunch to the finished dish, and if you happen to use red or rainbow chard, they add a lot of color too. // *Yield: 6 servings*

- **RECOMMENDED SKILLET:** 10¼ inch (26 cm)
- **COOKING METHOD:** Simmering/Broiling

1 ounce (2 tablespoons, or 28 g)
    unsalted butter, cut into 1-tablespoon
    (14-g) pieces
½ of a yellow onion, diced
2 cloves of garlic, minced
2 bunches of Swiss chard (about 1¼
    pounds, or 570 g total), stems and
    ribs diced and leaves cut into
    1-inch (2.5-cm) strips

1 cup (235 ml) heavy cream
Generous pinch of freshly grated nutmeg
Kosher salt
Freshly ground black pepper
3 ounces (85 g) shredded Gruyère
    (about 1 cup)

Preheat the broiler.

Preheat a cast iron skillet over medium heat. Add the butter, swirl to coat the inside of the skillet, and heat until the butter is melted and the foam subsides. Add the onion and sauté until it begins to soften, 3 to 4 minutes. Add the garlic and stir through. Add the chard stems and ribs and sauté until they begin to soften, 2 to 3 minutes. Add the chard leaves, cover the skillet, and cook, stirring occasionally, until wilted, 3 to 4 minutes. Add the cream and nutmeg, bring to a boil, and simmer, stirring occasionally, until the cream is thickened slightly, 10 to 12 minutes. Remove the skillet from the heat and season to taste with salt and pepper. Sprinkle with the Gruyère and broil until golden brown and bubbling, 3 to 4 minutes. Serve immediately.

Almond Green Beans

Green beans must be cooked through until they are tender—undercooked or al dente green beans taste starchy and have an unpleasantly squeaky chew. The steam from a little bit of water will help cook them through. After a few minutes, all of the water will reduce out and leave the green beans to sauté in the butter. // *Yield: 4 servings*

- **RECOMMENDED SKILLET:** 12 inch (30 cm)
- **COOKING METHOD:** Steaming/Sautéing

1 ounce (2 tablespoons, or 28 g)
    unsalted butter, cut into 1-tablespoon
    (14-g) pieces
2 shallots, sliced

1 pound (455 g) green beans,
    cut into 2-inch (5-cm) pieces
⅓ cup (31 g) sliced almonds, toasted
1½ teaspoons Lemon Pepper (page 250)
Kosher salt

Preheat a cast iron skillet over medium-low heat. Add the butter, swirl to coat the inside of the skillet, and heat until the butter is melted and the foam subsides. Add the shallots and sauté until they begin to soften, about 1 minute. Add the green beans and ¼ cup (60 ml) of water and cook, stirring occasionally, until the water reduced out and the green beans are tender, 8 to 12 minutes. Add the almonds and Lemon Pepper and stir through. Season to taste with salt and serve immediately.

Charred Broccoli with Meyer Lemon & Pine Nuts

Cooking in a cast iron skillet without any oil is slightly unconventional to be sure, but it's a nice method to try when you're in the mood for something completely different. Broccoli cooked in this manner is imbued with a lovely hint of bitterness and smokiness that really can't be achieved any other way.

This dish is equally delicious served hot right out of the skillet or as a salad at room temperature. // *Yield: 4 servings*

- **RECOMMENDED SKILLET:** 12 inch (30 cm)
- **COOKING METHOD:** Charring/Sautéing

(continued)

SIDES

10 ounces (280 g) broccoli florets
(1 to 1¼ quarts)
3 tablespoons (45 ml) extra virgin
olive oil, divided
2 tablespoons (18 g) pine nuts, toasted
1 green onion, sliced
Generous pinch of red chile flakes

½ teaspoon grated Meyer lemon zest
Supremes and juice from 2 Meyer lemons
Kosher salt
Freshly ground black pepper
½ ounce (15 g) shredded Parmigiano-
Reggiano (about 2 tablespoons)

Preheat a cast iron skillet over medium heat. Add the broccoli and cook, stirring occasionally (about 3 times), until bright green and charred in spots, 4 to 5 minutes. Add 2 tablespoons (30 ml) of the olive oil and continue to cook until tender-crisp, 2 to 3 minutes. Add the pine nuts, green onion, red chile flakes, and lemon zest and stir through. Remove the skillet from the heat. Add the remaining 1 tablespoon (15 ml) of olive oil and lemon supremes and juice and stir through. Season to taste with salt and pepper. Immediately transfer to a platter, sprinkle with the Parmigiano-Reggiano, and serve.

Whole Cauliflower Roast with Capers & Brown Butter

Rarely does a vegetable elicit such excitement as a cauliflower roasted whole. It makes for a stunning presentation, even if I do say so myself, so make a show of "carving" the roast and stirring it with the brown butter sauce at the table. The flesh will yield to the gentlest pressure and have a seductive silky texture.

To turn this side dish into a main course, simply toss it with freshly cooked linguini and top it with a generous grating of Parmigiano-Reggiano. // *Yield: 4 servings*

- **RECOMMENDED SKILLET:** 8 inch (20 cm)
- **COOKING METHOD:** Roasting

3 ounces (6 tablespoons, or 85 g)
unsalted butter, cut into 1-tablespoon
(14-g) pieces
1 small head of trimmed cauliflower
(about 1 pound, or 455 g)

1 shallot, minced
2 tablespoons (17 g) drained capers
2 tablespoons (8 g) minced Italian parsley
Kosher salt
Freshly ground black pepper

(continued)

Preheat the oven to 425°F (220°C, or gas mark 7).

Place the butter into a cast iron skillet and melt over low heat. Add the cauliflower and baste with the butter. Transfer the skillet to the oven and roast, basting every 10 to 15 minutes, until the cauliflower is dark golden brown and very tender, 40 to 45 minutes. A paring knife inserted in the center of the cauliflower will meet no resistance when it is done. Transfer the skillet back to the stovetop over medium heat, gently nudge the cauliflower to the side, and add the shallot and capers to the brown butter. Sauté until the shallot begins to soften, about 1 minute. Remove the skillet from the heat, add the parsley to the sauce, and spoon the sauce over the cauliflower. Nudge the cauliflower back into the center of the skillet, season generously with salt and pepper, and serve immediately.

Dilled Sautéed Cucumbers

Cucumbers are seldom enjoyed cooked, but they are just as delicious sautéed as they are in a salad. Since they are naturally watery, it's a good idea to scoop out the seeds before cooking. A melon baller is perfect for the job. // *Yield: 4 servings*

- **RECOMMENDED SKILLET:** 12 inch (30 cm)
- **COOKING METHOD:** Sautéing

2 tablespoons (30 ml) extra virgin olive oil
1 tablespoon (14 g) butter
2 English cucumbers, peeled, halved
    lengthwise, seeded, and cut into ¼-inch
    (6-mm) slices

3 tablespoons (12 g) minced fresh dill
Kosher salt
Freshly ground black pepper

Preheat a cast iron skillet over medium heat. Add the olive oil and butter, swirl to coat the inside of the skillet, and heat until the butter is melted and the foam subsides. Add the cucumbers and sauté until tender-crisp, about 2 minutes. Remove the skillet from the heat. Add the dill and stir through. Season to taste with salt and pepper, immediately transfer to a platter, and serve.

Summer Squash Fries

These chicken-fried zucchini and yellow squash sticks are just about as addictive as French fries, but I don't feel as guilty eating them because they count as a serving of vegetables!

For the best results, dredge the squash just moments before the oil reaches frying temperature. Serve with your choice of Fresh Herb Ranch Dipping Sauce (page 254), Buffalo Mayo (page 254), or Chipotle Dipping Sauce (page 255) on the side. // *Yield: 4 servings*

- **RECOMMENDED SKILLET:** Deep 10¼ inch (26 cm)*
- **COOKING METHOD:** Deep-Frying

2½ cups (313 g) all-purpose flour
2½ teaspoons (8 g) granulated garlic
1 teaspoon granulated onion
½ teaspoon cayenne pepper
Kosher salt
¾ cup (175 ml) buttermilk
1 egg

2 small zucchini (about 12 ounces, or 340 g total), cut into thirds crosswise and each third cut into 8 wedges
2 small yellow squash (about 12 ounces, or 340 g total), cut into thirds crosswise and each third cut into 8 wedges
1½ quarts (1.4 L) canola oil (enough to come to a depth of 1½ inches [3.5 cm])

Whisk together the flour, granulated garlic, granulated onion, cayenne, and several generous pinches of salt in a large bowl. Transfer about one-quarter of the flour mixture to a medium bowl. Whisk together the buttermilk, egg, and a generous pinch of salt in another medium bowl. Place the zucchini and yellow squash into a large bowl and toss until combined.

Pour the oil into a deep cast iron skillet and preheat over medium-high heat, starting over medium heat, until it registers 375°F (190°C) on a candy/jelly/deep-fry thermometer. Just before the oil comes to temperature, add about one-third of the squash to the smaller bowl of seasoned flour and toss to coat. Shake off any excess flour, transfer the squash to the buttermilk mixture, and stir to coat. Shake off any excess liquid, transfer the squash to the large bowl of seasoned flour, and toss to coat, separating any pieces that stick together. Shake off any excess flour, add the dredged squash to the skillet, and fry at a lively sizzle, stirring occasionally, until floating, golden brown, and crispy, 3 to 4 minutes. Using a wire skimmer, remove the squash to a paper towel–lined sheet tray and let drain for a moment. Season to taste with salt. Reheat the oil and dredge and fry the remaining squash in 2 more batches in the same manner. Serve hot.

*This can also be made in a deep 12-inch (30-cm) cast iron skillet.

Creamed Corn with Basil

Creamed corn is a favorite in the summertime, when corn is in season, and the unexpected addition of basil perks it up a bit. Many recipes for creamed corn rely on flour for thickening. I prefer to use a generous amount of sweet cream and simply simmer it until it reduces and thickens for a lighter and silkier texture. // *Yield: 4 to 6 servings*

- **RECOMMENDED SKILLET:** 10¼ inch (26 cm)
- **COOKING METHOD:** Simmering

4 ears of corn, shucked
1 ounce (2 tablespoons, or 28 g)
    unsalted butter, cut into 1-tablespoon
    (14-g) pieces
1 clove of garlic, minced

1 cup (235 ml) cream
Generous pinch of cayenne pepper
2 tablespoons (5 g) minced basil
Kosher salt
Freshly ground black pepper

Stand each ear of corn on its end on a cutting board and, using a sharp knife, cut the kernels off the ears. Scrape the cobs with the edge of the knife to remove any pulp that remains.

Preheat a cast iron skillet over medium-low heat. Add the butter, swirl to coat the inside of the skillet, and heat until the butter is melted and the foam subsides. Add the garlic and sauté until fragrant, about 15 seconds. Add the corn, cream, and cayenne and simmer, stirring occasionally, until thickened, 20 to 25 minutes. Remove the skillet from the heat, add the basil and stir through, and season to taste with salt and pepper. Serve hot.

Kale & Butternut Squash with Bacon & Toasted Garlic

This colorful dish will have you looking forward to the arrival of winter squash in the fall. It's hearty and satisfying and topped with a fried egg, it could even be served as a main course.

Starting sliced garlic in a cold skillet brings out its sweetness. The result is similar to roasted but in a fraction of the time. Removing the fried garlic and the bacon from the skillet and then reincorporating them later maintains their crunch in the finished dish. // *Yield: 4 to 6 servings*

- **RECOMMENDED SKILLET:** 12 inch (30 cm) with lid
- **COOKING METHOD:** Braising

SIDES

2 tablespoons (30 ml) extra virgin olive oil
3 cloves of garlic, sliced
2 thick-cut bacon strips, cut into thin strips
1 small butternut squash (about 1¾ pounds, or 795 g), cut into ½-inch (1-cm) cubes

1 bunch of Lacinato kale (about ¾ pound, or 340 g), stemmed and cut into 1-inch (2.5-cm) strips
Kosher salt
Freshly ground black pepper

Combine the olive oil and garlic in a cast iron skillet. Place over medium-low heat and cook, stirring occasionally, until the garlic is golden brown, 6 to 7 minutes. Using a slotted spoon, remove the garlic to a bowl. Add the bacon to the skillet and fry until golden brown, crispy, and rendered, 5 to 6 minutes. Using a slotted spoon, remove the bacon to the bowl with the garlic. Add the squash to the skillet and fry, stirring occasionally, until golden brown, translucent, and tender-crisp, 8 to 10 minutes. Add the kale and sauté until wilted, 2 to 3 minutes. Cover the skillet, decrease the heat to low, and simmer, stirring occasionally, until the squash and kale are tender, 10 to 12 minutes. Return the garlic and bacon to the skillet and stir through. Season to taste with salt and pepper and serve immediately.

Sorghum-Glazed Carrots & Parsnips

Set aside the sugar, honey, maple, and molasses. Carrots and parsnips are best paired with sorghum syrup. Thick, dark sorghum syrup, a staple of Southern cuisine, brings out the floral quality of the earthy root vegetables while enhancing their sweetness. Look for it at specialty markets or order it online.

Choose small top-on carrots for the best results. // *Yield: 4 to 6 servings*

- **RECOMMENDED SKILLET:** 10¼ inch (26 cm) with lid

- **COOKING METHOD:** Simmering

2 tablespoons (40 g) sorghum syrup
1 ounce (2 tablespoons, or 28 g) unsalted butter, cut into 1-tablespoon (14-g) pieces
6 small carrots (about 1 pound, or 455 g), peeled and halved lengthwise

4 small parsnips (about 1 pound, or 455 g), peeled and halved lengthwise
2 tablespoons (8 g) minced Italian parsley
Kosher salt
Freshly ground black pepper

(continued)

Combine the sorghum, butter, and ½ cup (120 ml) of water in a cast iron skillet. Place over medium heat and cook until the sorghum is dissolved and the butter is melted. Add the carrots and parsnips, bring to a boil, cover the skillet, and simmer until the carrots and parsnips are tender-crisp, 6 to 7 minutes. Uncover and simmer, stirring occasionally, until the carrots and parsnips are just tender and the glaze is thickened slightly, 5 to 6 minutes. Add the parsley and stir through. Season to taste with salt and pepper and serve immediately.

Skillet-Roasted Brussels Sprouts with Chestnuts, Shallots & Bacon

Enjoy this dish in the fall when both Brussels sprouts and chestnuts are in season. It's easy enough for a weeknight but special enough for the Thanksgiving table.

Chestnuts are easiest to peel while they're still warm. Be sure to remove the inner skin as well as the outer shell. // **Yield: 4 to 6 servings**

- **RECOMMENDED SKILLET:** 10¼ inch (26 cm)
- **COOKING METHOD:** Pan-Roasting

8 ounces (225 g) chestnuts
3 thick-cut bacon strips, cut into thin strips
2 ounces (4 tablespoons, or 55 g)
    unsalted butter, cut into 1-tablespoon
    (14-g) pieces

1¼ pounds (570 g) Brussels sprouts,
    trimmed and halved
8 small shallots, quartered
Kosher salt
Freshly ground black pepper

Preheat the oven to 400°F (200°C, or gas mark 6). Using a chestnut knife or bird's beak paring knife, cut an X into the cheek of each chestnut. Place the chestnuts into a skillet and roast until the chestnuts are tender when tested with the tip of a knife, 20 to 25 minutes. Set aside for a few minutes until just cool enough to handle and then peel and dice.

Preheat the skillet over medium heat. Add the bacon and fry until golden brown, crispy, and rendered, 7 to 8 minutes. Add the butter, Brussels sprouts, shallots, and chestnuts and stir through. Transfer the skillet to the oven and roast, stirring once or twice, until the Brussels sprouts are golden brown and tender, 35 to 40 minutes. Season to taste with salt and pepper and serve immediately.

SIDES

Quinoa Pilaf

Quinoa is a nice change of pace from the usual rice and potatoes. It's extremely easy to cook, it's delicious with a satisfying crunchy texture and a mildly nutty flavor, and it happens to be considered a "superfood" too.

You can tell quinoa is cooked through when it becomes tender and translucent and the curlicue-shaped germ is visible. // *Yield: 4 to 6 servings*

- **RECOMMENDED SKILLET:** 10¼ inch (26 cm) with lid
- **COOKING METHOD:** Simmering

2 tablespoons (30 ml) extra virgin olive oil
1 ounce (2 tablespoons, or 28 g)
  unsalted butter, cut into 1-tablespoon
  (14-g) pieces
1 leek, white part only, diced
2 stalks of celery, diced
1 carrot, diced

1½ cups (260 g) quinoa
2½ cups (570 ml) chicken stock
1 bay leaf
2 sprigs of fresh thyme
Kosher salt
Freshly ground black pepper
2 tablespoons (8 g) minced Italian parsley

Preheat a cast iron skillet over medium-low heat. Add the olive oil and butter, swirl to coat the inside, and heat until the butter is melted and the foam subsides. Add the leek and sauté until it begins to soften, 5 to 6 minutes. Add the celery and carrot and sauté until they begin to soften, 5 to 6 minutes. Add the quinoa and cook, stirring constantly, until toasted, about 2 minutes. Add the chicken stock, bay leaf, and thyme and season to taste with salt and pepper. The stock should taste a little salty now for perfectly sea-soned cooked quinoa later. Bring to a boil, cover the skillet, and simmer until the quinoa is tender and all the stock is absorbed, 16 to 18 minutes. Remove and discard the bay leaf and thyme. Fluff the quinoa with a fork and sprinkle with the parsley. Serve hot.

Sausage & Herb Cornbread Dressing

Here's a Southern-style dressing that's perfect to serve for the holidays or any other time of year. It's worth baking up a batch of cornbread just so you can make it—this dressing is so flavorful and rich and moist it doesn't even require gravy!

One whole loaf Sweet Onion Upside-Down Cornbread (page 225) yields approximately 10 cups (2 kg) crumbled. It can be made with or without the onion and baked in advance, stored in a zip-top bag in the freezer, and thawed before crumbling.

Store-bought sausage may be substituted for homemade. // *Yield: 8 servings*

- **RECOMMENDED SKILLET:** 12 inch (30 cm)

- **COOKING METHOD:** Sautéing/Baking

10 cups (2 kg) crumbled cornbread
2 ounces (4 tablespoons, or 55 g)
    unsalted butter, cut into 1-tablespoon
    (14-g) pieces
12 ounces (340 g) uncooked Homemade
    Sage Breakfast Sausage (page 56),
    broken up
1 yellow onion, diced
1 green bell pepper, diced

3 stalks of celery, diced
3 cloves of garlic, minced
3 tablespoons (8 g) minced fresh sage
1½ teaspoons minced fresh thyme
3 eggs
2¼ cups (535 ml) chicken stock
Kosher salt
Freshly ground black pepper

Preheat the oven to 350°F (180°C, or gas mark 4).

Spread the cornbread crumbs in a single layer on a sheet tray and bake until dry and light golden brown, 45 to 50 minutes. Let cool to room temperature.

Increase the oven temperature to 400°F (200°C, or gas mark 6).

Preheat a cast iron skillet over medium-low heat. Add the butter, swirl to coat the inside of the skillet, and heat until the butter is melted and the foam subsides. Add the sausage and cook, stirring occasionally, until golden brown but not necessarily cooked through, 6 to 8 minutes. Remove the sausage to a bowl. Add the onion to the skillet and sauté until soft, 7 to 8 minutes. Add the bell pepper and celery and sauté until soft, 14 to 16 minutes. Add the garlic and stir through and then add the sage and thyme and stir through.

Lightly beat the eggs in a large bowl. Add the chicken stock and whisk until combined. Add the cornbread crumbs, sausage, and onion mixture and toss gently to coat. Season to taste with salt and pepper. Transfer to the skillet and bake until light golden brown, 25 to 30 minutes. Serve hot.

Home Fries

The best home-fried potatoes come out of a cast iron skillet. They should cook up deep, dark golden brown and extremely crispy and have plenty of little bits of caramelized onions, and my version definitely lives up to those high expectations. While the recipe requires a bit of patience and attention, it's well worth the time and effort. It does, however, take one shortcut—par-cooking the potatoes in the microwave cuts down on the cooking time and the sticking as well.

Feel free to vary the recipe according to your mood and the ingredients you have on hand. You can use red or green bell peppers rather than jalapeño, substitute green onions for the red, or try bacon grease instead of canola oil.

These potatoes are equally good with scrambled eggs for breakfast and Constant Flip–Method Steaks with Butter, Frizzled Herbs & Garlic (page 119) for steak night. // *Yield: 4 servings*

- **RECOMMENDED SKILLET:** 12 inch (30 cm)
- **COOKING METHOD:** Pan-Frying

2 large russet potatoes (about 2 pounds, or 900 g total), peeled and cut into ½-inch (1-cm) cubes
⅓ cup (80 ml) canola oil

½ of a red onion, diced
1 jalapeño, seeded and minced
½ teaspoon Cajun Spice (page 250)
Kosher salt

Preheat a cast iron skillet over medium heat. Meanwhile, place the potatoes into a shallow microwave-safe dish, cover with plastic wrap, and microwave, stirring occasionally, until steamy, translucent, and tender-crisp, 5 to 6 minutes. Add the oil to the skillet and swirl to coat the inside. Add the potatoes and fry, stirring every 5 minutes or so, until golden brown, crispy, and nearly tender, 10 to 15 minutes. Add the onion and fry, stirring occasionally, until the potatoes are tender, 4 to 5 minutes. Add the jalapeño and fry, stirring occasionally, until soft, 3 to 5 minutes. Add the Cajun Spice and stir through. Season to taste with salt and serve immediately.

SIDES

Loaded Crispy Smashed Potatoes

Here's an upgrade on the ever-popular loaded potato skins. For more potato flavor in each bite, small yellow potatoes are boiled, smashed, and fried and only then piled high with toppings and baked. Diced fried bacon may be substituted for Andrew's Insta-Lardons (page 54).

These make a hearty side dish but may also be served as an appetizer or snack. // *Yield: 4 servings*

- **RECOMMENDED SKILLET:** 12 inch (30 cm)
- **COOKING METHOD:** Simmering/Pan-Frying

16 small yellow potatoes (about 1½ pounds, or 680 g total)
Kosher salt
½ cup (120 ml) canola oil and/or rendered Insta-Lardon fat

8 ounces (225 g) shredded sharp cheddar (about 2 cups)
8 ounces (225 g) cooked Andrew's Insta-Lardons (page 54)
3 green onions, sliced
½ cup (115 g) sour cream

Place the potatoes into a saucepot, add enough water to cover by about 2 inches (5 cm), and place over medium heat. Bring to a boil, add a generous pinch of salt, and simmer until cooked through, 16 to 18 minutes. A paring knife inserted in the center of a potato will meet no resistance when it is cooked through. Transfer the potatoes to a bowl and let cool slightly.

While still warm, place one potato onto a cutting board and press with the bottom of a small plate to smash until it is ⅜ to ½ inch (9 mm to 1 cm) thick. Transfer the potato to a sheet tray. Smash the remaining potatoes in the same manner.

Preheat the oven to 450°F (230°C, or gas mark 8).

Pour the oil into a cast iron skillet and preheat over medium heat until a crumb of potato sizzles immediately when added. Add half of the potatoes and fry until golden brown and crispy, 5 to 6 minutes. Flip the potatoes and fry until golden brown and crispy, 4 to 5 minutes. Remove the potatoes to a paper towel–lined sheet tray, let drain for a moment, and then transfer to a foil-lined sheet tray. Fry the remaining half of the potatoes in the same manner.

Season the potatoes generously with salt. Sprinkle with half of the cheese, then the lardons, then the green onions, and then the remaining half of the cheese. Bake until the cheese is melted, 5 to 6 minutes. Divide the sour cream among the potatoes and serve immediately.

SIDES

Sweet Potato Fries

Sweet potatoes, unlike starchy russet potatoes, do not really stay crisp when fried due to their high moisture content. The solution is cutting them into relatively thin sticks and coating them with a light cornstarch slurry batter.

Look for pure guajillo chile powder at Mexican markets or order online.

Serve these fries with Chipotle Dipping Sauce (page 255). // *Yield: 4 servings*

- **RECOMMENDED SKILLET:** Deep 10¼ inch (26 cm)*
- **COOKING METHOD:** Deep-Frying

½ cup (65 g) cornstarch
¾ cup (175 ml) pilsner beer or soda water
Kosher salt
½ teaspoon guajillo chile powder
¼ teaspoon granulated garlic

1½ quarts (1.4 L) canola oil (enough to come to a depth of 1½ inches [3.5 cm])
3 small orange- or red-fleshed sweet potatoes (about 1½ pounds, or 680 g total), cut into ¼ x ¼ x 4- to 5-inch (6 x 6-mm x 10- to 13-cm) sticks

Whisk together the cornstarch, beer or soda water, and a generous pinch of salt in a large bowl. Mix together the guajillo chile powder and granulated garlic in a small bowl.

Pour the oil into a deep cast iron skillet and preheat over medium-high heat, starting over medium heat, until it registers 375°F (190°C) on a candy/jelly/deep-fry thermometer. Just before the oil comes to temperature, give the cornstarch mixture one final whisk to recombine, add about one-quarter of the sweet potatoes, and stir to coat. Shake off any excess batter, add the dredged sweet potatoes to the skillet, and fry at a lively sizzle, stirring occasionally, until floating, golden brown, and crispy, 4 to 5 minutes. Using a wire skimmer, remove the sweet potatoes to a paper towel–lined sheet tray and let drain for a moment. Transfer the sweet potatoes to a large bowl, sprinkle with about one-quarter of the chile powder mixture, toss to coat, and season to taste with salt. Reheat the oil and batter, fry, and season the remaining sweet potatoes in 3 more batches in the same manner. Serve hot.

*This can also be made in a deep 12-inch (30-cm) cast iron skillet.

Onion Strings

This style of onion rings, which is lightly dredged in a combination of flour and cornstarch, becomes light and crispy and quite sweet when deep-fried. It is a perfect side for steaks and Smash Burgers (page 115).

For the best results, dredge the onions just moments before the oil reaches frying temperature. Serve with your choice of Fresh Herb Ranch Dipping Sauce (page 254), Buffalo Mayo (page 254), or Chipotle Dipping Sauce (page 255) on the side. // *Yield: 4 servings*

- **RECOMMENDED SKILLET:** Deep 10¼ inch (26 cm)*
- **COOKING METHOD:** Deep-Frying

1 cup (235 ml) buttermilk
Kosher salt
2 cups (250 g) all-purpose flour
¼ cup (32 g) cornstarch
2 teaspoons granulated garlic
1 teaspoon paprika

1½ quarts (1.4 L) canola oil (enough to come to a depth of 1½ inches [3.5 cm])
2 large yellow onions (about 1½ pounds, or 680 g total), cut into ¼-inch (6-mm) thick slices and rings separated

Whisk together the buttermilk and a generous pinch of salt in a medium bowl. Whisk together the flour, cornstarch, granulated garlic, paprika, and several generous pinches of salt in a large bowl.

Pour the oil into a deep cast iron skillet and preheat over medium-high heat, starting over medium heat, until it registers 375°F (190°C) on a candy/jelly/deep-fry thermometer. Just before the oil comes to temperature, add about one-quarter of the onions to the buttermilk mixture and stir to coat. Shake off any excess buttermilk, transfer the onions to the bowl of seasoned flour, and toss to coat, separating any pieces that stick together. Shake off any excess flour, add the dredged onions to the skillet, and fry at a lively sizzle, stirring occasionally, until floating, golden brown, and crispy, 4 to 5 minutes. Using a wire skimmer, remove the onions to a paper towel–lined sheet tray and let drain for a moment. Season to taste with salt. Reheat the oil and dredge and fry the remaining onions in 3 more batches in the same manner. Serve hot.

*This can also be made in a deep 12-inch (30-cm) cast iron skillet.

Southern-Fried Okra

If you are an okra lover like I am, this cornmeal-crusted okra recipe is for you. It cooks up light and crispy without a hint of sliminess. Large okra can be tough and stringy, so select small okra pods no larger than your pinkie finger. When in doubt, test by breaking the tip—it will snap off cleanly and easily on tender okra. Fresh okra, in season during the summertime, is best in this recipe, but you can substitute 1 pound (455 g) bag of frozen okra, partially thawed, with good results.

Since okra exudes a sticky slime when cut, the cornmeal coating sticks quite nicely without a preliminary layer of flour. For the best results, dredge the okra just moments before the oil reaches the frying temperature. Gently toss the okra with the cornmeal mixture to coat, as stirring the two together can result in a thick, heavy coating.

Serve with your choice of Fresh Herb Ranch Dipping Sauce (page 254), Buffalo Mayo (page 254), or Chipotle Dipping Sauce (page 255) on the side. // *Yield: 4 to 6 servings*

- **RECOMMENDED SKILLET:** Deep 12 inch (30 cm)*
- **COOKING METHOD:** Deep-Frying

½ cup (120 ml) buttermilk
Kosher salt
¾ cup (105 g) fine cornmeal
⅓ cup (42 g) all-purpose flour
1 tablespoon (10 g) granulated garlic
¼ teaspoon cayenne pepper

Freshly ground black pepper
1 quart (946 ml) canola oil (enough to come
   to a depth of ¾ inch [2 cm])
¾ pound (340 g) okra, cut into ¾-inch
   (2-cm) pieces

Whisk together the buttermilk and a generous pinch of salt in a medium bowl. Whisk together the cornmeal, flour, granulated garlic, cayenne, and several generous pinches of salt and pepper in a large bowl.

Pour the oil into a deep cast iron skillet and preheat over medium-high heat, starting over medium heat, until it registers 375°F (190°C) on a candy/jelly/deep-fry thermometer. Just before the oil comes to temperature, add half of the okra to the buttermilk and stir to coat. Shake off any excess buttermilk, transfer the okra to the bowl with the cornmeal mixture, and toss to coat, separating any pieces that stick together. Shake off any excess cornmeal, add the dredged okra to the skillet, and fry at a lively sizzle, stirring occasionally, until floating, golden brown, and crispy, 3 to 4 minutes. Using a wire skimmer, remove the okra to a paper towel–lined sheet tray and let drain for a moment. Season to taste with salt. Reheat the oil and dredge and fry the remaining okra in 1 more batch in the same manner. Serve hot.

*This can also be made in a deep 10¼-inch (26-cm) skillet.

Speedy Refried Pinto Beans

You can doctor up canned pintos when you don't have the time or inclination to cook refried beans from scratch from dried beans, and with this recipe, chances are nobody will ever know the difference. So that all of the flavors have plenty of time to simmer and come together, it starts off soupy but thickens up nicely.

Select canned pintos with nothing but beans and water on the ingredient list for the best results. Mexican oregano has a unique floral character. Omit it from the recipe if you can't find it; do not substitute Greek or Italian oregano. Cotija is a salty, hard cow's milk Mexican cheese. If you prefer, you can use cheddar to top the beans. Look for both Mexican oregano and cotija at Mexican markets. // *Yield: 4 to 6 servings*

- **RECOMMENDED SKILLET:** 9 inch (23 cm)
- **COOKING METHOD:** Pan-Frying/Simmering

¼ cup (52 g) lard or bacon grease
½ of a yellow onion, diced
1 small jalapeño, seeded and minced
2 cloves of garlic, minced
½ teaspoon ground cumin
¼ teaspoon dried Mexican oregano leaves

2 (15-ounce [425-g]) cans
   of pinto beans, drained
Kosher salt
Freshly ground black pepper
½ ounce (15 g) crumbled cotija
   (about 2 tablespoons)

Preheat a cast iron skillet over medium heat. Add the lard and swirl to coat the inside of the skillet. Add the onion and sauté until soft, 3 to 4 minutes. Add the jalapeño and garlic and sauté until soft, about 1 minute. Add the cumin and Mexican oregano and stir through. Add the beans and, using a potato masher, mash until coarsely pureed. Add 1 cup (235 ml) of water, stir through, and simmer, stirring frequently, until thick, 10 to 12 minutes. Season to taste with salt and pepper. Transfer to a bowl, sprinkle with the cotija, and serve.

Black Bean Variation: Substitute canned black beans for the canned pinto beans.

Elotes

Grilled corn on the cob slathered in mayo or crema, a thin type of sour cream, cheese, and chile is a popular street food in Mexico. It's easy to replicate at home using a mixture of sour cream and lime. The tanginess of the sauce, the saltiness of the cheese, and the chile's heat are a great contrast to the sweetness of the corn.

Cotija is a salty, hard cow's milk Mexican cheese. Look for it at Mexican markets. // **Yield: 4 servings**

- **RECOMMENDED SKILLET:** 12 inch (30 cm)
- **COOKING METHOD:** Pan-Frying

⅔ cup (154 g) sour cream
1 clove of garlic, grated on a Microplane
1 teaspoon grated lime zest
Freshly squeezed juice of 1 large lime
Kosher salt
2 tablespoons (30 ml) canola oil

4 ears of corn, shucked
1 ounce (about ⅓ cup, or 28 g)
 shredded cotija
½ teaspoon chipotle powder
2 tablespoons (2 g) minced cilantro

Whisk together the sour cream, garlic, lime zest, and lime juice in a medium bowl and season to taste with salt.

Preheat a cast iron skillet over medium heat. Add the oil and swirl to coat the inside of the skillet. Add the corn and cook, flipping occasionally, until bright yellow and golden brown in spots, 10 to 12 minutes. Transfer the corn to a platter and drizzle with the sour cream mixture and then sprinkle with the cotija, chipotle powder, and cilantro. Serve immediately.

SIDES

Flour Tortillas

Homemade flour tortillas are infinitely better than store-bought. They have a buttery flavor and wonderfully supple texture, plus they are great fun to make.

Good tortillas are made from a relatively wet dough. The dough will seem quite sticky and hard to manage, especially at first. Resist the temptation to add flour and persevere in kneading it, and it will become significantly less sticky after several minutes as the gluten develops. Even then the dough should be quite soft. Stick with it—no pun intended—and you'll be rewarded with tortillas that puff like balloons as they cook and are superbly more moist and tender.

Solid rendered lard may be substituted for the butter.

A clean kitchen towel is good for keeping tortillas warm as it insulates and at the same time absorbs moisture, keeping condensation at bay. You can also use a tortilla warmer lined with a towel or napkin.

In the unlikely event you have leftovers, homemade tortillas can be stored between sheets of parchment paper in a zip-top bag in the freezer. Thaw and then refresh them one at a time directly over a gas burner set to high, flipping frequently, until they are supple and brown spots appear, 20 to 25 seconds.

If you're taking the time to make tortillas, consider reserving a few for Sopaipillas with Honey & Cinnamon (page 246). // *Yield: 8 tortillas*

- **RECOMMENDED SKILLET:** 12 inch (30 cm)
- **COOKING METHOD:** Griddling

2½ cups (313 g) all-purpose flour,
   plus more for dusting
½ teaspoon kosher salt

¼ teaspoon baking powder
2 ounces (4 tablespoons, or 55 g)
   unsalted butter, cold

Whisk together the flour, salt, and baking powder in a large bowl.

Working quickly and with a light touch to prevent the butter from melting, shred the butter into the flour mixture. Stir through and, using your fingertips, rub the butter into the flour until the mixture resembles coarse crumbs. Add 1 cup (235 ml) minus 1 tablespoon (15 ml) of cool water and, using a spoon, mix until a sticky dough forms. Knead until no longer sticky but not necessarily smooth, 4 to 5 minutes. Cover and let rest for 15 to 20 minutes.

Cut the dough into eighths and form each portion into a ball. Cover and let rest for 5 to 10 minutes.

Using a small rolling pin, roll out each ball of dough to a 7- to 8-inch (18- to 20-cm) wide tortilla on a lightly floured surface. As you work, stack the tortillas, shaking off any excess flour, on a plate between sheets of parchment paper to keep them from sticking to each other.

Cook the tortillas in the same order as you rolled them: Preheat a cast iron skillet over medium heat. Add 1 tortilla and cook without disturbing until set, about 30 seconds. Using a spatula, flip the tortilla and cook until brown spots form, about 30 seconds. Flip the tortilla again and cook until puffed and brown spots form, about 30 seconds. Remove the tortilla to a clean kitchen towel and wrap to keep warm. Cook the remaining tortillas in the same manner and serve hot.

Duck Fat–Fried Potatoes

These fried potatoes are a real treat—they cook up crispy on the outside and creamy on the inside, and duck fat lends a fantastic savory quality. And they are surprisingly easy to make. Ordinary French-fried potatoes require two separate trips into the fryer, but this approach is a lot less fuss. In fact, they're so forgiving that as long as you watch that the oil keeps at a lively sizzle, you don't even need to bother with a thermometer.

Duck fat is available at gourmet markets and butcher shops. It's pricey, but it can be reused a number of times. Strain it through a fine-mesh sieve once it has cooled to room temperature and store in a tightly sealed container in the freezer for several months.

If you don't happen to have duck fat on hand, don't let that stop you from frying potatoes in this manner. You'll still have some tasty fries if you substitute canola oil. // *Yield: 4 servings*

- **RECOMMENDED SKILLET:** Deep 12 inch (30 cm)*
- **COOKING METHOD:** Deep-Frying

16 ounces (475 ml) duck fat (enough to come to a depth of ½ inch [1 cm])
2 medium russet potatoes (about 1¾ pounds, or 795 g total), peeled, cut into ¾-inch (2-cm) cubes, rinsed until the water runs clear, drained, and dried thoroughly on paper towels

1 large clove of garlic, minced
½ teaspoon minced fresh thyme
½ teaspoon coarse ground black pepper
Kosher salt

(continued)

Place the duck fat into a deep cast iron skillet and preheat over medium heat until a cube of potato sizzles immediately when added. Add the potatoes and fry at a lively sizzle, stirring occasionally, until floating, golden brown, crispy, and tender, 16 to 18 minutes. Using a wire skimmer, remove the potatoes to a paper towel–lined sheet tray and let drain for a moment. Transfer to a bowl and add the garlic, thyme, and pepper and stir through. Season to taste with salt and serve hot.

*This can also be made in a deep 10¼-inch (26-cm) skillet.

Sautéed Cabbage with Pancetta

This recipe has an Italian accent, but I do endless variations on garlicky sautéed cabbage depending on what I'm in the mood for. I may use canola instead of olive oil, skip the rosemary, or throw in bacon instead of pancetta. Sometimes, I omit the pork all together for a lighter dish. From time to time, I add some onions. If I'm serving it with Asian food, I season with soy sauce rather than salt. Whatever the flavoring, no cabbage is more compelling than that given the quick cast iron skillet treatment. // *Yield: 4 servings*

- **RECOMMENDED SKILLET:** 10¼ inch (26 cm)
- **COOKING METHOD:** Sautéing

2 ounces (55 g) sliced pancetta,
   cut into thin strips
2 tablespoons (30 ml) extra virgin olive oil
½ of a medium green cabbage
   (about 1 pound, or 455 g), cut into
   1½-inch (3.5-cm) pieces

2 cloves of garlic, minced
½ teaspoon minced fresh rosemary
Kosher salt
Freshly ground black pepper

Preheat a cast iron skillet over medium heat. Add the pancetta and sauté until golden brown, crispy, and rendered, 2 to 3 minutes. Add the olive oil and stir through. Add the cabbage and sauté until it begins to soften, 3 to 4 minutes. Add the garlic and rosemary and sauté until the cabbage is tender-crisp, 2 to 3 minutes. Season to taste with salt and pepper. Transfer to a bowl and serve immediately.

Toasted Orzo with Salami & Asparagus

Here's an orzo dish that seems to have more in common with risotto than it does with pasta. Toasting dry orzo in butter until it's golden brown gives it a complex, nutty aroma and flavor.

// *Yield: 4 servings*

- **RECOMMENDED SKILLET:** 10¼ inch (26 cm)
- **COOKING METHOD:** Simmering

1½ ounces (3 tablespoons, or 42 g) unsalted butter, cut into 1-tablespoon (14-g) pieces
8 ounces (225 g) orzo
2 cloves of garlic, minced
2½ cups (570 ml) chicken stock
½ of a bunch of asparagus (about 8 ounces, or 225 g), trimmed and cut into ½-inch (1-cm) pieces

3 ounces (85 g) diced Italian salami
2 ounces (55 g) shredded Parmigiano-Reggiano (about ½ cup)
Kosher salt
Freshly ground black pepper

Preheat a cast iron skillet over medium heat. Add the butter, swirl to coat the inside of the skillet, and heat until the butter is melted and the foam subsides. Add the orzo and cook, stirring constantly, until golden brown and toasted, 3 to 4 minutes. Add the garlic and stir through. Add the chicken stock, bring to a boil, and simmer, stirring frequently, until the orzo is nearly al dente, 10 to 12 minutes. Add the asparagus and simmer, stirring constantly, until tender-crisp, the orzo is al dente, and most of the stock is absorbed, about 2 minutes. Remove the skillet from the heat and add the salami and Parmigiano-Reggiano and stir through. Season to taste with salt and pepper and serve immediately.

Risotto Milanese with Peas & Prosciutto

A cast iron skillet is the perfect cooking vessel for risotto. The heat capacity maintains a steady simmer, while the broad surface area allows stock to reduce readily.

This particular flavor of risotto is a classic of Italian cuisine. Make a big batch so that you have enough leftovers to make Mozzarella-Stuffed Arancini (page 82) later. // *Yield: 4 servings*

- **RECOMMENDED SKILLET:** 10¼ inch (26 cm)

- **COOKING METHOD:** Simmering

1½ quarts (1.4 L) chicken stock
Large pinch of saffron threads
2 tablespoons (30 ml) extra virgin olive oil
½ of a yellow onion, diced
2 cups (400 g) Arborio rice
⅓ cup (80 ml) white wine
⅓ cup (43 g) frozen peas, thawed

1½ ounces (3 tablespoons, or 42 g) unsalted butter, cut into 1-tablespoon (14-g) pieces
3 ounces (85 g) shredded Parmigiano-Reggiano (about ¾ cup)
3 ounces (85 g) thinly sliced prosciutto
Kosher salt
Freshly ground black pepper

Combine the chicken stock and saffron in a small sauce pot, bring to a boil, and reduce to a bare simmer.

Preheat a cast iron skillet over medium-low heat. Add the olive oil and swirl to coat the inside of the skillet. Add the onion and sauté until it begins to soften, 3 to 4 minutes. Add the rice and cook, stirring constantly, until toasted, about 2 minutes. Add the wine and simmer, stirring constantly, until nearly dry, 1 to 2 minutes. Using a ladle, add enough of the hot stock to cover the rice by 1 inch (2.5 cm) and simmer, stirring constantly and adding more stock a ladleful at a time as the liquid reduces below the level of the rice, until it is creamy and the rice is nearly tender, 18 to 20 minutes. Add the peas and simmer, stirring constantly, until the rice is tender but toothsome and the peas are heated through, 1 to 2 minutes. Remove the skillet from the heat, add the butter, Parmigiano-Reggiano, and prosciutto and stir through. Season to taste with salt and pepper and serve immediately.

SIDES

Charred Eggplant Baba Ganoush

Eggplant for baba ganoush is usually roasted in the oven but charring it in a skillet on the stove-top seems to make for less water-logged eggplant and therefore fluffier baba ganoush.

This baba ganoush is best the day after it's made. Store in a tightly sealed container in the refrigerator.

Whether you're serving this on its own or as a part of a mezze platter, possibly with hummus and Falafel with Lemon-Yogurt Dipping Sauce (page 88), offer plenty of warm pita bread for dipping. // *Yield: about 1 quart (946 ml) or 8 servings*

- **RECOMMENDED SKILLET:** 12 inch (30 cm)

- **COOKING METHOD:** Charring

2 large globe eggplants (1 pound to 1 pound 2 ounces, or 455 to 510 g each)

3 large cloves of garlic, minced

¼ cup (60 g) tahini

3 tablespoons (45 ml) extra virgin olive oil, plus more for serving

Freshly squeezed juice of 2 large lemons

Kosher salt

Freshly ground black pepper

Aleppo pepper, for serving

Preheat a cast iron skillet over medium-low heat. Add the eggplants and cook, flipping occasionally, until charred all over and quite soft, 40 to 60 minutes. Transfer to a bowl and let cool to room temperature.

Trim the stems off the eggplants and peel. Combine the eggplants, garlic, tahini, olive oil, and lemon juice in a food processor and process until smooth. Season to taste with salt and pepper. Transfer to a tightly sealed container and refrigerate overnight for the flavors to come together.

Transfer to a serving bowl and drizzle with additional olive oil and sprinkle with Aleppo pepper.

Dry-Fried Okra with Curry Powder & Cilantro

Here's a recipe for what is essentially okra chips with Indian spices. Serve it along with Indian Chicken Stir-Fry (page 188) or Lamb Chukka (page 189). It also makes a fantastic snack or appetizer all by itself.

Large okra can be tough and stringy, so select small okra pods no larger than your pinkie finger. When in doubt, test by breaking the tip—it will snap off cleanly and easily on tender okra.

Mildly hot Kashmiri chile powder is available at Indian markets. // *Yield: 4 servings*

- **RECOMMENDED SKILLET:** Deep 12 inch (30 cm)*
- **COOKING METHOD:** Deep-Frying

1 quart (946 ml) canola oil (enough to come to a depth of ¾ inch [2 cm])
1 pound (455 g) okra, cut on a bias into ⅛- to ³⁄₁₆-inch (3- to 5-mm) thick slices
½ teaspoon Curry Powder (page 252)

½ teaspoon Kashmiri chile powder
3 tablespoons (3 g) minced cilantro
Kosher salt
1 lime, cut into 8 wedges

Pour the oil into a deep cast iron skillet and preheat over medium-high heat, starting over medium heat, until it registers 375°F (190°C) on a candy/jelly/deep-fry thermometer. Add half of the okra to the skillet and fry at a lively sizzle, stirring occasionally, until floating, light golden brown, and crispy, 4 to 5 minutes. Using a wire skimmer, remove the okra to a paper towel–lined sheet tray and let drain. Reheat the oil and fry the remaining okra in 1 more batch in the same manner. Transfer the okra to a large bowl, sprinkle with the Curry Powder, Kashmiri chile powder, and cilantro. Toss to coat, and season to taste with salt. Serve hot with the lime wedges.

*This can also be made in a deep 10¼-inch (26-cm) skillet.

SIDES

Dal with Caramelized Onions

Dried, split legumes and the dishes made with them are both known as *dal* in Indian. This particular dal is made with quick-cooking, earthy split red lentils along with caramelized onions (page 68) for sweetness.

Red lentils should be picked over for any stones and then rinsed before cooking, but they do not require presoaking. Since their hulls have been removed, they fall apart as they cook, resulting in a dish with a coarse puree-like texture.

This dal should be accompanied by some steamy, fragrant basmati rice. The combination makes a great side for Saag Paneer (page 186), Indian Chicken Stir-Fry (page 188), Lamb Chukka (page 189), or Dry-Fried Okra with Curry Powder & Cilantro (page 222).

// *Yield: 4 servings*

- **RECOMMENDED SKILLET:** 10¼ inch (26 cm)
- **COOKING METHOD:** Sautéing/Simmering

3 tablespoons (45 ml) canola oil
1 small yellow onion, julienned
½ teaspoon mustard seeds
Kosher salt
2 cloves of garlic, minced

1 teaspoon minced ginger
½ teaspoon ground cumin
1 cup (192 g) split red lentils, picked over
Freshly squeezed juice of ½ of a lime

Preheat a cast iron skillet over medium-low heat. Add the oil and swirl to coat the inside. Add the onion, mustard seeds, and a generous pinch of salt and cook, stirring frequently, until the onion is golden brown, 35 to 40 minutes. Add the garlic and ginger and stir through. Add the cumin and stir through. Add the lentils and 1 quart (946 ml) of water, bring to a boil, and simmer, stirring frequently, until the lentils fall apart and most of the water is absorbed, 40 to 45 minutes. Add the lime juice and stir through and season to taste with salt and serve hot.

5

SWEETS AND BAKES

Sweet Onion Upside-Down Cornbread

Make the most of sweet onion season with this twist on classic cornbread. The onions soften and caramelize slightly as the cornbread bakes, making for a presentation that's as attractive as it is delicious.

It's a good idea to try to lay out the onion slices in the skillet before heating it up to get a sense of how they'll fit, since there isn't much time to play around once the skillet is hot. If the slices don't fit a single layer, simply remove as many of the outer rings as necessary to make it work. // *Yield: 6 to 8 servings*

- **RECOMMENDED SKILLET:** 9 inch (23 cm)
- **COOKING METHOD:** Pan-Frying/Baking

1½ cups (210 g) coarse ground cornmeal
½ cup (63 g) all-purpose flour
1 tablespoon (13 g) sugar
2 teaspoons baking powder
½ teaspoon baking soda
¾ teaspoon kosher salt
2 large eggs, at room temperature

1½ cups (355 ml) buttermilk,
    at room temperature
1½ ounces (3 tablespoons, or 42 g)
    unsalted butter, melted
3 tablespoons (42 g) bacon grease
1 small sweet onion, cut into ½-inch
    (1-cm) thick slices

Preheat the oven to 425°F (220°C, or gas mark 7).

Whisk together the cornmeal, flour, sugar, baking powder, baking soda, and salt in a large bowl. Whisk together the eggs, buttermilk, and butter in a medium bowl.

(continued)

Preheat a cast iron skillet over medium heat. Right before the skillet is ready, add the egg mixture to the cornmeal mixture and whisk until just combined and all of the ingredients are moistened. Add the bacon grease to the skillet and swirl to coat the inside. Add the onion slices, arranging them in a single layer. Add the batter and fry until the edges begin to set, about 2 minutes. Transfer the skillet to the oven and bake until the cornbread is golden brown, the edges start to shrink away from the skillet, and a toothpick inserted into the center comes out with moist crumbs, 22 to 26 minutes. Let cool in the skillet for at least 15 minutes. Place a platter over the skillet and invert to unmold the cornbread, cut into wedges, and serve warm.

Masa Cornbread

One day I was getting ready to make a batch of cornbread when I took it into my head to use masa harina, typically used for making corn tortillas and tamales, instead of cornmeal. Southern-cooking purists may frown upon my reckless experimentation, but it resulted in a moist cornbread with far more earthy, corny flavor than I'd ever tasted before. Then, I gave my unorthodox recipe another upgrade and baked it in a cast iron skillet instead of a glass baking dish, and that's when I really achieved my idea of cornbread perfection. Starting the cornbread in a cast iron skillet on the stovetop essentially fries the edges, giving the cornbread a substantial dark, golden-brown, crispy crust on the bottom.

In my experience, Bob's Red Mill masa harina is far superior to other widely available brands and worth seeking out for use in this recipe. If you can't find it, opt for masa for tamales, which has a coarser texture than masa for tortillas.

The masa makes this recipe a fusion of Southern, Southwestern, and Mexican cuisines. Serve it with anything from barbecue to chili to mole. // *Yield: 6 to 8 servings*

- **RECOMMENDED SKILLET:** 9 inch (23 cm)
- **COOKING METHOD:** Pan-Frying/Baking

(continued)

1¼ cups (145 g) masa harina
¾ cup (94 g) all-purpose flour
2 teaspoons sugar
2 teaspoons baking powder
½ teaspoon baking soda
¾ teaspoon kosher salt
2 large eggs, at room temperature

¾ cup (175 ml) milk, at room temperature
¾ cup (175 ml) buttermilk, at room temperature
1½ ounces (3 tablespoons, or 42 g) unsalted butter, melted
3 tablespoons (42 g) bacon grease

Preheat the oven to 425°F (220°C, or gas mark 7).

Whisk together the masa harina, flour, sugar, baking powder, baking soda, and salt in a large bowl. Whisk together the eggs, milk, buttermilk, and butter in a medium bowl.

Preheat a 9-inch (23-cm) cast iron skillet over medium heat. Right before the skillet is ready, add the egg mixture to the masa harina mixture and whisk until just combined and all of the ingredients are moistened. Add the bacon grease to the skillet and swirl to coat the inside. Add the batter, spreading it evenly, and fry until the edges begin to set, about 2 minutes. Transfer the skillet to the oven and bake until the cornbread is golden brown, the edges start to shrink away from the skillet, and a toothpick inserted into the center comes out with moist crumbs, 22 to 26 minutes. Let cool in the skillet for at least 15 minutes. Cut into wedges and serve warm.

Jalapeño-Cheddar Variation: Immediately after spreading the batter into the skillet, scatter 2 sliced jalapeños and then 4 to 6 ounces (115 to 170 g) shredded sharp cheddar (about 1 to 1½ cups) over the top.

Buttermilk Biscuits

These biscuits, which develop a lovely golden-brown crust on the bottom from being baked in CI, take almost no time or effort to mix together. The less you work the dough, the more tender the biscuits will be, so minimize kneading as much as possible and don't try to make biscuits cut from scrap dough as pretty as those cut in the first round.

Use the basic recipe for serving with butter and jam or for making breakfast sandwiches, Biscuits & Sausage Gravy (page 60), and Chicken-Fried Chicken Biscuit Sandwiches (page 102).

The savory variation with cheese and nigella is an absolute favorite of mine. Nigella, which has a flavor similar to that of thyme, is also known as *kalonji* or *charnushka* and available at spice shops and Indian markets.

If you will be serving the biscuits split, do it gently with a serrated knife. Otherwise, they may fall apart because they are so delicate. // ***Yield: 10 biscuits***

- **RECOMMENDED SKILLET:** 12 inch (30 cm)
- **COOKING METHOD:** Baking

4 cups (500 g) all-purpose flour,
   plus more for dusting
2 tablespoons (28 g) baking powder
1¼ teaspoons kosher salt

7 ounces (14 tablespoons, or 200 g)
   unsalted butter, cold
1¾ (410 ml) cups buttermilk, cold

Preheat the oven to 425°F (220°C, or gas mark 7).

Whisk together the flour, baking powder, and kosher salt in a large bowl.

Working quickly and with a light touch to prevent the butter from melting, shred the butter into the flour mixture. Stir through and, using your fingertips, rub the butter into the flour until the mixture resembles coarse crumbs. Add the buttermilk and, using a spoon, stir until a shaggy dough forms. Knead lightly a few times just until any loose bits hold together. Gently pat the dough into a 2-inch (5-cm) thick circle on a lightly floured surface. Using a 2½-inch (6-cm) round cutter dipped in flour, cut biscuits as close together as possible. Gently pat the scraps together into a 2-inch (5-cm) thick circle and cut additional biscuits in the same manner.

Arrange the biscuits evenly in a 12-inch (30-cm) cast iron skillet and bake until light golden brown, 24 to 28 minutes.

Serve warm.

Cheddar & Nigella Variation: Stir 8 ounces (225 g) of shredded sharp cheddar (about 2 cups), 2 tablespoons (6 g) of minced fresh chives, 2 teaspoons of nigella seeds, and 1 teaspoon of freshly ground coarse black pepper into the flour mixture before shredding in the butter. Though they need no accompaniment, these are fantastic split and filled with a slice of Black Forest ham.

Twenty-Four-Hour Salted Rye Chocolate Chunk Skookie

In the case of this skillet cookie, bigger really is better! It's sure to please kids because of its giant proportions and adults with its sophisticated and slightly less sweet flavor compared to the classic. The savory rye flour balances all the sugar as does the flaky salt, and resting the dough overnight before baking hydrates the flour and develops more complex, caramel-like notes. But if you need some immediate gratification and just can't bear to wait 24 hours to satisfy your sweet tooth, go ahead and bake the skookie right away—it'll still be absolutely delicious!

The skookie is even better the day after it's baked. Keep it in a tightly sealed container for 2 to 3 days. // *Yield: 12 to 16 servings*

- **RECOMMENDED SKILLET:** 12 inch (30 cm)
- **COOKING METHOD:** Baking

1½ cups (188 g) all-purpose flour
½ cup (64 g) dark rye flour
⅓ cup (45 g) cake flour, sifted
1¼ teaspoons kosher salt
1 teaspoon baking soda
8 ounces (16 tablespoons, or 225 g)
    unsalted butter, preferably European
    style, softened

¾ cup (170 g) packed light brown sugar
⅔ cup (133 g) sugar
2 eggs, at room temperature
2 teaspoons pure vanilla extract
10 ounces (280 g) chopped bittersweet
    chocolate (about 1⅔ cups)
Flaky sea salt, such as fleur de sel
    or Maldon

Whisk together the all-purpose flour, rye flour, cake flour, kosher salt, and baking soda in a medium bowl. In a mixer fitted with a paddle attachment, beat together the butter, brown sugar, and sugar on low speed until just creamed, 3 to 4 minutes. Beat in the eggs one at a time until thoroughly combined and then beat in the vanilla extract. Add the flour mixture and mix on low until the dough comes together. Stop the mixer occasionally during the mixing process and scrape down the sides and bottom of the bowl to ensure that everything is well blended. Add the chocolate and mix until incorporated. Transfer the dough to a zip-top bag, seal, and refrigerate overnight.

Preheat the oven to 350°F (180°C, or gas mark 4).

Press the cookie dough evenly into a 12-inch (30-cm) cast iron skillet and sprinkle with a generous pinch of sea salt. Bake until the skookie is golden brown, the edges start to shrink away from the skillet, and a toothpick inserted into the center comes out with moist crumbs, 35 to 40 minutes. Let cool in the skillet for at least 15 minutes. Cut into wedges and serve warm or at room temperature.

Chocolate Buttermilk Skake with Ganache Frosting

This is, in my humble opinion, the quintessential chocolate cake. It is exceptionally chocolatey and fluffy and moist and tender and without a doubt my ultimate, all-time favorite. It's special enough for a birthday but quick and easy enough for any day. It is a lot like devil's food cake but much simpler to make—you don't have to remember to bring butter and eggs to room temperature in advance and you don't have to cream a finicky batter.

I adapted the recipe from the commercial-quantity one that we used for layer cakes when I was teaching in the Clark College bakery program.

When heating the cream for the ganache, it is ready the moment it comes to a boil. Do not let it boil for any length of time because if it starts to reduce, you run the risk of breaking the ganache.

Due to the buttermilk and oil in the batter, this cake keeps quite well and is still delicious a day or two after it's baked. // *Yield: 8 servings*

- **RECOMMENDED SKILLET:** 10¼ inch (26 cm)

- **COOKING METHOD:** Baking

Unsalted butter, for greasing the skillet
1¾ cups (238 g) cake flour
1⅓ cups (267 g) sugar
½ cup (40 g) plus 2 tablespoons (10 g)
   cocoa powder
2 teaspoons baking soda
¼ teaspoon kosher salt
1 egg

½ cup (120 ml) canola oil
1 cup (235 ml) buttermilk
¾ cup (175 ml) coffee, at room temperature
6 ounces (170 g) chopped semisweet
   chocolate (about 1 cup)
½ cup (120 ml) cream
2 teaspoons light corn syrup
¼ teaspoon pure vanilla extract

Preheat the oven to 350°F (180°C, or gas mark 4).

Butter a 10¼-inch (26-cm) cast iron skillet, line the bottom with parchment, and butter the parchment.

Sift together the cake flour, sugar, cocoa powder, baking soda, and salt into a mixer bowl. Whisk together the egg and oil in a medium bowl. Whisk together the buttermilk and coffee in another medium bowl.

Add the egg mixture to the flour mixture and, using a paddle attachment, mix on low speed until thoroughly combined. Add the buttermilk mixture a little bit at a time, mixing on low speed after each addition until smooth. If you add the wet ingredients to the flour mixture all at once, you'll inevitably wind up with a lumpy batter. Stop the mixer occasionally during the mixing process and scrape down the sides and bottom of the bowl to ensure that everything is well blended. Transfer the batter to the skillet and bake until the edges start to shrink away from the skillet and a toothpick inserted into the center comes out with moist crumbs, 55 to 60 minutes. Let cool in the skillet for 20 to 30 minutes. Place a piece of parchment and then a sheet tray over the skillet and invert to unmold the cake. Peel off the parchment from the bottom. Place a cooling rack over the cake and invert again to turn the cake right-side up. Peel off the parchment from the top and let cool to room temperature on the cooling rack.

Place the chocolate into a medium bowl. Combine the cream and corn syrup in a small saucepan. Bring to a boil, stirring to dissolve the corn syrup. Immediately pour the cream mixture over the chocolate, add the vanilla, and whisk slowly until smooth. Let cool, stirring occasionally, until thickened but still spreadable, 25 to 30 minutes.

Transfer the cake to a cake plate. Pour the ganache on the cake and spread over the top, swirling decoratively. Cut into wedges and serve.

Hazelnut-Spice Cake

A quick and easy treat for a coffee or tea break, this aromatic cake is moist and tender with a bit of crunch from ground hazelnuts. Though it needs no frosting, I won't object if you top it with a bit of chocolate-hazelnut spread.

Adding sugar to the food processor when grinding the hazelnuts helps to keep them from turning into nut butter. Using the same skillet that you melted the butter in to bake the cake means you can skip the greasing step.

For the best flavor and texture, enjoy this cake the same day it's made. It's especially delightful still warm from the oven. // **Yield: 8 servings**

- **RECOMMENDED SKILLET:** 9 inch (23 cm)
- **COOKING METHOD:** Roasting/Baking

¾ cup (101 g) hazelnuts	2 teaspoons baking powder
4 ounces (8 tablespoons, or 112 g) unsalted butter, cut into 1-tablespoon (14-g) pieces	1 teaspoon kosher salt
	1 teaspoon ground cinnamon
	½ teaspoon freshly grated nutmeg
⅓ cup (67 g) sugar	2 eggs, at room temperature
⅓ cup (75 g) packed light brown sugar	1 cup (235 ml) milk, at room temperature
1¾ cups (219 g) all-purpose flour	½ teaspoon pure vanilla extract

Preheat the oven to 350°F (180°C, or gas mark 4).

Place the hazelnuts into a 9-inch (23-cm) cast iron skillet and bake until light golden brown, 14 to 16 minutes. Immediately transfer to a bowl and let cool completely. Add the butter to the hot skillet and set aside to melt. Swirl to coat the inside of the skillet.

Transfer the hazelnuts to a clean kitchen towel. Fold the towel over them and rub to loosen the skins. Pick the skinned hazelnuts out of the towel and transfer to a food processor. Add the sugar and brown sugar and pulse until finely ground.

Whisk together the flour, baking powder, salt, cinnamon, nutmeg, and hazelnut mixture in a large bowl. Whisk together the eggs, milk, vanilla, and butter in a medium bowl.

Add the egg mixture to the flour mixture and whisk until just combined and all of the ingredients are moistened. Transfer the batter to the skillet and bake until the cake is golden brown, the edges start to shrink away from the skillet, and a toothpick inserted into the center comes out with moist crumbs, 45 to 50 minutes. Let cool in the skillet for at least 15 minutes. Cut into wedges and serve warm.

Triple Ginger Gingerbread

With dried ground, fresh grated, and chewy diced candied ginger, this fluffy, tender, and moist gingerbread has a triple punch of spicy ginger flavor.

Using the same skillet that you melted the butter in to bake the cake means you can skip the greasing step. // **Yield: 8 servings**

- **RECOMMENDED SKILLET:** 10¼ inch (26 cm)
- **COOKING METHOD:** Baking

4 ounces (8 tablespoons, or 112 g) unsalted butter, cut into 1-tablespoon (14-g) pieces
2 cups (250 g) all-purpose flour
¾ cup (150 g) sugar
1 teaspoon baking powder
¼ teaspoon baking soda
¼ teaspoon kosher salt
2 teaspoons ground cinnamon

1 teaspoon ground ginger
¼ teaspoon ground cloves
1½ ounces (42 g) candied ginger, diced (about ¼ cup)
2 eggs, at room temperature
1¼ cups (295 ml) milk, at room temperature
¼ cup (85 g) molasses
1½ teaspoons Microplane-grated ginger

Preheat the oven to 350°F (180°C, or gas mark 4).

Place the butter into a 10¼-inch (26-cm) cast iron skillet and melt over low heat. Swirl to coat the inside of the skillet.

Whisk together the flour, sugar, baking powder, baking soda, salt, cinnamon, ground ginger, and ground cloves in a large bowl. Add the candied ginger and stir through. Whisk together the eggs, milk, molasses, grated ginger, and butter in a medium bowl.

Add the egg mixture to the flour mixture and whisk until just combined and all of the ingredients are moistened. Transfer the batter to the skillet and bake until the gingerbread is golden brown, the edges start to shrink away from the skillet, and a toothpick inserted into the center comes out with moist crumbs, 45 to 50 minutes. Let cool in the skillet for at least 15 minutes. Cut into wedges and serve warm.

Funnel Cakes

You don't have to wait for the fair to come around to get your funnel cake fix. The favorite carnival treats can be whipped up in a jiffy as they are made from what is essentially a thin pancake batter and take just moments to deep-fry. Making them at home is great fun as spiraling the batter from a funnel into the hot oil and watching the instant transformation as it fries up is captivating!

Since funnel cakes are so light and there's almost nothing to them, they float on the surface of the oil from the moment they are added to the skillet and they hardly make the temperature fall. So keep a close eye on the thermometer as you cook and decrease the heat if necessary.

// *Yield: 4 servings*

- **RECOMMENDED SKILLET:** Deep 12 inch (30 cm)
- **COOKING METHOD:** Deep-Frying

1½ cups (188 g) all-purpose flour
¼ cup (50 g) sugar
2 teaspoons baking powder
½ teaspoon kosher salt
2 eggs

1½ cups (355 ml) milk
1 teaspoon pure vanilla extract
1½ quarts (1.4 L) canola oil (enough to come to a depth of 1 inch [2.5 cm])
½ cup (60 g) powdered sugar

Whisk together the flour, sugar, baking powder, and salt in a large bowl. Whisk together the eggs, milk, and vanilla in a medium bowl.

Pour the oil into a deep cast iron skillet and preheat over medium-high heat, starting over medium heat, until it registers 375°F (190°C) on a candy/jelly/deep-fry thermometer. Just before the oil comes to temperature, add the egg mixture to the flour mixture and whisk until smooth. Pour a heaping ½ cup (115 g) batter into a funnel with a ½-inch (1-cm) spout while holding the spout closed with a finger. Hold the funnel over the center of the skillet, release your finger, and let the batter pour into the oil while quickly moving the funnel in a tight spiral motion. Fry the funnel cake until golden brown, about 1 minute. Using tongs, flip the funnel cake and fry until golden brown, about 45 seconds. Remove the funnel cake to a paper towel–lined sheet tray and let drain. Reheat the oil and make 3 more funnel cakes with the remaining batter in the same manner.

Transfer the funnel cakes to a platter and, using a fine-mesh sieve, dust with the powdered sugar. Serve immediately.

Chocolate-Berry Cobbler

This cobbler is made with mixed berries and a chocolate–chocolate chip biscuit topping. The berries are only lightly sweetened and lightly thickened and very juicy.

The juices tend to bubble over a bit, so it's a good idea to line the oven rack below it with foil to catch any spills and make for easy cleanup.

Judging when the cobbler is golden brown and done can be somewhat tricky since the chocolate biscuit topping is already brown. So don't hesitate to peak under one of the center biscuits to see if it's set.

Serve it à la mode, with either chocolate or vanilla ice cream (or a little scoop of both!) or with lightly sweetened vanilla whipped cream. // *Yield: 6 to 8 servings*

- **RECOMMENDED SKILLET:** 10¼ inch (26 cm)

- **COOKING METHOD:** Baking

3 ounces (6 tablespoons, or 85 g) unsalted butter, cold, plus more for greasing the skillet
1¾ cups (219 g) all-purpose flour
¼ cup (20 g) cocoa powder, sifted
⅔ cup (133 g) sugar, divided
1 tablespoon (14 g) baking powder
½ teaspoon kosher salt
1 egg, cold
½ cup (120 ml) cream, cold
⅓ cup (80 ml) buttermilk, cold
½ teaspoon pure vanilla extract

12 ounces (340 g) strawberries (about 3 cups), sliced
6 ounces (170 g) raspberries (about 2 cups)
6 ounces (170 g) blackberries (about 1½ cups)
6 ounces (170 g) blueberries (about 1½ cups)
1½ tablespoons (12 g) cornstarch
3 ounces (85 g) chopped bittersweet chocolate (about ½ cup)

Preheat the oven to 425°F (220°C, or gas mark 7).

Butter a 10¼-inch (26-cm) cast iron skillet.

Whisk together the flour, cocoa powder, ⅓ cup (67 g) of the sugar, baking powder, and salt in a large bowl. Whisk together the egg, cream, buttermilk, and vanilla in a medium bowl.

Mix together the strawberries, raspberries, blackberries, blueberries, cornstarch, and the remaining ⅓ cup (67 g) of sugar in a large bowl until all of the dry ingredients are moistened. Transfer the berry mixture to the skillet.

(continued)

Working quickly and with a light touch to prevent the butter from melting, shred the butter into the flour mixture. Stir through and, using your fingertips, rub the butter into the flour until the mixture resembles coarse crumbs. Add the chocolate and stir through. Add the egg mixture and, using a spoon, stir just until a dough forms and all of the ingredients are moistened. Scoop the dough onto the filling in the skillet by the heaping tablespoon (15 g), spacing it evenly. Bake until the filling is bubbling around the edges and the biscuit topping is dark golden brown, 35 to 40 minutes. Serve hot.

Raspberry-Almond Tea Cake

This cake is inspired by French financiers, which are brown butter and almond cakes shaped like little bars of gold. They are traditionally baked in tiny rectangular tins, which are a real pain to grease and flour before baking. So, I figured why not just skip the whole process of preparing the baking molds by making one large cake in the very same pan that's used to brown the butter? After all, it's already greased! I used a cast iron skillet, of course, and it worked beautifully. The cake slid out like a dream, and the edges came out extra crisp and even more delicious than usual. // *Yield: 6 to 8 servings*

- **RECOMMENDED SKILLET:** 9 inch (23 cm)

- **COOKING METHOD:** Baking

5 ounces (10 tablespoons, or 140 g)
    unsalted butter, cut into 1-tablespoon
    (14-g) pieces
¾ cup (150 g) sugar
¾ cup (71 g) almond meal

½ cup (63 g) all-purpose flour
¼ teaspoon kosher salt
5 egg whites, at room temperature
5 ounces (140 g) raspberries
    (about 1 heaping cup)

Place the butter into a 9-inch (23-cm) cast iron skillet. Place over medium heat and cook, stirring constantly, until golden brown and nutty, 5 to 6 minutes. Swirl to coat the inside of the skillet and immediately pour the butter into a small bowl and let cool slightly.

Whisk together the sugar, almond meal, flour, and salt in a medium bowl. Add the egg whites and whisk until smooth. Add the butter and whisk until smooth. Cover and let rest for 1 to 2 hours.

Preheat the oven to 350°F (180°C, or gas mark 4).

Transfer the batter to the skillet and arrange the raspberries over the top of it, poking each one down into the batter just slightly. Bake until the cake is golden brown, the edges start to shrink away from the skillet, and a toothpick inserted into the center comes out with moist crumbs, 55 to 60 minutes. Let cool in the skillet for at least 15 minutes. Cut into wedges and serve warm or at room temperature.

Peach Shortcakes

Shortcakes are the perfect way to showcase ripe summertime fruit. Feel free to vary the filling according to what's in season. Strawberries, mixed berries, and nectarines are all good choices. Taste the fruit for sweetness and adjust the amount of sugar you add to it accordingly.

Tahitian vanilla has a uniquely floral character that pairs nicely with fruit. It's available at gourmet markets and online. // *Yield: 8 servings*

- **RECOMMENDED SKILLET:** 10¼ inch (26 cm)
- **COOKING METHOD:** Baking

2 cups (250 g) all-purpose flour
⅓ cup (75 g) packed light brown sugar
1 tablespoon (14 g) baking powder
½ teaspoon kosher salt
¼ teaspoon ground cinnamon
Pinch of freshly grated nutmeg
Pinch of ground cardamom
1 egg, cold
1½ cups (355 ml) plus 1 tablespoon
    (15 ml) cream, cold, divided

3 ounces (6 tablespoons, or 85 g)
    unsalted butter, cold
2 teaspoons turbinado sugar
8 peaches, peeled, pitted,
    and cut into 8 wedges
¼ cup (50 g) sugar
¼ cup (30 g) powdered sugar
¼ teaspoon pure vanilla extract,
    preferably Tahitian

Preheat the oven to 425°F (220°C, or gas mark 7).

Whisk together the flour, brown sugar, baking powder, and salt in a large bowl. Whisk together the cinnamon, nutmeg, and cardamom in a small bowl. Whisk together the egg and ½ cup (120 ml) of the cream in a medium bowl.

(continued)

Working quickly and with a light touch to prevent the butter from melting, shred the butter into the flour mixture. Stir through and, using your fingertips, rub the butter into the flour until the mixture resembles coarse crumbs. Add the egg mixture and, using a spoon, stir until a shaggy dough forms. Knead lightly a few times just until any loose bits hold together. Gently pat the dough into a 1¼-inch (3-cm) thick circle on a lightly floured surface. Cut the dough into 8 even wedges.

Arrange the shortcakes evenly in a 10¼-inch (26-cm) cast iron skillet. Brush the tops with 1 tablespoon (15 ml) of the cream. Sprinkle with the turbinado sugar and then sprinkle with the cinnamon mixture. Bake until golden brown, 22 to 24 minutes. Let cool to room temperature.

Meanwhile, mix together the peaches and sugar in a large bowl and let macerate, stirring occasionally, until juicy, 15 to 20 minutes.

Whip the remaining 1 cup (235 ml) of cream, powdered sugar, and vanilla together to medium peaks.

Using a serrated knife, cut the shortcakes in half horizontally. Arrange the shortcake bottoms, cut-side up, on individual plates. Divide the sugared peaches along with their juices and then the whipped cream among them. Top with the shortcake tops cut-side down. Serve immediately.

Free-Form Apple Pie

This particular pastry is more closely related to the type of tart known as a *galette* in French or a *crostata* in Italian than it is to the classic American apple pie. The pastry crust is rolled out, filled, and then the edges are simply folded over the fruit. The filling is unthickened, barely sweetened, and arranged in a relatively thin but decorative manner. Though the results are strikingly beautiful, this sort of free-form pie is deceptively easy to make. You don't have to fuss over rolling out perfect circles of pastry or crimping the edges as any irregularities only enhance its rustic charm.

Use Braeburn apples if you prefer a tart filling, Honeycrisps if you prefer it on the sweeter side, or feel free to experiment with other cooking apples as you like. Leave the peels on the apples for a more decorative presentation. Peel the apples if you prefer a smoother texture. // *Yield: 6 to 8 servings*

- **RECOMMENDED SKILLET:** 12 inch (30 cm)
- **COOKING METHOD:** Baking

2 cups (250 g) all-purpose flour,
  plus more for dusting
½ teaspoon kosher salt
7 ounces (14 tablespoons, or 200 g)
  unsalted butter, cold, divided

¼ cup (60 g) packed brown sugar
½ teaspoon ground cinnamon
4 Braeburn or Honeycrisp apples

Whisk together the flour and salt in a large bowl.

Working quickly and with a light touch to prevent the butter from melting, shred 6 ounces (12 tablespoons, or 170 g) of the butter into the flour mixture. Stir through and, using your fingertips, rub the butter into the flour until the mixture resembles coarse crumbs. Add ¼ cup (60 ml) plus 2 tablespoons (30 ml) of cold water and, using a spoon, stir until a shaggy dough forms. Knead lightly a few times just until any loose bits hold together. Gently pat the dough into a circle, wrap with plastic wrap, and refrigerate until firm but still malleable, 35 to 40 minutes.

Preheat the oven to 425°F (220°C, or gas mark 7).

Meanwhile, whisk together the brown sugar and cinnamon in a small bowl. Cut the remaining 1 ounce (2 tablespoons, or 28 g) of the butter into eighths. Peel the apples, if desired, and cut them in half. Using a melon baller, remove the seeds and then, using a paring knife, remove the remainder of the cores. Carefully cut the apples crosswise into ⅛-inch (3-mm) thick slices, keeping the slices together to keep each apple half intact.

Using a large rolling pin, roll out the dough to a 14-inch (36-cm) wide circle on a lightly floured surface. Gently fold it into quarters, transfer it into a 12-inch (30-cm) cast iron skillet, and then unfold it, centering it and easing the dough into the corners and up the sides of the skillet. Add the sliced apple halves, arranging them in a single layer, and then press down gently on each one to fan out the slices slightly. Sprinkle the apples evenly with the brown sugar mixture and then top each one with a piece of diced butter. Fold the edge of the dough over the apples. Bake until the crust is golden brown, the apples are tender, and the juices are thickened, 50 to 55 minutes. Let cool in the skillet for at least 15 minutes. Cut into wedges and serve warm or at room temperature.

Pear Tarte Tatin

The traditional French tarte tatin is made with apples, but it's equally delicious and possibly even more beautiful with pears.

Be careful not to burn yourself when adding the pears to the caramel as it is extremely hot and will bubble up on contact with the fruit.

Unmold this tart soon after it comes out of the oven. If you let it cool in the skillet, the caramel will harden and it will stick. In the event that the tart does cool in the skillet, simply heat it for a few moments on the stovetop to remelt the caramel. Also, serve the tart soon after unmolding it, or the pear juice–tinged caramel sauce can cause the crust to go soggy. // **Yield: 8 servings**

- **RECOMMENDED SKILLET:** 10¼ inch (26 cm)
- **COOKING METHOD:** Baking

1½ cups (188 g) all-purpose flour,
   plus more for dusting
½ teaspoon kosher salt
5 ounces (10 tablespoons, or 140 g)
   unsalted butter, cold, plus 2 ounces
   (4 tablespoons, or 55 g) unsalted butter,
   cut into 1-tablespoon (14-g) pieces,
   divided

5 ripe but firm large Bartlett pears
Freshly squeezed juice of 1 lemon
1 cup (200 g) sugar

Whisk together the flour and salt in a large bowl.

Working quickly and with a light touch to prevent the butter from melting, shred the cold butter into the flour mixture. Stir through and, using your fingertips, rub the butter into the flour until the mixture resembles coarse crumbs. Add ¼ cup (60 ml) plus 1½ teaspoons cold water and, using a spoon, stir until a shaggy dough forms. Knead lightly a few times just until any loose bits hold together. Gently pat the dough into a circle, wrap with plastic wrap, and refrigerate until firm but still malleable, 35 to 40 minutes.

Preheat the oven to 425°F (220°C, or gas mark 7).

Peel the pears and cut them in half. Using a melon baller, remove the seeds, and then using a paring knife, remove the remainder of the cores. Drizzle the pears with the lemon juice.

(continued)

Combine the sugar, butter cut into 1-tablespoon (14-g) pieces, and ⅓ cup (80 ml) water in a 10¼-inch (26-cm) cast iron skillet. Bring to a boil, stirring slowly just until the sugar is dissolved. Using a pastry brush, brush down the sides of the skillet with water and boil until dark golden brown and caramelized, 13 to 15 minutes, swirling the skillet frequently once the sugar begins to brown. Add the pear halves, cut-side up, and with the stem ends toward the center of the skillet, arranging them in a single layer, and simmer until they begin to soften, 25 to 30 minutes.

Meanwhile, using a large rolling pin, roll out the dough to an 11½- to 12-inch (29- to 30-cm) wide circle on a lightly floured surface. Using a paring knife, cut out an 11-inch (28-cm) circle, reserving the scraps for another use. Gently fold the dough circle into quarters, transfer to a plate, cover with plastic wrap, and refrigerate until ready to use.

Remove the skillet from the heat and let cool 5 to 10 minutes. Working quickly, transfer the dough to the skillet and then unfold it, centering it and gently tucking the edges down between the pears and the sides of the skillet. Bake until the crust is golden brown, 30 to 35 minutes. Place a cake plate over the skillet and invert to unmold the tart. Cut into wedges and serve warm.

Fresh Pineapple Upside-Down Cake

In the Cast Iron Cooking Group on Facebook, it seems like making a pineapple upside-down cake and sharing a photo of it is a rite of passage for new members. Old members share theirs all the time too. I don't have any statistics, but I'm guessing it's the single most shared dish in the group.

After seeing dozens of pineapple upside-down cake pics, I finally had to get in on the action myself. So here's my version of the classic dessert, which is made from scratch with fresh ingredients. It's hardly any more trouble than using the boxed mix and canned pineapple, and I think you'll agree it is worth the extra little bit of effort.

Luxardo cherries are the original Italian maraschino cherries in syrup. They are free of red dye and almond flavoring and actually taste like cherries, and they are the extra-special finishing touch on this cake. Luxardo cherries are available in gourmet shops and online. If you cannot find them, substitute dried sour cherries rather than the commonly available variety.

Unmold this cake soon after it comes out of the oven. If you let it cool in the skillet, the brown sugar topping will harden and it will stick. In the event that the cake does cool in the skillet, simply heat it for a few moments on the stovetop to remelt the sugar. // *Yield: 8 servings*

- **RECOMMENDED SKILLET:** 10¼ inch (26 cm)

- **COOKING METHOD:** Baking

1½ cups (188 g) all-purpose flour
1½ teaspoons baking powder
½ teaspoon kosher salt
4 ounces (8 tablespoons, or 112 g)
   unsalted butter, softened, divided
½ cup (115 g) packed light brown sugar
1 small pineapple, peeled, cut into ½-inch
   (1-cm) thick slices, and cored

Luxardo maraschino cherries
¾ cup (150 g) sugar
2 eggs, at room temperature
1½ teaspoons pure vanilla extract
½ cup (120 ml) pineapple juice

Preheat the oven to 350°F (180°C, or gas mark 4).

Sift together the flour, baking powder, and salt into a medium bowl.

Place 1 ounce (2 tablespoons, or 28 g) of the butter into a 10¼-inch (26-cm) cast iron skillet and melt over low heat. Swirl to coat the inside of the skillet. Spread the brown sugar evenly in the bottom of the skillet. Arrange as many pineapple slices as will fit in a single layer decoratively atop the brown sugar, cutting them as necessary, and reserve any remaining pineapple for another use. Place a cherry into the center of each pineapple slice and into each of the smaller gaps.

In a mixer fitted with a paddle attachment, beat together the remaining 3 ounces (6 tablespoons, or 85 g) of butter and sugar on medium speed until light and fluffy, 5 to 6 minutes. Beat in the eggs one at a time on low speed until thoroughly combined and then beat in the vanilla extract. Add one-third of the flour mixture, then one-half of the pineapple juice, then one-third of the flour mixture, then the remaining one-half of the pineapple juice, and finally the remaining one-third of the flour mixture, beating on low speed after each addition until just combined. Stop the mixer occasionally during the mixing process and scrape down the sides and bottom of the bowl to ensure that everything is well blended. Transfer the batter to the skillet and spread evenly, being careful not to disturb the pineapples and cherries. Bake until the edges start to shrink away from the skillet and a toothpick inserted into the center comes out with moist crumbs, 45 to 50 minutes. Let cool in the skillet for 5 to 10 minutes. Place a cake plate over the skillet and invert to unmold the cake. Cut into wedges and serve warm or at room temperature.

Sopaipillas with Honey & Cinnamon

These crispy, fried pastries are a favorite in the Southwest. Once you make and roll out some tortilla dough, they fry up in a jiffy, and they puff up like pillows as they do.

Freshly fried sopaipillas are often rolled in cinnamon sugar or drizzled with honey and then sprinkled with cinnamon. Personally, I enjoy the sticky honey variation but don't much care for mouthfuls of dry raw cinnamon, so I prefer to warm the two together for nicer texture and more intense red hot–like flavor. I also like to play up the cinnamon's heat with a little pinch of cayenne.

Since sopaipillas are so light and there's almost nothing to them, they float on the surface of the oil from the moment they are added to the skillet and they hardly make the temperature fall. So keep a close eye on the thermometer as you cook and decrease the heat if necessary.

// *Yield: 4 servings*

- **RECOMMENDED SKILLETS:** 8 inch (20 cm) plus deep 10¼ inch (26 cm)*
- **COOKING METHOD:** Deep-Frying

½ cup (170 g) honey
1 teaspoon cinnamon
Generous pinch of cayenne pepper, optional

½ batch of Flour Tortillas (page 216),
    rolled out and quartered but not cooked
1½ quarts (1.4 L) canola oil (enough to
    come to a depth of 1½ inches [3.5 cm])

Whisk together the honey, cinnamon, and cayenne, if desired, in a cast iron skillet.

Pour the oil into a deep cast iron skillet and preheat over medium heat until it registers 375°F (190°C) on a candy/jelly/deep-fry thermometer. Add 4 of the sopaipillas and fry at a lively sizzle, flipping once or twice, until golden brown and crisp, 2 to 3 minutes. Using a wire skimmer, remove the sopaipillas to a paper towel–lined sheet tray and let drain. Reheat the oil and fry the remaining sopaipillas in 3 more batches of 4 in the same manner. Transfer the sopaipillas to a large platter.

Place the skillet with the honey mixture over low heat, whisking occasionally, until it is warm and thin, 3 to 4 minutes. Drizzle the sopaipillas with the honey mixture and serve immediately.

*This can also be made in a deep 12-inch (30-cm) cast iron skillet.

Lemon-Honey-Olive Oil Cake

The rich flavor of olive oil is front and center in this unusual cake. It's extremely tender and stays moist longer than most and may be even better the day after it's baked. // *Yield: 8 servings*

- **RECOMMENDED SKILLET:** 10¼ inch (26 cm)
- **COOKING METHOD:** Baking

Unsalted butter, for greasing the skillet
1¾ cups (219 g) all-purpose flour
½ teaspoon baking powder
½ teaspoon kosher salt
½ cup (100 g) plus 2 tablespoons
   (26 g) sugar
Grated zest of 1 large lemon
2 eggs, at room temperature

½ cup (170 g) honey, preferably
   citrus blossom
¾ cup (175 ml) plus 2 tablespoons
   (30 ml) extra virgin olive oil, divided
¼ teaspoon pure vanilla extract
½ cup (120 ml) milk
¼ cup (60 ml) freshly squeezed
   lemon juice, divided
1 cup (120 g) powdered sugar

Preheat the oven to 350°F (180°C, or gas mark 4). Butter a 10¼-inch (26-cm) cast iron skillet, line the bottom with parchment, and butter the parchment.

Sift together the flour, baking powder, and salt into a medium bowl.

Whisk together the sugar and lemon zest until very fragrant. Add the eggs and whisk until light and fluffy, 3 to 4 minutes. Add the honey and whisk until thoroughly combined and then add ¾ cup (175 ml) of the olive oil and vanilla extract and whisk until thoroughly combined. Add one-third of the flour mixture, then one-half of the milk, then one-third of the flour mixture, then the remaining one-half of the milk and 2 tablespoons (30 ml) of the lemon juice, and finally the remaining one-third of the flour mixture, whisking after each addition until just combined. Transfer the batter to the skillet and bake until the edges start to shrink away from the skillet and a toothpick inserted into the center comes out with moist crumbs, 50 to 55 minutes. Let cool in the skillet for 20 to 30 minutes. Place a piece of parchment and then a sheet tray over the skillet and invert to unmold the cake. Peel off the parchment from the bottom. Place a cooling rack over the cake and invert again to turn the cake right-side up. Peel off the parchment from the top and let cool on the cooling rack.

Transfer the cake to a cake plate. Whisk together the powdered sugar, remaining 2 tablespoons (30 ml) of olive oil, and remaining 2 tablespoons (30 ml) of lemon juice until smooth. Pour the icing on the cake and spread over the top, letting some drip down the sides. Cut into wedges and serve warm or at room temperature.

6

SPICES AND SAUCES

Lucy's Seasoned Salt

I almost never use processed foods or ingredients because I like to know exactly what I'm feeding my family. Product labels listing such mysterious ingredients such as "spices" don't pass my test. But I have to admit that I like the flavor of the seasoned salt with the orange cap and the big red *L* on the label—you know the one I'm talking about. It's a must for proper diner-style burgers, chicken-fried steak, and Salisbury steak, so I re-created it from scratch. My knock-off version has the same flavor profile but is less salty and less harsh so that it can be used generously. // *Yield: about ⅓ cup (80 g)*

3 tablespoons (45 g) fine sea salt
2 teaspoons paprika
2 teaspoons granulated garlic
1 teaspoon onion powder
½ teaspoon ground turmeric

½ teaspoon sugar
¼ teaspoon celery seeds, ground
¼ teaspoon cayenne pepper
¼ teaspoon freshly ground black pepper

Whisk together all of the ingredients in a medium bowl. Store in a tightly sealed container in the pantry for several months.

Lemon Pepper

Many recipes for this common spice blend exist, but most miss the critical sour component that's present in the popular store-bought lemon pepper with the big red *L* on the label. So, I developed a knock-off version that includes citric acid for the necessary tartness. Citric acid, which comes in powder form, is inexpensive and readily available online and wherever candy-making supplies are sold. // *Yield: generous ⅓ cup (35 g)*

Microplane-grated zest of 3 large lemons
3 tablespoons (18 g) freshly ground
    black pepper
1 tablespoon (15 g) plus 1 teaspoon
    kosher salt

2 teaspoons citric acid
2 teaspoons granulated garlic
1 teaspoon granulated onion
1 teaspoon sugar

Spread the lemon zest in a single layer on a parchment paper–lined cooling rack on a sheet tray and let dry at room temperature for about 24 hours.

Transfer the dried lemon zest to a medium bowl and add the pepper, salt, citric acid, granulated garlic, granulated onion, and sugar and stir through. Store in a tightly sealed container in the pantry for several months.

Cajun Spice

The beauty of this homemade spice mix is that you can adjust the heat level to your liking. Also, store-bought blends are expensive and often contain too much salt. Use this blend for seared or blackened steaks or fish, home fries, and anywhere else you want to add some spicy zing. // *Yield: scant ½ cup (65 g)*

2 tablespoons (14 g) paprika
2 tablespoons (20 g) granulated garlic
1 tablespoon (10 g) granulated onion
1 tablespoon (6 g) freshly ground
    black pepper

2 teaspoons dried thyme leaves
1½ teaspoons dried basil
1½ teaspoons cayenne pepper, or to taste
1 teaspoon freshly ground white pepper

Whisk together all of the ingredients in a medium bowl. Store in a tightly sealed container in the pantry for several months.

Curry Powder

No store-bought curry powder is as aromatic and flavorful as that made from freshly toasted and ground spices. // *Yield: about ½ cup (50 g)*

- **RECOMMENDED SKILLET:** 8 inch (20 cm)
- **COOKING METHOD:** Toasting

3 tablespoons (15 g) coriander seeds
1 tablespoon (6 g) cumin seeds
1 teaspoon fenugreek seeds
1 teaspoon fennel seeds
1 teaspoon yellow mustard seeds
1 teaspoon black peppercorns

1 teaspoon white peppercorns
5 whole cloves
1-inch (2.5-cm) cinnamon stick, crushed
2 tablespoons (14 g) ground turmeric
1 tablespoon (5 g) cayenne pepper

Combine the coriander, cumin, fenugreek, fennel, and mustard seeds, black and white peppercorns, whole cloves, and cinnamon in a cast iron skillet. Place over medium-low heat and toast, stirring constantly, until fragrant, golden brown, and crackling, 6 to 8 minutes. Immediately transfer to a bowl and let cool completely.

Using a spice mill, grind the toasted spices to a powder. Transfer to a medium bowl and add the turmeric and cayenne and stir through. Store in a tightly sealed container in the pantry for several months.

Garam Masala

Garam masala is an Indian blend of warm spices. Toasting the spices intensifies their fragrance and flavor and results in a mix that's far superior to store-bought. // *Yield: about ½ cup (50 g)*

- **RECOMMENDED SKILLET:** 8 inch (20 cm)
- **COOKING METHOD:** Toasting

2 tablespoons (16 g) green cardamom pods,
     peeled
5½-inch (14-cm) cinnamon stick, crushed
2 tablespoons (10 g) coriander seeds

2 tablespoons (12 g) cumin seeds
2 tablespoons (10 g) black peppercorns
2 teaspoons whole cloves

Combine the cardamom, cinnamon, coriander and cumin seeds, black peppercorns, and whole cloves in a cast iron skillet. Place over medium-low heat and toast, stirring constantly, until fragrant, golden brown, and crackling, 6 to 8 minutes. Immediately transfer to a bowl and let cool completely.

Using a spice mill, grind the toasted spices to a powder. Store in a tightly sealed container in the pantry for several months.

Creamy Horseradish Sauce

Serve a spoonful of this zippy sauce with any seared steak or chop. // *Yield: ¾ cup (175 g)*

½ cup (115 g) mayonnaise, preferably
     Best Foods
¼ cup (60 g) prepared horseradish

1 tablespoon (11 g) Dijon mustard
¼ teaspoon Worcestershire sauce

Whisk together all of the ingredients in a medium bowl. Store in a tightly sealed container in the refrigerator for about a week.

Tartar Sauce

This sauce is the perfect accompaniment to fried fish or seafood. // *Yield: 1½ cups (340 g)*

¾ cup (175 g) mayonnaise, preferably
     Best Foods
½ of a yellow onion, grated
1 small pickle, grated
2 tablespoons (8 g) minced Italian parsley

Freshly squeezed juice of 1 lemon
½ teaspoon Tabasco sauce
Kosher salt
Freshly ground black pepper

Whisk together all of the ingredients in a medium bowl. Store in a tightly sealed container in the refrigerator for about a week.

Fresh Herb Ranch Dipping Sauce

This recipe is thick enough to serve as a dipping sauce and thin enough to serve as a salad dressing. The flavors improve with time, so if at all possible, make it the day before you plan to serve it. // *Yield: a generous ¾ cup (180 g)*

½ cup (115 g) sour cream
¼ cup (60 ml) buttermilk
3 tablespoons (9 g) minced fresh chives
2 tablespoons (8 g) minced Italian parsley

1 teaspoon minced fresh thyme
3 cloves of garlic, grated on a Microplane
¼ teaspoon freshly ground black pepper
Kosher salt

Whisk together the sour cream, buttermilk, chives, parsley, thyme, garlic, and black pepper in a medium bowl. Season to taste with salt.

Store in a tightly sealed container in the refrigerator for several days.

Buffalo Mayo

This simple spicy and vinegary mayo makes a great dipping sauce or sandwich spread. // *Yield: 1 cup (225 g)*

¾ cup (175 g) mayonnaise, preferably
    Best Foods

¼ cup (60 ml) Tabasco sauce
½ teaspoon Worcestershire sauce

Whisk together all of the ingredients in a medium bowl.

Store in a tightly sealed container in the refrigerator for about a week.

Chipotle Dipping Sauce

This spicy and smoky sauce is fantastic as a dipping sauce or as a sandwich spread. Use more or less chipotles as you wish to adjust the heat level. Leftover chipotles keep well in the freezer. // *Yield: a generous 1¼ cups (285 g)*

6 canned chipotles in adobo sauce
1 cup (225 g) mayonnaise, preferably Best Foods
2 cloves of garlic, grated on a Microplane

2 tablespoons (30 ml) freshly squeezed lime juice
Kosher salt, to taste

Force the chipotles through a fine-mesh sieve to remove the skins and seeds. Whisk together the chipotle puree, mayonnaise, garlic, and lime juice in a medium bowl. Season to taste with salt and pepper.

Store in a tightly sealed container in the refrigerator for about a week.

Lemon-Yogurt Dipping Sauce

This simple and zesty sauce couldn't be easier to make. Feel free to stir in some minced fresh mint or sprinkle it with a pinch of Aleppo pepper or toasted ground cumin. Serve it as a dip for falafel and Middle Eastern spiced chicken, beef, and especially lamb or use it as a spread for pita sandwiches. // *Yield: 1¼ cups (290 g)*

1 cup (230 g) Greek yogurt
Freshly squeezed juice of 1 large lemon

2 cloves of garlic, grated on a Microplane
Kosher salt

Whisk together the Greek yogurt, lemon juice, and garlic in a medium bowl. Season to taste with salt.

Store in a tightly sealed container in the refrigerator for about a week.

Charred Tomatillo Salsa

This green salsa is mildly spicy, but you can vary the heat level by adding more or less serrano chiles as you wish. Serve it warm or at room temperature as a dip for tortilla chips or as a topping for tacos, fajitas, quesadillas, and other Tex-Mex and Mexican-inspired dishes.

To make easy work of trimming the cilantro, simply grab the entire bunch with both hands and give a firm twist in opposite directions to break off the bottoms of all the stems in one go. Use the entirety of the leafy portion and discard the stem ends.

The salsa is delicious as soon as it's made, but it is even better if it's refrigerated overnight, which allows the flavors time to marry.

Roma tomatoes may be given the same type of treatment to make red salsa. // *Yield: about 1 quart (946 ml)*

SPICES AND SAUCES

- **RECOMMENDED SKILLET:** 12 inch (30 cm)

- **COOKING METHOD:** Charring

1½ pounds (680 g) tomatillos
(about 16 medium to large)
4 to 6 serrano chiles
1 large clove of garlic
1 yellow onion, coarsely diced

1 small bunch of cilantro, stems trimmed
Freshly squeezed juice of 1 large lime
⅛ teaspoon ground cumin
Kosher salt

Preheat a cast iron skillet over medium heat. Add the tomatillos, serrano chiles, and garlic and cook, flipping occasionally and removing the garlic after 6 to 7 minutes when it is charred in spots and removing the serrano chiles after 10 to 12 minutes when they are army green and charred in spots, until the tomatillos are charred in spots, soft, and pale green, 15 to 18 minutes.

Trim the stems off the serrano chiles and discard them. Combine the chiles with the tomatillos, garlic, onion, cilantro, lime juice, and cumin in a blender and blend until pureed. Season to taste with salt.

Store in a tightly sealed container in the refrigerator for about a week.

Charred Tomato Sauce

This sauce has a lot of body and a bright, fresh tomato flavor with a hint of smokiness imparted from charring the tomatoes on the stovetop in a cast iron skillet. Use it as you would a long-simmered red sauce to toss with pasta, to top Chicken Parmesan (page 151) or pizza (page 149), or for a base for Shakshuka (page 63).

Leftover accumulated tomato juices may be used in soups and sauces. // *Yield: about 1 to 1¼ quarts (946 ml to 1.2 L)*

- **RECOMMENDED SKILLET:** 12 inch (30 cm)
- **COOKING METHOD:** Charring

3 pounds (1.3 kg) Roma tomatoes
 (about 14 large)
2 large cloves of garlic, minced
¼ teaspoon red chile flakes

3 tablespoons (45 ml) extra virgin olive oil
¼ cup (10 g) minced basil
Kosher salt
Freshly ground black pepper

Preheat a cast iron skillet over medium heat. Add the tomatoes and cook, flipping occasionally, until charred all over and quite soft, 22 to 26 minutes. Transfer to a bowl and let cool to room temperature.

Peel the tomatoes. Combine the tomatoes, reserving any accumulated juices, garlic, red chile flakes, and olive oil in a blender and blend until a pureed. Add the basil and stir through. Season to taste with salt and pepper. Transfer to a tightly sealed container and refrigerate overnight for the flavors to come together.

Reincorporate part or all of the reserved tomato juice as desired for a thinner sauce and re-season with salt and pepper.

Store in a tightly sealed container in the refrigerator for about a week.

Resources

Hungry Cravings
www.hungrycravings.com
For tutorials demonstrating techniques used for recipes in this book, cooking inspiration and recipes, and the latest news on my culinary adventures, please visit my blog *Hungry Cravings*.

The Cast Iron Collector
www.castironcollector.com
This website offers in-depth information on cast iron collecting and maintenance and restoration.

Facebook Cast Iron Cooking Group
www.facebook.com/groups/CastIronSkillet/
This website offers lots of great information on cast iron cooking, collecting, and maintenance and restoration, tons of friendly folks willing to share their experiences and answer questions, lots of animated and opinionated discussion on all things related to cast iron cooking, and most importantly an endless stream of cast iron cooking photos to make you hungry and inspire you to get in the kitchen. It's a closed and carefully policed group that will admit you if you ask.

JBR Jeffrey B. Rogers The Culinary Fanatic
http://theculinaryfanatic.com/ and https://www.youtube.com/user/TheCulinaryFanatic
Here you will find excellent videos on cast iron cooking, collecting, and maintenance and restoration from a widely accepted authority on the subject.

Acknowledgments

Thank you to my editor, Dan Rosenberg, for recognizing that the moment was right for a cast iron skillet cookbook and then entrusting me to write it. At the time, Dan had no way to know about the depth of my obsession with cast iron cookware and cast iron cooking, and yet somehow, he was able to foresee that this would be the perfect subject for me.

Thank you to my art director, Marissa Giambrone, for allowing me to pursue my creative vision and do the photography for the book.

And thank you to the entire crew at Quarto for making this book possible.

Thank you to my husband, Barry, for acting as my resident science expert, taste tester, guinea pig, time taker, scribe, proofreader, personal assistant, personal shopper, chauffeur, barista, sommelier, personal trainer, therapist, and cheerleader during this time. I couldn't have done this without you.

Thank you to my little brother Andrew for being my collaborator, consultant, and comic relief. I couldn't have written this book in just three and a half months without you.

Thank you to my mom and dad, Irina and Tony, for being my proofreaders, recipe testers, and cheerleaders.

And thank you to the following for providing cast iron skillets for my use:

- Kara Sharpe and Field Company

- Michael Griffin and FINEX

- Patrick Kohm and Greater Goods

- Katie Caniglia, Cadie Pittman, and GRIZZLY Cast Iron Cookware

- Ryan Martin and John Wright Company

- Arda Koch and KochCookware

- Mark Kelly and Lodge Manufacturing

- Steve Koleno, Matt Morris, and Lucky Decade Foundry

- Eric Steckling and Marquette Castings

- Peter Huntley and Stargazer Cast Iron

- Bibi Nucci and Victoria

About the Author

Lucy Vaserfirer is a culinary educator, chef, recipe developer, food blogger, food stylist, food photographer, and the author of *Marinades: The Quick-Fix Way to Turn Everyday Food Into Exceptional Fare, with 400 Recipes; Flavored Butters: How to Make Them, Shape Them, and Use Them as Spreads, Toppings, and Sauces; Seared to Perfection: The Simple Art of Sealing in Flavor;* and the entertaining and educational food blog *Hungry Cravings,* an online resource demystifying complicated cooking and baking techniques and offering delicious, foolproof recipes. A Le Cordon Bleu graduate with degrees in both culinary arts and patisserie and baking, she lives with her husband in Vancouver, Washington.

Index

For all the cooks who adopt a cast iron skillet. Take care of it and it will take care of you.

Brimming with creative inspiration, how-to projects, and useful information to enrich your everyday life, Quarto Knows is a favorite destination for those pursuing their interests and passions. Visit our site and dig deeper with our books into your area of interest: Quarto Creates, Quarto Cooks, Quarto Homes, Quarto Lives, Quarto Drives, Quarto Explores, Quarto Gifts, or Quarto Kids.

First Published in 2018 by The Harvard Common Press, an imprint of The Quarto Group, 100 Cummings Center, Suite 265-D, Beverly, MA 01915, USA.
T (978) 282-9590 F (978) 283-2742 QuartoKnows.com

The Harvard Common Press titles are also available at discount for retail, wholesale, promotional, and bulk purchase. For details, contact the Special Sales Manager by email at specialsales@quarto.com or by mail at The Quarto Group, Attn: Special Sales Manager, 401 Second Avenue North, Suite 310, Minneapolis, MN 55401, USA.

22 21 20 19 18   1 2 3 4 5

ISBN: 978-1-55832-929-4

Digital edition published in 2018

Library of Congress Cataloging-in-Publication Data available

Design and Page Layout: Megan Jones Design
Food Styling and Photography: Lucy Vaserfirer

Printed in China